BORN TO PLAY

BORN TO PLAY
The Eric Davis Story

LIFE LESSONS

IN OVERCOMING

ADVERSITY ON AND

OFF THE FIELD

Eric Davis

WITH RALPH WILEY

VIKING

VIKING
Published by the Penguin Group
Penguin Putnam Inc., 375 Hudson Street,
New York, New York 10014, U.S.A.
Penguin Books Ltd, 27 Wrights Lane,
London W8 5TZ, England
Penguin Books Australia Ltd, Ringwood,
Victoria, Australia
Penguin Books Canada Ltd, 10 Alcorn Avenue,
Toronto, Ontario, Canada M4V 3B2
Penguin Books (N.Z.) Ltd, 182–190 Wairau Road,
Auckland 10, New Zealand

Penguin Books Ltd, Registered Offices:
Harmondsworth, Middlesex, England

First published in 1999 by Viking Penguin,
a member of Penguin Putnam Inc.

1   3   5   7   9   10   8   6   4   2

Illustration credits
In photo section, page 3: John Dennis Hanlon/*Sports Illustrated*;
6: Los Angeles Dodgers, Inc.; 8 (below): Jerry Wachter Photo.
All other photographs courtesy of Eric Davis.

LIBRARY OF CONGRESS CATALOGING-IN-PUBLICATION DATA

Davis, Eric. 1962–
Born to play : the Eric Davis story : life lessons in overcoming adversity
on and off the field / by Eric Davis with Ralph Wiley.
p.   cm.
ISBN 0-670-88511-8
1. Davis, Eric, 1962–   .   2. Baseball players—United States—Biography.
I. Wiley, Ralph.   II. Title.   III. Title: Eric Davis story.
GV865.D297A3   1999
796.357'092—dc21   98–35636

This book is printed on acid-free paper.
∞

Printed in the United States of America
Set in Stemple Garamond
Designed by Jaye Zimet

And Jesus said unto them, Because of your unbelief: for verily I say unto you, If ye have faith as a grain of mustard seed, ye shall say unto this mountain, Remove hence to yonder place; and it shall remove; and nothing shall be impossible unto you.

—Matthew 17:20

For we walk by faith, not by sight.

—2 Corinthians 5:7

First, I want to give all the praise and honor to God for His healing hands in my life. I thank Him for having provided me with such wonderful doctors and nurses, whose compassion, skill, knowledge, and expertise were available to assist me in my fight against cancer. Words cannot express my appreciation to them for their genuine concern and care.

I especially thank God for my loving wife and daughters, my wonderful Mom and family. You all have been a pillar of strength for me and I am blessed to have you on my team. I especially want to thank my fans and friends whose support and prayers sustained me through the struggle. You are all truly special to me and I thank God for you.

In addition, I'd like to thank my marketing and public relations representative, Angela Hunt, of Celebrity Images, who has been instrumental in seeing that this book became a reality and whose assistance has been invaluable to me. I also want to thank my literary agent, Gail Ross, of Lichtman, Singer and Ross, for her tenacity and professionalism in seeing this project through. And to Viking, thank you for believing enough in my story to make it available to the public.

Finally, to my friend and coauthor, Mr. Ralph Wiley, who helped bring my story to life. Your gift is peerless. God bless you brother.

—Eric Davis

CONTENTS

BORN TO PLAY

PART I
Spring

ONE / SPRING 1998

ADVERSITY/BLESSING

Trouble at Work

STRATEGY/LIFE LESSON

Know Your Craft and Personnel

My whole life's been a trial and a blessing. I've lived and learned that a bad thing can turn out to be a good thing, and a good thing can become a learning experience. That's the way it often is. It's important to see things as they are, as well as how you wish they would be. I've been a professional ballplayer for eighteen years now, here in the spring of 1998, and a major leaguer for thirteen. Few things that I know of feel better than hitting a home run in the big leagues. If there was a way to tell you how that feels, to put wood on a big-league pitch and knock it out of the ballpark, then I'd share it with you, because, bottom out, that's just the kind of person I am. If everyone could know how it feels . . . but there isn't a way to describe it. You have to feel it.

I'll tell you what you *can* do. You can listen to the sound, and by that know the feeling is there. The louder the knock, the better a ball's been hit. When you hear that sound, it means another spring training, then another grind—162 games to see who can play best. I'm still getting around on the cheese—the ball still jumps off my bat as colors spin around me. Orange uniform numbers. White bases. Blue sky. Brown dirt. Green grass. I'm

grateful to be here in Fort Lauderdale with the Baltimore Orioles baseball club. This is what I know, love, do—have done for
a while. This is me.

It's probably similar for my teammates this season. All of us
are back for one more go-round. That's getting rarer these days.
Teams don't stay together. Now, not only can you get traded;
you can walk free agent. Or your time may be up. Happens to
everybody eventually.

Sooner or later it'll happen to me. But not today.

I'm in the cage, taking my cuts. Scotty Erickson is bringing
it. Scott throws a heavy ball. Can splinter your bat almost just
by looking at it. I line one out the opposite way anyhow. Fans
in the stands cheer and call my name. "Eric! Good hit, Eric!"
"Hey, Eric! Nice job!" "We love you!"

Teammates will say just about anything to one another, kidding around. Outfielder Tony Tarasco, who ain't gonna make
this club and knows it—Joe Carter's here, over from Toronto—
just said to me that my chemotherapy "aroused" him, made him
"want" me. Said it gave him a "tingle."

"Funny guy." I sneered, snorted, then smiled. I ain't mad at
him. I jump back in the cage.

" 'Oh Eric, we love you Eric,' " Joe mocks me in a falsetto
voice as a few Baltimore-based TV cameras film us. Joe smiles.
Got one of those disarming lightbulb smiles. Joe says, "Oh, so
you're a *movie star* now. Ah, Eric Davis is old news. There's a
new guy in town. 'Oh, we love you Eric.' "

Joe's kidding. Maybe he doesn't know that the fans appreciate
me coming back from cancer. Joe was adored by the Toronto fans
in his day because he produced—354 career homers and the walk-
off job to win the World Series in '93. Maybe being adored is ad-
dictive and you get to wanting it all the time. But when that grind
gets to grinding, when the days get muggy and long and that
Lamp, the sun, beams down in the dog days of July and August,
then it'll be all about production, smiling or not. Cancer or not.
Quietly I say to Joe, "It's just one day, Joe. Let me have my day."

I feel lucky—no, not lucky, *blessed*—to be back among top-end big leaguers. I had cancer, a malignant tumor, and I'm lucky to be alive. I didn't have to be alive, let alone facing big-league pitching. There's an art and a science to facing big-league pitching, and also a ritual—things that take years to learn. If you haven't learned, the pitchers know you don't know. I've been buzzed chin-high by the best, at the highest level. Sometimes they got me, sometimes I got them. It's been a battle. Can't say if I won their respect. They won mine. Not for throwing at me; that only gets my blood going. No, I respect them for getting me out, because I'm not an easy guy to get.

But I *fear* no pitcher. I've already faced tough situations, not just in the big leagues. Grew up in what turned out to be a tough 'hood in L.A. Lost a loved one to it. Smashed up my kidney something terrible during the 1990 World Series. Nearly died. Spent years in the minors. Had nine surgeries. And just last year, in '97, I had colon cancer. A malignant tumor the size of an orange, or a baseball, was removed from me, along with a third of my colon. I took 36 chemotherapy treatments prior to the spring of '98. But I still come to the post. They'll have to tear this uniform off me one day. And only God determines when the harvest time has come.

I just keep on plugging, and let His will be done.

A week ago, on February 11, I drove from our home in Woodland Hills to the treatment facility at the UCLA Medical Center. I took the Ventura Freeway to the 405, to Westwood. I didn't want to go, didn't feel up to it, but I *had* to go. Once in there I smiled at the other patients. Some smiled back, even some too weak to hold a smile very long. I know how they felt. I was with 'em, part of a battle that's unspectacular, not so crowd-pleasing as what I do for a living. No less of a battle than facing 97-m.p.h. cheese. I was taking my last chemo treatment. (Rather face the cheese.)

Chemo is like—well, snakebite, I guess. Glass bottles of Leucovorin and volatile 5FU hung over me as I sipped the tea

my wife, Sherrie, made from herbs she got from Robin Anthony, wife of the ex-Dodger outfielder Eric Anthony. As usual
I didn't watch as the urine-colored 5FU dripped into my arm.
Focused elsewhere. Sometimes I brought videos of movies.
Two-hour movies. Two-hour treatments. If you don't occupy
yourself during chemo, each drip seems to take forever and each
drop is like a big gong going off inside you. Now the Leucovorin. It's clear, colorless. Then I was finally done. The reactions I
developed when I first began treatment last July—the height-
ened, sickening sense of smell, the queasiness—had subsided a
great deal by then but were still there. I'd taken the full cycle,
was thankful the side effects were no worse. Dr. William Isakoff
said we'd continue monitoring for five years for reappearance of
the cancer. But as far as I was concerned this was it, the last
treatment. After eight months, the ordeal was over. Made it with
prayer—*fierce* prayer, a prayer *party*—God's help, and that of
my mother, father, sister, wife, and family.

It was hard mentally to go from Woodland Hills to the
medical facility over in Westwood. Adjuvant chemotherapy, begun six weeks after my surgery on June 13, 1997, at Johns Hopkins University Hospital in Baltimore. Some of my old guts are
gone; I've still got some left. I had to take chemotherapy, not
just for my sake but for my daughters, Erica, Sacha; for my wife,
Sherrie; my mother, Shirley—for my whole family. People do
look up to me. Some I know, some I don't. Some I met in the
cancer wards. Some come to the ballpark, even in pain. When I
hit a ball, as long as that ball's in flight, their pain is suspended.
People with handicaps are more passionate about the players
than Joe Average. Joe Average mulls over all that glue, the
money ballplayers make. People in wheelchairs, heads made
bald by radiation or chemo—they admire the skill, the battle.
Money can't help you get a hit off the Big Unit—or cancer. So
cancer survivors can relate, know without speaking that we
share a battle. If I'm in there playing, I don't want to be seen as
damaged goods, or a symbol. But that's probably the case. *Invite*

him back because he showed courage, but don't depend on him. Get Joe in here. One of the minor-league outfielders is almost ready. Joe is older, even more grizzled than me. He can take care of himself. But comparing a young player like Jeffrey Hammonds to me isn't fair to Jeffrey. I remember when I came up and was compared to Willie Mays. I was able to do things, but I couldn't carry Willie Mays, and Jeffrey can't carry Eric Davis. Being a symbol isn't why I play. I play because I love to, always did, always could, and I took on baseball as a job years ago. Do what you love. It'll still become a job, but that love will still be in there. I once heard a definition for the most unforgettable love of your life—great sex, and great heartache and pain. I think of hitting a homer, or about striking out, or about nine surgeries, and I like that definition. I'd like to think all this time I spent playing wasn't wasted. People in chemo, who cheer or who wait at the ramps, my family, my girls—by them being there, they tell me, "It wasn't wasted time."

Hope my teammates don't doubt me—especially not after what happened last season.

Feels good to be back with Baltimore, back in the Show, period. I want my teammates to know I'm good, that ol' E.D. won't let 'em down. I worked out in a different way this off-season, due to the chemotherapy. No weight training. Instead I worked in the martial arts, deep thinking, meditation, stretching, yogalike activity, working both inside and out. And now I want 'em to know they don't have to treat me different, or expect any less than my usual. I'm healthy, 100 percent—maybe 99 $^{44}\!/_{100}$ percent if you count my being 35, soon to be 36, then 37, and missing a section of intestine. Other than that, I feel strong. What else could it be *but* the grace of God?

I let my personality out. When you join a club, you get to see how another big leaguer gets his numbers. You know him then. You can read box scores, watch highlights, but that doesn't tell you how a guy gets his numbers, where his mass is, off what pitches he thrives, in what situations he's comfortable, how the umpiring affects him, what he believes in, how he came up in the game, what he can joke about, or can't, all kinda stuff. You want to know, so you can complement him within your own game, if you can. How to best set him up to be successful. Within a couple of months of joining the Orioles, I could imitate perfectly the batting stances of all my teammates.

"This is Harold," I say, assuming Harold Baines's stance. I exaggerate it some. Everyone smiles. Bainesy laughs. Then I do Roberto Alomar's stance. He laughs. I do Hammer, jumping up, turning in a circle, saying "Aw c'mon, Blue!" Hammer says, "Pops, that's not me," but he's smiling, because he knows it is. I jump back in the cage, set another one off to right-center, a drive deep into the bleacher seats. They're made of metal. The ball bangs off them loudly. Somebody barks like a hungry dog. *"Let the big dog eat!"* That's how it starts for me. Right-center-field bleachers on a line. When I go deep in the spring, it's to right-center. As summer arrives, I'll drop an ounce on the bat, to 31. Then I'll be pulling—taking pitches to the back wall of many an AL bullpen.

That night I fix a big meal for some of my teammates. Cook oxtails in a pressure cooker 'til the meat is falling off the bone, whip up some greens (turkey is lean, you can season it to taste, but honestly? I slipped some ham in the greens), candied sweet potatoes, macaroni and cheese. I can eat like that again, occasionally, even with a third of my large intestine gone. Guys stop by—Lenny Webster, Hammer, Eddie Murray—eat like there's no tomorrow. We talk about Mike Mussina's knuckle-curve, that Frisbee of his, and other things that oughta be illegal. Before dropping off to sleep, I lie alone in my bed, listening to my body. Feels quiet. Healed. God brought me back for something.

Jupiter, Florida—early March. Standing in against some kid for the Montreal Expos. Don't know who he is. If he makes it, I'll learn him. Montreal is always beating the bushes, finding a live arm from Dominica or Venezuela who the Expos can squeeze wins from before he goes free agent and Montreal loses him to the Yankees, Dodgers, Braves, Orioles, Indians, some team that can afford him if he's worth it. The big leagues weed them out. Right now, this is just some kid trying to make the club, rushing it up there for all he's worth. I stand in calm, hands twisting around the bat handle, held in front of and just below the Oriole insignia on the uniform top.

Everything upright. Relaxed. Deep in the box.

The rookie's arm whips forward and I see the release point clearly; he brings me belt-high gas. I turn. Helps to be strong in the gut. Bomb contact—feels like it always does when you catch one on the sweet spot, in your wheelhouse. Like feeling a color. Like you swallowed the Lamp, but it don't burn bad, burns good. I don't watch it. I look in our dugout. I like to see their faces when I take a guy deep. Plus I don't want to show pitch up. May have to face him again, next time with something on the line. I want him to think he can get me. The pitcher has his hands on his hips. I don't know him. But he knows me, now.

"Hey Keith man, you're Eric Davis!"

There's a reason I lasted, a reason I survived in the big leagues, and survived cancer. A strategy was developed, and a lot of lessons learned. There's a plan. What is the plan? Well, it's God's Plan *first,* that has to be acknowledged *first,* in order for anything else good to happen in your life. That ain't just a loose excuse, that's my life, the reality of my life. God has always been my manager. My job is to play what he deals. Sometimes you just have to go on faith.

I hit .474 the first seven games. Three homers. I worked. I prayed. I got dog tired of being in Florida. Ray Miller, the new manager, says I've got nothing to prove. Says he wants me in 100 games. My wonder is not whether I can play 100. I wonder whether that's all we'll need for us to win. I don't wonder if the cancer cells have been removed from my body. I give that one to God.

* * *

In an early season April home game, three of us threw out the ceremonial first pitch—me; Boog Powell, the old Orioles' first baseman; and a player from the minor leagues named Joel Stephens. Boog is in his fifties, I'm in my deep thirties, Joel is in his early twenties. We all have had colon cancer. We can't ask "Why me?" because why *not* me? That's your first thought, and for some that's the first answer. Boog played first base in Baltimore for years. Joel has been an outfielder in the minors for two and a half years. He said he paid attention to how I handled the cancer. He said he had a goal now, to get in an at-bat during the upcoming season. I told him I understood that, and would pray he'd do it.

Mr. Angelos says, "Once an Oriole always an Oriole." I've learned to take the man at his word. Not that he's above making mistakes. We're all only human, but for a ball club owner, I don't think I've met anyone better than Mr. Angelos. Watching this organization run when I first came here in '97 was like watching a Ferrari in a Grand Prix. All the pieces fit in a machine with a lot of horsepower: mechanics, great; pit people, great; car owner, great. All we need is a driver.

Ray Miller, pitching coach last year, is taking over for Davey Johnson, a great manager, one of the best that ever came down the pike, as far as I know. Davey believed in me. When I came back from cancer surgery and chemo last year, he gave me every opportunity to hit my way onto the playoff roster—when I did it, he didn't resent it, he was happy for me. He knew I could help him and the ball club. That's supposed to be the bottom line. The Orioles were all about winning, an organization dedicated to providing a community service, and they did it with a lot of class and style. That doesn't mean mistakes wouldn't be made. We all make outs.

We started off business as usual. For other teams that would mean a house afire. A 10–2 record out the gate was not crazy good for us, not if we pitched well. In baseball, pitching is everything. Pitching is key. And pitching is delicate. It dictates winning and losing; can make or break a streak. You can go to Atlanta (or New York in the '98 season) and come out of there 0-for-19 *real* easy. And after that quick start, we began to wobble, badly. Ray used 20 different batting orders barely a month into the season. Seemed to favor hitting me or Joe Carter second, behind slumping Brady Anderson. He hit me or Joe second 30 times. A waste. In the bullpen, we had arms, but no proven closer. Last season's closer, Randy Myers, went over to Toronto, after Davey Johnson stepped down as manager after winning 98 games. Manager of the Year one day, gone the next. Armando Benitez has the stuff but not the experience. Thinks being closer means staying in the clubhouse working out until the sixth inning, like Myers. That's not it at all. It's just as simple and as hard as getting big-league hitters out. Got a pitching coach as a manager now. Last season, 1997, with Mike Mussina, Erickson, and Jimmy Key being right on the beam as starters, pitching good all year, we were strong. In 1998: What's wrong with this picture? If anything happens to Mussina, Erickson, or Key—trouble. In the 162-game grind, wherever you're short, it comes out.

The funny thing about Davey Johnson is, he's been with all these teams, everybody says how good they were—how lucky he was to be managing the Mets in the '80s, the Reds in the mid-'90s, Baltimore the last couple of years—but when he leaves, those teams don't do so well for a while. I don't know if Pat Gillick and Kevin Malone, the Oriole general manager and assistant, wanted Ray Miller to manage. It'll take time for him. Managing's a whole other gig—keeping everybody ready, using 'em right, playing to their strengths, handling different game situations. Sometimes the best managing is no managing. Especially with talented veterans. Ray was Mr. Angelos's call, they say, so it's hard. Never played for an owner in baseball that I respect in the same way I do Peter Angelos. And I'll never forget what he did for me. I owe him my best efforts to get a World Series title.

But with the shape of our pitching in early 1998, seems like the best we can do is .500.

Over in the National League, you carry 10, 11 pitchers on a roster, tops, or that's been my experience. This season, we have a short bench of everyday players because we are carrying 12 pitchers. Twelve arms on a 25-man roster. Carrying 12, pitching better be a strength. We have three legit starters—Mussina, Erickson, and Key. Two of them got hurt in May. DL—disabled list. Got four lefties, but none of them are starters. As for Ray, he's a good pitching coach, but sometimes you can be good at one thing, then take on more responsibilities and lose the edge on the very thing you're good at. Ray's been using a lot of experimental batting orders, hitting Brady leadoff, then me or Joe, maybe B.J., Raffy, then Robby, then Cal—it's been throwing guys off. Robby's a number two hitter. You can hit him leadoff, even third, but ideally he's a number two hitter. As we struggled in May and June, Ray had Robby hitting fifth—supposedly protecting Rafael Palmeiro. But Bay-Bay don't have the pop to protect nobody. He's not that kind of hitter. Robby's more a table setter. Hitting second changes my approach, my preparation. You look to advance runners, hit to right. By the All Star break I had 11 homers. Ten were solo. Joe had 10 homers. *All* of his were solo. My at-bats were short, but I understood that everybody wanted to play. I think we'll win if I'm in there. As a big leaguer, it's the only way to think. If you ever stop thinking that, it's time to go home.

So what do we do? We get swept by the *Tampa Bay Devil Rays*, at home, four games! Swept by Devil Rays?! Drabek took the last loss, May 18. Gave up five in four frames. Hit rock bottom. I tossed and turned that night. Davey Johnson was in Florida, laughing probably. I take that back. Davey was probably mad, probably felt he should be at the helm of the club right now.

Early June. We haven't seen .500 since Mike Mussina got hit in the face by a line drive off Sandy Alomar's bat on May 14, suffering a broken nose and bad facial lacerations. He's gonna miss some turns, and when he does come back it'll take a while for him to be Moose again.

Jimmy Key went on the 60-day DL a few days later. Bad rotator cuff.

Now Ray has taken to pinch-hitting for me in late-game situations. Happened in Anaheim, with my family in the stands. Then in Tampa, against Esteban Yan. I don't care anything about any Esteban Yan. Mariano Rivera either. Ray still pinch-hit me with Harold Baines. H.B.'s a great hitter. I don't particularly like being pinch-hit for, just to get a lefty-righty matchup. I understand it more with Bainesy—as a hitter he's my equal. Or better. Well . . . sometimes. When Tampa Bay came into Baltimore, I faced Yan and took him to the back of the bullpen for a home run. Just to try and clear up misgivings Ray might have about me. Right now there appears to be many.

The batting order is still not set. Brady's still struggling. Took 80 games for Ray to move B.A. out of leadoff. Hitting second— safe to say I never hit second before. I'm an RBI guy, my bat can protect another RBI guy, I'm going to get numbers if I'm healthy. The book says .269 lifetime hitter, but that's not me. I shouldn't have even been out there from 1991 through 1994 with that damaged kidney. I'm .290. A *hard* .290. Batting average is overrated anyway. Reggie Jackson is lifetime .263, anyway. It's all about run production. Do you score, drive runs home? Although I had 25 extra-base hits at the All Star break, I only had 28 RBI. Batting second, nobody on.

As a big leaguer, you *have* to get your numbers in order to stay around. Knowing that can cause funny things to happen sometimes. Just that little bit of selfishness—like, a base hit up the middle with a runner on second. Say the runner on second is, ah, unfast, like quite a few of our guys are. You want that guy to get around with your RBI, so maybe you steam in toward second base to draw the throw from the cutoff man, making sure the run scores but also running into an out, killing a rally for the team, maybe. Or say a guy's running, got second base stolen, but you swing anyway 'cause there's a hole where a middle infielder went to cover the bag. Maybe you do this when the hit-and-run's not on. Maybe a 3–1 pitch, runners at second and third, and it figures to be the cheese, so you swing over the top of it because it's actually a splitter; but see, you want those ribbies, instead of taking the walk, letting the guy behind you put in some work. Subtle things.

No one has really accepted the reason why the Orioles are losing this year. I don't think they want to accept it. Our manager is trying to prove he can manage, instead of just letting the club play; the starting pitching is short due to injury; some arms in the rotation and the pen can't get big-league hitters out anymore. We aren't good enough. The batting order is all out of whack. Nothing's going right. After Rafael Palmeiro went deep against the Yankees on June 15 during the first game of a three-game set at Camden Yards against New York, Yankee pitcher Mike Stanton came back and immediately hit me dead square in the back with a fastball. It did hurt—don't *ever* think that ball doesn't hurt—but I didn't charge the mound. Didn't know if our pitchers would protect me or not. Tino Martinez got hit in the back by Armando Benitez at Yankee Stadium, after a Bernie Williams three-run homer, precipitating a brawl. I knew how to answer. Go deep. Let your pitchers handle the rest. Later I was asked if I thought Stanton tried to hit me. I couldn't say. Looking at the video, at his release point, let's just say I don't think he was trying to miss me.

On Wednesday, June 17, the largest crowd in the history of Camden Yards shows up for the Yankees. I'm in right field. Mussina is pitching, but he's not right yet. He walks the light-hitting Luis Sojo, so Darryl Strawberry comes up in the first inning. Straw gets a change-up and takes it out—high, deep, way beyond the center-field wall, a *towering* drive, moon shot; it lands 467 feet away at the base of the ivy-covered hitter's backdrop behind center. I stand in right. That's the longest ball that's been hit at Camden Yards. I had the third-longest hit there.

Now I had number four. I hit it in '94, when I was with Sparky Anderson's Detroit Tigers. Dead center too. Straw's bomb gives the Yanks a 3–0 lead. We've been battling since we were boys, me and Straw, so it was just a matter of time before my turn came. Straw and me, we go back. We competed against each other in Little League. Usually it's been, he makes a play, I make a play. Or, vice versa. My turn.

In the eighth inning, with Joe aboard, I'm due up. Yankee manager Joe Torre comes out of the dugout immediately. Some people think because I had cancer I'm weaker now. But I notice managers like Joe Torre will have a mound meeting on me in a minute. They still call the bullpen for me. Torre doesn't want Andy Pettitte facing me a third time: 5–2 Yankees. This is my element, the late-game RBI spot. I'm not punching out often in that spot. I'm looking for something I can drive, but I'll chip the good pitch down the right-field line, go up the middle if I need to. We need something to win this game. I'm standing in the on-deck circle; Raffy behind me. Torre brings in Mariano Rivera, fastballer, the ninth-inning closer, even though it's only the eighth inning.

"You're gonna take him out, kid," Raffy says to me.

"If he brings me the cheese, he's mine, kid," I say, swinging an iron rod around as we talk.

Ray pinch-hits for me. At first I think, 'Oh, okay, Bainesy.' Then I frown. Bainesy is on the DL. So Ray hits for me with Rich Becker, an outfielder we picked up off waivers from the Mets. Pinch-hitting for me, in a late-game home-run situation? With Rich? He's a legitimate big leaguer, but I had to look down at my own self, to see if I was still me. I didn't want to see what happened. I went into the clubhouse alone, took a shower, dressed. Rich grounded out to second. We lost. Again. I left without a word. Didn't sleep. Tossed and turned. I *hate* losing. For my own manager to have no faith in me, not to believe in my baseball ability—it hurt. I didn't get here hitting lefty pitchers only. Ain't no specialty players coming up to the big leagues.

Ain't happening. You don't make it to the big leagues as a pinch hitter extraordinaire. Late-game situations are what I've spent my life preparing for. That's *me*. The season's going down the tubes. We're giving in to the grind already. Some guys are signed, some are comfortable, and some are struggling. In our clubhouse something's missing. I know what it is. Faith. Somebody's got to battle back.

I know I've got to try and lead, somehow.

The next day, I got to the park at 2 P.M., even though a night game was scheduled.

I went directly into Ray's office. "What's going on, Ray?" I asked.

"I knew you'd come in first thing, E.D.," Ray said. Said he didn't sleep good last night. I said that I didn't either. He said if a home run could've tied the game he would've let me hit. I said we scored a run in the ninth and lost 5–3, so if I *had* homered, it would've meant a tie game. He said the book showed righthanders were 4-for-40 off Rivera, and lefties (Becker is a lefty hitter) were 7-for-30, that Becker was a good high-fastball hitter. I said if Becker was *that* good he wouldn't have been waived. I'd never faced Rivera. I had no fear of him. I'm the one with the bat. If he missed his spot or if I was hot, I didn't care who he was—but he'd care about me. I've faced the best in the big leagues for 13 years. Mariano Rivera isn't any better than Clemens, Ryan, Lee Smith—I could name 'em for you if we had time. Absently, Ray said he shouldn't have pinch-hit me.

Didn't Ray have any confidence in me? The thing about Davey Johnson was that he had that faith, that confidence in you, or made you think so. There's a point the game goes beyond numbers, things you have to *know.* I don't see it with Ray. Davey showed confidence even if you didn't have confidence. You don't have confidence every time you go to the mound, or to the plate. You might have gotten beat up the last couple of times. You might be 2-for-40, bases loaded, in the ninth. Davey's going to let you hit because he's saying, "You can do it. You can get this guy."

I hadn't gotten pinch-hit for much since my rookie years in the big leagues, in '84 and '85. When I came up, in the mid-'80s, you didn't have printouts hanging on the walls of the dugouts. You had vets and you listened to 'em. A computer might say I'm 3-for-14 off Denny Naegle, 1-for-4 the last time I faced him. What the computer doesn't say is I put a charge into all four balls I hit off Denny—four bullets, three chased down, one outta here, not a cheap home run but a rocket into the right-center stands. The 1-for-4 is deceiving. If I've got confidence in you, doesn't matter if Babe Ruth's up, or if Bob Gibson is on the mound. If I have confidence in you—if you've proven it—I'm going with you. That's what bonds teams. That's how cliques are stopped, by guys getting a chance to do what they do best, then doing it. We're playing to the opposition's strengths.

"Ray, you can't do that to people who have been through the wars, and won. I'm a warrior, Ray." I was pleading with the manager. I know how I respond. I respond to faith. "You can't *not* have confidence in me, Ray. I've come too far. I can still do it, Ray."

"I know you can, E.D.," Ray said. He seemed distracted.

"Ray . . . *I can do it.*"

Ray said, sure I could. Said he had confidence in me. All the confidence in the world. But I didn't get the feeling of confidence from him. You never know what's in the back of somebody's mind. There have been players who've come back from cancer, played cameo roles—pitcher Dave Dravecky with the San Francisco Giants in the '80s, the Dodgers' Brett Butler a couple years ago. Butler called after I was diagnosed and had surgery last year. He was kind, but I don't know of anyone who came back from cancer to the same level of productivity on the field. I can do it. I *feel* it. Doesn't mean Ray can feel it. He's a pitching coach. If I was a manager, I'd hire him as a pitching coach myself. He was pitching coach last year when we won 98 games, beat the breaks off the whole AL East, led wire to wire. But managing everyday players over 162 games is different.

Baseball is fluid in this way—if you're in the big leagues long enough, you run across the same guys again and again. In 1990 I was the Man in Cincinnati. Ray Miller was pitching coach in Pittsburgh. The Pirates also had Barry Bonds, and if they beat us in the playoffs, they would get to play the defending champion, Oakland A's, in the World Series. It doesn't get much better than Barry Bonds as a player, Jim Leyland as a manager. But the Cincinnati Reds played well, and we won that National League Championship Series. I made plays. You can beat a guy and end up playing with him and you're teammates. To me, Bonds is at this point still the best player, and Leyland may be the best manager. They hold no grudge because we won that playoff in '90. I can't really say what's bothering Ray about me. If Ray can't see what I'm capable of, if the decision is made to trade me, there's nothing I can do, not with Ray Miller pinch-hitting for me with Rich Becker.

The Lord restoreth my soul, my body, and my faculties. God didn't go halfway. How can I? He brought me back from so much. He allowed me to still be able to run. He left me still able to swing a bat. In spite of all I'd done in baseball, it seemed people appreciated me only when I got cancer. But I had given it all before and produced. All you can do is give to the game. You can't take. You're going to do well, you're going to struggle. You're going to get sick, but God willing, you're going to get well again. There's a divine plan. God's will is in baseball too. You can't take from God. You can't take from the game. All you can do is give. Then you'll get.

"Ray, you just don't realize what you have here in this clubhouse."

Never . . . say . . . die.

* * *

So we went up to Shea, and I got hit with a pitch again, this time by Rick Reed. Right on the elbow. The bursa had to be drained. We had our bench coach, Eddie Murray, a should-be Hall of Famer, showing outfielders how to throw because he felt like he didn't have anything else to do, and because we were losing. I'd never had an elbow problem before. By us having a veteran team, there's not much for a coach to do in terms of instruction. It's all deployment. Ray asked if the outfielders would work with Ed. Ed felt he wasn't contributing. Nobody picks up a pitcher's tendencies like Ed, or lifts a sign like Ed. But as far as playing defensive outfield, there ain't a lot Eddie Murray can do coaching my defensive technique. Ed was a first baseman. Brilliant as Ed is about the infield game, we had him coaching the outfielders. Ed tried to change my arm action, wanting me throwing over the top. As an outfielder, I don't throw like that. I throw three-quarter, to get carry. I messed up my elbow some more. My elbow hurt so bad I had to run the ball back into the infield after a base hit. The brass said I might go on the DL. They said it with long faces. I met with Ray and Kevin Malone in the visiting clubhouse in Montreal, on Sunday, June 29. Montreal was busy sweeping us three games. Kevin Malone, with a long glum face, asked me if I thought that going DL was a good idea. "Tuesday," I said to him and Ray. "I'll be ready Tuesday."

Finally, on Tuesday, July 1, Ray changed the batting order to Alomar first, Brady second, me number three, Raffy at cleanup. We went to New York, lost 3 one-run games, hit the All Star break 38–50. We were playing mule-ugly until those three in New York. The Yankees were 61–20—a modern-day record for a first half, .753 ball—after beating us 1–0 on Sunday, July 5. In the fifth, I hit a hard single off David Cone. Raffy lifted an opposite-field fly ball down the left-field line. A rookie named Ledee seemed to catch it, then dropped it. I couldn't tell if the ump called Raffy out. We'd lost 4–3 the day before on a blown call. Scott Brosius dropped a throw, but the third-base umpire called an out. I see Ledee drop it; I look at Blue, who very leisurely drops his arm. Now I've got to make third from a standstill halfway between first and second. For having just turned 36, I get to third quick. So does the ball. Blue pulls the chain, we end up losing, 1–0.

The very same guys managed by Davey Johnson, who won 98 games last season, have now disintegrated into cliques. Losing does that. The question is, Can I put this club on my back and carry it for a month? And will I get the chance? I've done it before—before the cancer was diagnosed. People are saying it's too late for us. No. We're just in an impossible situation. That's my specialty.

The Yankees were out of sight now—30 games up. We were 15 ½ games behind the Red Sox for the wild-card spot—17 in the loss column. The Orioles weren't as bad as we were playing. The Yankees and Red Sox were good, but not as good as they were playing. Nobody's .750 in the big leagues. It'll all even out. Just may not even out this year. In times of trouble, work harder. As my mother says, "He may not be there when you want Him, but He's always right on time."

At the All Star break, I was hitting .287, with 34 runs scored, 13 doubles, 11 home runs, a triple, 25 extra-base hits, and only 28 RBI. The Orioles were fractured, going nowhere. D.O.A.

Sherrie, Erica, and Sacha came to Baltimore after the break. I do love my girls so. Anybody who knows me knows that. I come from a praying family—a praying father, a praying mother, and a praying sister. I pray often myself. I prayed now, for the ability to be me again in baseball. I didn't pray to win. I prayed to be me. I knew by then that sometimes winning is all on the outside, and sometimes it's all on the inside. Sometimes a cancer is outside, sometimes inside. Sometimes a big leaguer can be special, but we all are special, sometimes. Some of us just happen to play this great game of big-league baseball for a living while we're young enough and able. In the major leagues, there are many life lessons for everybody. It's just a question of which spring.

TWO / SPRING 1980

ADVERSITY/BLESSING

Youth

STRATEGY/LIFE LESSON

Be Grounded, Study Models, Keep Living

It started back before I can remember, from the first games of tag I played with my brother. I just had the knack. I was four or five years old, chasing Jim and being chased around the five rooms we grew up in, hollering and screaming like banshees as we ran around the apartment. I could always catch him. I had a better burst—movement from a standstill. He couldn't get away from me, even though he was a year older. Sometimes I worried him—he wanted to get away but couldn't. I was too fast, too quick, always around. He moved as fast as he could, but sometimes it seemed as if he was slowing down for me. Laughing, carefree, running wide open, I reached out to tag him—and tripped over the phone cord and went headfirst into the edge of the coffee table. I can't remember the pain now, but it must have been bad. I do remember the blood, and getting stitched up. The evidence is over the right corner of my mouth until this day. Scarred for life.

In the spring of '80, and for all 18 years of my life prior to that, my mother, father, sister, and brother were the center of my universe, all of us cozy in apartment number 1, inside a dune-colored, four-unit, stucco two-story at 6606 Denver Avenue, the heart of central Los Angeles, in eternal sunshine, and my life had been quite happy. Denver is a residential street running parallel to the main thoroughfares of Figueroa to the east, Hoover and Vermont due west. In the heart of what is now called the ghetto—that was my refuge, my safety net, my home.

My parents were home. And on this May morning, in the spring of 1980, they were beside themselves.

My mother, Shirley, kept saying, "I can't believe it. Praise God, I can't believe it."

I looked over at my father, Jimmy Davis Sr., and we shared a smile.

"I don't know why you can't believe it, Mom. It's me. Ain't that right . . . Ham?"

Larry Barton Jr. had just left the same five rooms where I'd grown up. He was there to get my signature on a professional baseball contract with the Cincinnati Reds organization. I'd just graduated from John C. Fremont High a few blocks away. Did what I had to do because Shirley wasn't hearing otherwise. I thought that school was not for everybody—that meant me—and the sooner we learned that, the better off we'd be. But I wasn't allowed my opinion. Shirley stayed at home with us, trained us to be respectful, taught us to cook, clean, sew, believe in God, take care of ourselves, write legibly, do our multiplication tables, shop thrifty, squeeze a buck until it hollered like we did when we played, get the most from what we had, see Mt. Moriah Baptist Church as our home away from home, do what we said we would, keep our own counsel, look out for one another.

I was the youngest of three. My sister, Sharletha Rochea, who we called Rochea, was born on October 6, 1959, back in Natchez, Mississippi, my parents' hometown. My brother, Jimmy Jr., we called Li'l Jim, and then Jim Bean, and then just

Bean as we grew older; he was born March 15, 1961, in L.A. I was born there as well, May 29, 1962. I was a fresh 18 in the spring of 1980. I walked back to our bedroom, Jim's and mine. I sat on his twin bed—his side was always kept a little neater than mine—and saw in my mind a wire hoop hanging on the door, and heard the three of us laughing, me, my brother, and my father, playing ball, right there, even where we slept. We played for hours until my mother was reduced to screaming.

"Will you all *PLEASE STOP IT!?*"

And then we played on until she stormed into our bedroom, snatched the wire hoop down, stormed back into my parents' bedroom, then slammed and locked the door. We stood there frozen in our action poses, Jim and me out of breath from sheer exertion, my father holding his breath at the same time. The three of us looked at one another in something like shame—but it was happy shame.

"Uh-oh. What 'chu gonna do *now*, Dad?"

"I'm not gonna do *nothin'*. What are you gonna do?" he said.

My mother used to say she didn't have a husband as much as she had three sons. My father was 18 and my mother 17 when they started courting back in Natchez, where my father was a star high school athlete. He'd gone to a junior college for a year. Then my sister was born and he had to find work, more future than he saw in Natchez, so he moved to California. Months later my mother and Rochea followed, my mother's belly big with Jim. My father came to the land of milk and honey in 1960. He started working at a Boys Market warehouse in Hawthorne, as a grocery stock warehouseman. Worked that job the next 37 years—as long as I've been alive. It provided enough to keep us hopping. We moved around at first; lived in an apartment at 48th and Vermont for about two years, until I was born, then moved to East 28th Street, then to 49th and Compton Avenue, and then, finally, to the four-unit stucco apartment building on the east side of Denver Avenue.

My father found a second job at Center Drug Store in Manhattan Beach. He worked that job for over twenty years, until the proprietor, Ray Lazar, sold out to a larger drugstore chain. They didn't keep my dad on. Said they didn't know if he would be dependable. Once when I was very young, I rode over to Center Drug Store with my father to pick up his pay. It was evening. I could smell salt in the air. We sat outside in a little blue Mercury Comet he had. He was a Chevy man at heart, later had one or two of those. A black-and-white cruised by with two policemen in it. It rode by again. My father said, "I'll be glad when Mr. Lazar gets here." Soon he got there, through the back, and he let us in. I looked around, thought it smelled funny. I'd never been in a drugstore. Then the two policemen entered in a slight crouch, but they straightened up when they saw Mr. Lazar smiling. "Thanks for stopping by," said Mr. Lazar to the policemen. "Can't be too careful. I want you to meet Jimmy Davis. He works for me. If you ever see him around here, it's all right."

"Oh . . . just making sure, sir."

"Fellas, lemme tell you something," said Mr. Lazar. "If this man right here ever did something wrong, something even halfway bad, I'd lose confidence in the whole human race."

I wasn't surprised to hear this. But I *was* surprised that this stranger knew it, too.

I recall another time, back when I was 11, my father took me with him to pick up his paycheck, this time at the Boys Market in Hawthorne. While he was inside, I watched these kids playing in the park, on a gridiron. They had on purple football uniforms, like the Minnesota Vikings. Gold face masks. Made me want to wear one. I'm sitting there looking at the kids thinking they were moving in slow motion, compared to the way my father moved; these kids wouldn't be much of an issue for me. By then I had been playing with my father outdoors on the play fields, and also with boys who were six and seven years older than me. I didn't find it odd that they always picked me first: "I got Keith!" (I was called by my middle name, Keith, just as my sister was called by her middle name, Rochea. Even today, I like calling Hall of Fame ballplayers by their first and middle names. Hank Aaron would be Henry Louis, for example.)

Anyway, these boys in the Viking uniforms were my age, and I'm saying to myself, "They can't play better than me." I just wanted to wear one of those sweet Viking unis. I asked my father about it and kept after him until finally he took me and Jim Bean around there one day, and they said we came too late to sign up. I don't recall Ham dwelling on it later. He might have, but not with us. He was a protective sort when it came to real-world stuff. He just said, "Aw, they probably just didn't want you boys showing them up." I thought I wanted it so bad—but not getting it was the best thing that could've happened. Baseball was my destiny.

It wasn't until years later that I could fully appreciate my father's life. He moved his family to California, saw Watts burning in '65 behind a police brutality incident, saw riots after Martin Luther King was killed in '68, then Black Panther–police shootouts. Being a black man, a family man, and going in and working day after day through it all, God only knows what it did to his work environment, the backlash, then he watched his neighborhood decline as children unluckier than us in the way of fathers went straight gank, gangster, O.G.—they had a lot of names for it by the time I got to high school. It happened right outside our door as I was growing up, yet I wasn't aware of how bad it was until I reached junior high. That's how strong my parents were.

We attended church on Sunday and gave credit where it was due because no matter what else, we had each other, health, youth, and God to thank for it all. So Mt. Moriah was one of two activities that were not optional. The other was schoolwork. Like most children, Jim and I played hard all day on Saturdays, and occasionally felt we were too tired to get up early Sunday morning, get scrubbed, brushed, and dressed to go to Mt. Moriah Baptist Church, at the corner of 43rd and Figueroa, where we would have to keep still—hard to do back then—and listen to the Word, as given in the spiritual coaching of the Reverend Earl Pleasant, and then the Reverend Melvin V. Wade Sr., the man who performed Sherrie's and my wedding ceremony, years later. We went to church religiously because, as we felt then, we had no choice. But as the years passed the church became central to us. But back when we were boys, we begged off from going a few times. My mother and father didn't argue with us about it. My mother might have complained, said she didn't raise heathens, but Ham said, "All right, men, but if you don't go to church, if you don't take care of your spirit, then you know you can't play ball for the rest of this week, until next Sunday comes around."

That would seem like a good deal to us, until a few hours later, on Sunday afternoon, when the rest of the neighborhood boys had shed their Sunday best and come down to our place. Dad bought us every kind of equipment that was important to us: basketball, football, baseball gloves, a bat, nets for the playground rims. Ours was the sports equipment house for the neighborhood. I was the key attraction. People would come around asking for this ball or that ball, begging for the hoop nets, begging for Keith: "Let's go play!" And Jim Bean and I would ask, "Can we, Dad?"

"Y'all ain't goin' nowhere," Ham said. "You don't go to church, you don't play."

The next Sunday, Jim and me, we'd be waking *them* up to go to church.

The neighborhood games didn't really start until the Davis brothers came out. It was practically a responsibility for me to be good: I had the equipment. I had the father. And I had the tools.

"Let us borrow the baseball gloves! Give us the nets! Y'all football the one got laces on it!"

And so this was all linked together in my life and my mind— sports, religion, family, church, spirituality. Not in some pious, loud, attention-getting way. But it was still there. Clear. Strong.

Nobody understood more that I was born to play than my brother, Jim. I played with him, always on him to play more, and he would, but I was relentless, and good, from playing so much, from having my father's—and my mother's—physical traits, and my mentality. I played on teams and sometimes my brother would come and watch me. He's always been the sort to meet people. One day over at Baldwin Hills Park Recreation Center, I was playing as a 10-year-old on a 12-year-old basketball team, and Sam Watson, an 18-year-old, showed up with his hand-picked squad led by Walter Armstrong. Sam wasn't one of those guys who would say "Somebody ought to give those kids something to do"—he'd get a van and go *get* the kids, take them around. He knew that boys needed activity. Sam also liked to win. He brought Walter Armstrong with him. As a 12-year-old, Walter already had rep. He'd end up going to Crenshaw High, where Darryl Strawberry also went. My brother had met Sam, somehow, and as they were on their way into the gym one day, my brother told Sam, "You just don't know what's waiting for you in there." "What you mean, Jim?" "My brother Keith's in there." "That's nice your brother's playing, but we got Walter Armstrong here."

Jim said, "I don't care *who* you got. You just don't know what's waiting for you in there."

I was what was waiting in there.

Sam ended up screaming at Walter and his other guys, saying they were letting little number 10 beat them by himself. We did beat 'em, too, and Sam later said it was one of the great days of his life, just watching me play the first time, even though his squad got beat. Later, Walter Armstrong was a star at Crenshaw, and even later, when a so-called agent tried to get him to go overseas to play basketball, Walter said he had more money in his car than the agent was offering. Don't know what happened to Walter Armstrong after that. I do know that when he was 12, he had a lot of game. Almost as much as I had at age 10.

My favorite times of all were when we had barbecues in the backyard behind the apartment building that was our home. My parents were neighborly folks, communal. That's how they were raised. Our house was the sports house of the neighborhood, but mother wouldn't let us play with anybody she didn't know or whose parents she hadn't met. That's just how she was. She rode tight herd on us, never worked outside the home while we were growing up, but worked hard on us. Her school was the University of Home Training. Attendance was mandatory. And we didn't have trouble in the neighborhood as young kids—or I should say *I* didn't—because there were three of us. And because I could play. I could *really* play. I just could.

"Who you s'posed to be?" some new kids might ask.

"I'm Keith. And that . . ." Jim would step out, smiling challengingly, "is my brother, Jim."

"And I'm Rochea," my sister might say, sauntering up. "What you wanna do?"

The new kid (or kids) might say, "Nuttin'," or "Play some ball. You gotta ball?"

"Play ball? 'Gainst Keith? Hmph. Well, we got *all* the balls," Rochea would add.

My sister and brother paved the way for me, in the neighborhood, and later at Bethune Junior High and Fremont High. But when we were not yet in high school, still close to home, any conflicts were usually silently settled, and if not, we might go "head up." Fight or no fight, it all went by quickly, and soon after we'd all be friends again and they and their parent (or parents, if they were lucky like us) would be coming over to the famous Davis backyard barbecues. Some of these neighborhood friends did well later on and I still keep up with them, and some of them were our relatives, and some of them didn't do so well. It's hard to know what to do when some of the people you grew up with, liked, and played ball against—who are your brothers, sisters, and cousins—and who your parents fed, turn into Hoover Crips, or Broadway Crips, or Brims. You feel bad, but you don't forget when you were young and happy, and they came over for barbecue and fried fish.

I recall growing up in that community, South Central, when it wasn't bad, when it seemed to me that if you did something wrong, everybody knew about it. Back when I was growing up, everybody would discipline you. If you did something wrong and your parents were at work, the neighbors would let you have it and tell your mother and father when they came home so you got two whippings. My mother's sister Thelma, my aunt Tee, lived in the same unit as we did, and not only did Rochea baby-sit her two children, she kept an eagle eye out on us. My mother's first cousin lived not far away, and her son, Renard, was one of my running buddies and athletic competitors. That's what we're missing in society today. Back then, no one spoke of child abuse when it came to not sparing the rod. What I was getting at that particular time, by today's standards, may have prompted Social Services to take me from my parents. I was always rambunctious, and now I appreciate my parents for their lessons because they made me not only recognize right and wrong, but showed me that love can take different forms. My parents wanted us to do right. If you did wrong, you got a spanking. I discipline my girls. I don't abuse them, but if they do wrong I let them know it was wrong. "Time out" ain't gonna happen. There are phases you go through as a child. There was a phase when I thought I could do anything I wanted to do without any repercussions, followed by a phase in which I was scared to death of my mom and dad. That was the early manifestation of a fear of God—someone wiser, more powerful than you. I was blessed. I came up with two strong parents. That has a lot to do with my reservoir of strength today.

It all comes around, and you have to have experienced it to have it in you.

My mother cooked well and in vast amounts. She'd make all this good food—mountains of potato salad, coleslaw, barbecued ribs, barbecued or smothered chicken and rice and gravy, creamed or roasted corn, turnip greens, collards, macaroni and cheese, biscuits, rolls, any kind of cake. My father wouldn't break out beer but it was BYOB, and if you think our backyard wasn't full of aunts, cousins, neighbors—real and for-a-day— you are mistaken. My parents would put us children out in the front for a while as the adults played the Stylistics, Dramatics, Delfonics, Ohio Players, Dells, Isley Brothers, Isaac Hayes, Barry White, Marvin Gaye, Marvin and Tammi, Donny and Roberta, Sam and Dave, Johnnie Taylor, Tyrone Davis, Percy Sledge, Aretha Franklin, Ray Charles. Then as the years went by, it was the Watts 103rd Street Rhythm Band doing "Express Yourself," Bloodstone doing "Natural High," Sly and them singing "I Want to Take You Higher." We'd come in and put some Jackson 5 on the turntable and the adults would say, "Dance, Keith, Dance, Jim and Rochea. Y'all dance for us," and we would. My parents would soon be back to spinning Al Green. They loved some Al Green. No surprise to me now, that I love Al Green too, and know all his classic lyrics.

> I . . . I'm so in love with you
> Whatever you want to do
> Is uh-all right with me-eee-ee
> Cause youuuu . . . make me feel so brand-new-oo-oo
> And I . . . want to spend my life with you-oo-oo.
> Lets . . . do you want to stay together?
> Loving you whether, whether
> Times are good or bad, happy or sad . . .

I never thought I'd be a professional baseball player. Not at first. I was just trying to keep up with my father. That was a job.

We called him Ham. Still do. That's what he called us, me and Li'l Jim. We played ball with him all the time. He'd come to Bethune playground or 66th Street playground after he got off work and played with us in his work boots. We could not beat him. Sometimes he raced us in his work boots. We could not beat him. I couldn't outrun my father until I was 15. He was that fast and that quick. I'd have to make a serious move just to get by him. Most boys lucky enough to have and remember their fathers remember looking up to them, remember them as giants. I'm no different, I'm sure, only this is not just a childhood memory. The man could play. Learning how to compete with him was important in my athletic development.

Plus, he had character. You couldn't find the bottom of it. Would as soon miss breathing as miss work. When he got off the 4 A.M. to 1 P.M. shift at Boys warehouse, that's when we'd play. He showed my brother and me no mercy. Hip-checks, hand-checks, backing us down in the lane, going over us, ripping the ball away until we went home and told Mama, and she'd get on him.

"Jimmy, those boys are nine and ten years old, and you're down there pushing them and elbowing them, you know you ought to be ashamed of yourself!" And he would act like he was ashamed, briefly, for her benefit, but he knew what he was doing. Having fun. "If you're gonna play, play," he'd say to us, and wouldn't allow us to cry just because he was roughing us up.

Then at 7 P.M. he would go to his janitorial job at Center Drug Store in Manhattan Beach until midnight. He worked those two jobs for a combined 57 years. Still at the day job. May be over there right now, even as you read this. He worked odd jobs between shifts—helped neighbors and relatives paint, or remodel, or move. Ham was just a hard-working, everyday-type brother. By the time I was eleven, the older boys were always choosing me first for sports. I was good because that's how good I had to get to beat Ham. It was a challenge because of how great an athlete I believe my father was. I can recall him playing in softball leagues and basketball leagues and going to watch him with my brother when we were small. I knew he had ability, but at that time you don't even know what ability is, really. You just know results. I'm six years old, seeing my father beating the breaks off everybody he played. When we were young, he was still young, relatively, and ungodly quick, and *so* strong. They had a night summer basketball league at Jefferson High, and he'd go down there and abuse those dudes, and have people asking us who Ham was, and he'd just laugh and say he was our daddy, say his day was done and he was working two jobs for his family, was an old married man, but he had two young sons, and they'd be back around to Jeff one day soon, to kick tail and take names. Fast as lightning was Ham, and all of five eight. I never let him know how good I thought he was. Couldn't let him know that. But I believed it without thinking of it, the way I believed in the way the sun rose each morning over the San Bernadinos. Ham would open the blinds and say, "Sun shines over here just like it do in Beverly Hills. Let some of the Lord's light in here."

By the time I could beat him, I was already a neighborhood attraction. I was playing on raw ability. Ham watched me mature. He saw us playing pick-up games at the parks and playgrounds, and he often played with us over in them, too. So Ham still might be the greatest competitor I've ever known. He got me my first glove, he got us old tennis balls we taped up, a wooden bat we drove nails into every time we'd crack it. We hit tennis balls until we had to bind 'em with black electrical tape. Never thought at the time it was unusual, being able to knock a cover off a ball.

Ham came home one afternoon ready to hoop with us. I was hitting. I must have been, oh, 10. Hit one pretty good. Jim laid it in there and I hit it. Ham hit his right fist in his left hand like he had on a glove, which he didn't, and faded back, and then he turned and ran, but he still didn't catch the ball on the fly. Jim and I were laughing as he jogged up with the warped tennis ball. He was laughing, too. But different. He looked at me in a way he never had before.

He said, "Boy . . . you're a natural. You are a natural born, son."

I didn't know precisely what that meant, but I did know that generally it was a good thing, being a natural, and I also knew that whatever it was, if my father said it, then it was true. But I had a twinkle in my eye I'm sure as I said, "Izzat anything like a ham, Ham?"

My father laughed. "That's . . . a li'l bit better'n a ham, Ham. But you're still a ham, now."

Even as I grew taller and finally was able to outrun him, Ham never sat at the kitchen table saying, "Keith, you got a chance of going pro." He wasn't stern although he could put something on your behind if he felt you were wrong; he could sling electrical cords, man, he could do that, not as hard as he backed us down under the wire rim on the bedroom door when we were young. Out on the playground, we'd play for hours, until my father got there too. Don't know if you'd call it play. It was fun, but it was work. I know he was playing tired after working a shift at the Boys Market in Hawthorne or the one in Gardena, or at the Center Drug Store. By the time we were 12 he'd play on the other team when we played at the playground. He wouldn't guard me, or usually not even Jim. But if I drove, my father would be there collapsing in the middle, giving me nothing easy—"Turn him, stop his dribble, don't give him room, don't give him room!" It seemed like he had more energy at forty years old than I've ever had in my life. By 14, I was five ten on my way to six three. I took after my mother in some ways. She was tall, coordinated, a looker too, clothes horse, had a closet full of clothes. She was independent. With what I'd gotten from God, Ham, and Shirley, I played. Between 14 and 15, I found I could dunk the basketball. That's when I started to beat Ham, when I could finally outrun and outjump him, being quicker even than he was now.

When I got to be 15, I was able to beat Ham, and that meant I could beat all of them, there in the 'hood. I beat the collapsing defense with a feint, a quick step-through, then rose, and to my joy and surprise I kept going up. I dunked hard, on game point, for the first time. I was thrilled.

"Hey! Hey, Ham! That's what I'm talkin' 'bout!"

Ham's teammates said, "You walked! You *had* to travel! Mr. Davis, didn't he walk?"

My father shook his head, as if to get water out of his ears.

"Naw, I don't think he did that time." That night at the dinner table, I gave it to Ham like he had given it to me. I had always liked him calling me "ham," as in, "You ain't nothing but a ham, pressure will cook a ham." Jim never liked it. But Ham says I always smiled, as if to say, "Good. Challenge me. Make me go higher." Jim and I were different. At each other's throats, although we only physically fought one time. He was a good athlete, an inch shorter than me, even thinner, but in basketball he was a better shooter. I may have had more athletic ability, all-around, but he could stroke it. He had ability. He just didn't apply himself to it as hard as I did, or for as long. He loved to play, but it never became his home away from home. We grew up in that apartment, that three-bedroom apartment. It wasn't large, but it was home. And to me it was a mansion. It was home. My father provided the best furniture he could and my mom wasn't settling for anything less, and she made it cozy. Everybody came to our house. We were close-knit and we did a lot of things together. There were those fish fries every Friday. The adults would get their party on and have Al Green and Marvin Gaye going, and they would have us dancing. But the weekend cookouts always had to come to an end, eventually, and the weeks between them got grimmer as years went by. But there was always sports, athletics, and I was growing ever more talented. Dunking on Ham proved it to me.

"Who's the ham now, Ham?" I said to my father, smiling over my mother's dinner. Ham's smile was faint. Said he didn't sleep well that night. Me, I slept like a rock. Soon I was starring in basketball and baseball at Fremont High in tenth grade. It was so easy with boys my age, after playing all those years with Ham and older boys and men, with my cousin Renard, my friends like Cubby, and friendly rivals, like Byron Scott and Walter Armstrong in basketball, and a lanky first baseman with a looping left-handed swing from over by the Crenshaw district with a funny name:

Strawberry. Darryl. D. Straw.

It quickly became habit, linking up Eric Davis and Darryl Strawberry. It's *been* habit for 25 years. Darryl was from around the way, over west. I knew him ever since we were 11, and Baldwin Hills Park and Recreation Center, my park team, was playing Jesse Owens Park and Recreation, Straw's team, for the Little League title, back in '73. I was playing shortstop at the time (I was an infielder until my second year in the minor leagues). I was leading my squad, playing hard, like Ham taught me, playing on athletic ability, not technique. Wasn't thinking pro. Darryl was playing center, first base sometimes. We knew about Darryl. Hit lefty. A bomber. We'd heard about him already. I guess they knew about us too. Darryl hit a home run that day. Come to think of it, he may have hit two. But we beat the breaks off of 'em, 14–6. What did I do? Well, let's just say they didn't get me out much in Little League, and I think I was in my second year of organized ball with the Reds' organization before I was ever caught stealing a base.

After the game in the handshake line, when Straw and I got to each other, I looked at him, and he looked at me and gave me a goofy smile that makes you smile when you see it. I just said, "Darryl Strawberry, right?" He just said, "Eric Davis, right?" And we slapped palms and moved down the line. Then I heard Straw's voice. "Hey!" I turned around. "See you later?" he asked.

"Definitely," I said, remembering the monster shots he had hit in the game.

And we did. Soon we were playing on the same team; Earl Brown coached the Compton Moose, a Connie Mack team. We had some other good players like Chris Brown, who later played with the Giants, but Straw, he'd always say, "It's me and you, E. We're the ones going." And by that he meant to the major leagues. But Straw and I were very different. Straw lived for it. He lived to make the major leagues. That was life to him. That was reality to him. To me, it was a game. I played baseball because I could play it well, and because I loved to play. Straw always was dreaming of playing in the big leagues. I had no notion of even being drafted at the time.

My mother was the one who took me around to the baseball games in Little League in Baldwin Hills, then to Connie Mark League games in Compton. Ham was busy working. Shirley was the team mother who baked cupcakes, brought the cold drinks for us. I even had a couple of birthday parties at the Baldwin Hill Recreation Center field. I gave my mother the ribbons I won.

In elementary school, the teachers were more hands-on. I was terribly shy when I wasn't at 6606 or on the playground playing ball; I noticed everything—an athlete's eyes and his mind are his greatest secrets, Ham always said that—but I was painfully shy and I think my stuttering was just shyness. It kept me from having to say anything. If you wanted to see my expression, pass me the rock and let's go. Sometimes I wanted to say so much so fast, I just got in the habit of stuttering. Shirley would tell me to slow down, think first. Another person helped me, too, with that and other socialization. My fifth-grade teacher at 66th Street Elementary School became my godmother. Her name is Diane Marshall. She took to me like I was her own son, and she got me to do a lot of different things and motivated me to do a lot *more* things, and I guess she saw a lot of things in me that I didn't even see in myself. Her confidence and that of my siblings and my parents were important. Now my mother had already stressed the value of education to me. Ms. Marshall reinforced that by telling me I had a good mind and could go a long way in athletics, and that was a good combination for a young man to have, and it could take me interesting places where I could learn valuable lessons and help my folks out. I liked the way she talked to me. To have someone else outside my home care that much, especially looking back now, knowing that everybody else saw just another black kid from South Central. She was a white teacher driving in every day, and she said, "You have a chance to do great things, Eric. Greater than even you or I know."

Ms. Diane Marshall lived over by Westwood and would take me over there for tennis lessons. For three years I took tennis lessons from Arthur Ashe. I don't know how Ms. Marshall convinced him to spend so much precious time with a kid like me, but she did, and she'd come and get me every Saturday and we'd spend the day together, and Arthur Ashe would work with me on my groundstrokes and footwork and volleying. I liked spending time with her. She got me my own tennis gear. These were the short-pants days. I was playing in white Daisy Dukes. I thought I looked . . . kinda soft. I was no bigger than an average child my age. I was too macho to stay with it, and I think this disappointed Arthur a little, but he had so many other things going on it probably didn't disappoint him much. He did say I could win at tennis. Mostly it was gratifying because Ms. Marshall was proud of me, and I was able to participate in something outside of the sports that a kid like me was supposed to play. I dropped tennis, but until this day, I see Ms. Marshall. I've never asked her why she did those things for me, but she saw something in me, she said.

I went to Bethune Junior High School. My elementary school was just a block away from home, and Bethune was four blocks away. By the time I got to junior high, it was on. It was the first time I'd gone to a school where I didn't know everybody, had to blend in. Initially, I felt I had to establish myself athletically, which was tough, because everyone would rather get their props that way and not have to deal with the alternatives. I quickly discovered that the teachers didn't care as much as they did in elementary school. It was more of a business. I quickly established myself as one of the leaders at Bethune. I always was a leader. My brother was a year ahead of me and he made it easier for me. Both my brother and my sister established themselves before I got there, so when I came along people said, "That's Sharletha's little brother; you know Sharletha, the one who likes to hang with low riders. Low riders only. Oh, that's Jimmy's little brother, you know Jimmy, he hoops on the team, a little undercover gangster" (this last part made me frown). I was the baby boy, so they paved the way for me, and I continued to play all the sports, so I was way cool.

By the time I was in high school, it was *really* on. Jefferson High, one of Fremont High's big rivals, was prone to fighting after the city league games because they usually lost, so they were well practiced at fighting. Then the Crips came up out of Washington High, and they didn't fight, they shot. And we were in Hoover 'hood—Hoover Crips territory. That's where we were. We had to keep living. My father and mother and sister and brother and my God-given ability shielded me from the violence to a degree. Through all that, my father worked the same two jobs a combined total of 57 years—37 on one, 20 on the other. Not making enough to move us away yet never so little to do without. I think I'll probably never be able to thank him enough for that. So as far as showing up for work goes, being professional about going to work, doing the work, or working in a hostile environment, I have no excuses. I come to the post. Every day.

I may have been five ten, 140 pounds soaking wet in the ninth grade. The ninth-graders played the faculty in football and I scored five touchdowns. But I was going to Fremont to hoop and play baseball. I played varsity basketball, started at point guard. We went to the city semifinals against Crenshaw at the L.A. Sports Arena, and that was a very big deal for a tenth-grader. Even for me.

The baseball coach's name at Fremont was William Dickson—he was the junior varsity coach prior to me coming to Fremont

BORN TO PLAY / 39

for my sophomore year. The guy who coached Chet Lemon and all them at Fremont was Chuck Arwine. He had resigned, I suppose because he didn't think any more talent was coming through Fremont. A lot of talent already had. Fremont was the baseball powerhouse in the city league of L.A. We had Chili Davis, who'd become a longtime, veteran big-league switch-hitter, with power to all fields, one of the '98–'99 Yankees, a stand-up kind of guy, and a class act. And yet, Chili Davis couldn't even make the starting varsity at Fremont, so he transferred over to Dorsey High. Fremont High was where Chet Lemon, George Hendrick, Bobby Tolan of the Big Red Machine, Bob Watson, William Crawford, and Danny Ford, all legit, productive big leaguers, came before me and played. Gene Mauch, the manager, went to Fremont.

I went out for baseball cold. Coach Dickson had no idea who I was. But that was all right. I figured he would pretty soon. But he fooled me. He told me I couldn't even try out for the varsity baseball team, that he couldn't waste his time with a basketball player, and to go down to the JV field. Meanwhile, I see two guys out there that played Little league with me all the way through in Baldwin Hills and I knew they couldn't play better than me. They were on varsity as tenth-graders, and you're going to tell me I've got to play JV? So I went down to the JV field for one day. Took batting practice—and disrupted the varsity practice. I'm trying to reach that varsity field with a line drive on every swing, and accomplishing it more than a few times. They're all going, "Look out!" "Heads up!" "Who's that?" I went home upset. Ham asked why. I said they wouldn't let me try for varsity. Coach said I was a basketball player. Said only real baseball players played for Fremont.

I told Jim, "I'm not playing baseball, then." But he knew me, so he said "Okay, Keith, if you don't want to play, don't play. But you can *play* some baseball, bro."

My brother talked to Coach Dickson the next day without my knowledge. I don't know what he said, but after that and batting practice the day before, when I went back out there—I was just *drawn* to the baseball field—coach not only had me with var, he had my game gear.

Coaches Arwine and Dickson coached pretty much all those players I named, all those major leaguers who came before me at Fremont High, but none of those guys ever came back, and me being so young, not knowing, having coaches telling me about these guys, and watching them only a little—most of them were in the big leagues at that time, or just leaving—I didn't care about them because I couldn't see them. Okay, they went to my school. So what? Where are they now? Can't they see what's happening here? Don't they know I'm here? And I vowed to myself at that time that if I made it, I would come back to at least let the next Eric Davis know who I was. And I have. I donate uniforms, and I go back. I let them see me. I know they still play baseball over there. They know who I am and deserve to see me because I'm an alum, and maybe seeing me will be all it takes to have them visualize a different future than the one they think is in store.

I played third base my sophomore year at Fremont. Big Mark Fulcher, six four, 230 pounds, was playing shortstop. Great athlete. His little brother, David Fulcher, was later a big free safety who played in the 1989 Super Bowl with the Cincinnati Bengals. Mark made him look little. Coach Dickson said he sent me down to JV the first day because he didn't want me to be big-headed, but I've never had a big head. I just always wanted to play at the top level. I always considered the top level to be my level. I've never been overly cocky but I've always been totally confident. Took me a long time to realize that baseball is a game of hierarchy, and a lot of times it's just not about ability. Having too much ability can be trouble. But I just always wanted to show what I've got, what God gave me. I didn't, couldn't, see that as being some kind of sin, the fact that I could play. In basketball, I was dribbling, passing the ball, scoring, eventually averaging 14 points a game my junior year, with Dane Suttle and another guy getting most of the shots, and my brother, another senior, playing behind me. I never really thought about it at the time; I always knew Jim Bean was proud of me, but the fact is, he was the older brother, and he was backing me up, he was my caddy, he was the one giving me a blow when I needed a little rest. We started 15–2 my junior year when I was running point, but then Coach Sullivan said he didn't want anybody shooting but the two stars, and that sort of put a damper on it for me. I went through the motions in some practices until coach said, "You can go home if you want," and I told him, "I was waiting for you to say that—I can go play baseball," and I left. Fremont lost three straight games, including one to Crenshaw, which had Walter Armstrong coming off the bench. My brother got more playing time. That part of it was good. I could've stayed out, but the players were coming by the house. I asked Jim Bean what I should do. Even though he was playing more with me gone, he said, "You know what I think, Keith? I think you should play. Who's better?"

So I came back and played. And at the end of the season, seven schools from out in the valley were coming to our house, asking me to transfer out, including Kennedy High, where the big seven-foot center, Stuart Gray, who would go to UCLA, was a senior. My brother had graduated and gotten a basketball scholarship to a small school, Northern Nazarene, in Idaho. I didn't want to get up early and go out to the valley. People said I was crazy to stay at Fremont. But I did stay. I averaged 29.2 points a game my senior year. The basketball player I admired growing up was Walt Frazier. He had the classiest game in the NBA at that time to me, back in the early and mid-seventies. All you heard were good things about him. I liked his demeanor. I wore number 10 in high school because of Walt Frazier. But I never got a chance to *watch* much baseball. Baseball was a game I grew to love by *playing,* not watching. Maybe that's why my style of doing things is unique, individual. I never really copied anybody. Ham held his hands in front of him and kind of low when he hit in softball. So did Muhammad Ali when he boxed. I liked Ali. I loved Ham.

Ham expected me to play well and didn't think much of it otherwise, until the baseball scouts started calling for me when I was in the tenth grade. I can remember the first time Larry Barton Jr. of the Reds called my house, wanting me to play on one of their winter teams. My father said, in a vacant voice, that would be fine by him as long as it was fine by me, and then he hung up. He looked at me in a way he hadn't done since I hit that ball over his head in the street five years before. I guess it dawned on him that he'd been the first one who said, "Hey, this boy is a natural." It was then Ham could really see it, when scouts from the Reds were calling his house for his 15-year-old son to play against local college teams. My father probably still thinks I could've been a college basketball star, or even an NBA player. Since my brother hooped at Fremont High, and had gotten a basketball scholarship to Northern Nazarene up in Idaho, Ham probably thought I was going to hoop my way through college, too. He never saw me play organized baseball until I was a bona fide big leaguer, a *real* Cincinnati Red, playing at Dodger Stadium, in 1984.

Athletic competition at the high school level in L.A. was fierce and raw. Butch Johnson, the ex–Dallas Cowboy receiver, went to Dorsey High. Sparky Anderson went there. Warren Moon went to Hamilton. Freeman Williams, a star basketball player, went to Manual Arts. Back in the day, Paul Blair, the Orioles center fielder, went to Manual Arts as well. James Lofton, Green Bay Packer wide receiver, went to Washington. When I came through, Ralph Jackson, UCLA guard, and Byron Scott, Laker guard, went to Inglewood, Morningside. Jay Humphries. Kenny Fields was at Verbum Dei, near Watts, where Roy Hamilton and David Greenwood went; they went to UCLA, later played in the NBA. Crenshaw was a new school when I was getting ready to come through the preps. Wendell Tyler, the UCLA, Rams, and 49ers running back, went there. As far as Fremont goes, Ricky Bell, the USC and Tampa Bay Bucs tailback, had gone there. Just as pivotal, Ricardo Sims had gone to Washington

High. Ricardo Sims was the big Crip. *The* O.G. Ham asked if we wanted to transfer to the valley after schools called 6606 with promises of this and that. You could bus out. There was good competition out there too. John Elway, Jay Schroeder, Grenada Hills, Pacific Palisades, respectively. Darren Daye, Stuart Gray, heading to UCLA for basketball, were then playing in the valley too. Ham asked if I wanted to go, said they had better equipment, better fields out there. He didn't say it would be an easier battle. Just a different battle.

Like I said—Jefferson High was an "if we can't win the game we'll win the fight" school. The Crips came up around Washington High, and they recruited as hard as the scouts from valley high schools and Division 1-A colleges. If you weren't good, or lucky . . . the Crips, they got their share, too. Yeah, they did. Even sometimes when the player had ability. I had something else. I could always say, "I'll go home" and mean it. I had a home to go to.

By the time the spring of '80 rolled around, we were graduating from high school, Darryl from Crenshaw High, me from Fremont. Straw may have been the premier ballplayer in greater L.A., and that was saying a mouthful. In hoop, I finished second in the city in scoring to Sam Potter, who went to Cal. Played L.A. High the last game of my senior year. Sam was averaging 29.6 points a game and I was averaging 29.2. He'd scored 28 points in his last game, and I needed to score 40 to be leading scorer in the city. I scored 21 in the first quarter—then L.A. High quit. Their coach took them off the court. He felt the calls were going against them. They forfeited the game, and so I lost the scoring title to Sam Potter, and ended my basketball career. I thought it was funny. Baseball season was around the corner. I wondered if Sam was going to play baseball. The last I heard, he went up to Berkeley on a basketball scholarship.

I'd started playing with the Reds' winter team when I was in tenth grade. The Reds had a scout team that played UCLA, USC, Cal-State Fullerton, junior colleges in Southern California. We were like young princes of the diamond. Joe Price, who later pitched for the Reds and Giants, was on that team. Frank Pastore, who pitched in the big leagues, was with us. It was a stay-in-shape thing for some of us, but also an opportunity for high school players to use wooden bats, and it was a *great* opportunity for a lean brown kid like me to be known, because I didn't come out of the valley. But I never looked at it as an opportunity to get *drafted*. Coming from inner-city L.A., who knows about the amateur baseball draft? I sure didn't. What are the chances of a skinny city kid who plays hoop with such a vengeance and so well getting drafted by the big leagues?

It wasn't until my senior year that it began to hit me full force—that this would be my life. Scouts were coming not only to all the games but our practices. Coach Dickson told me to stay at home on draft day. "They'll call you at home," he said. I believed him, because by then people had timed me, pinched me, poked me, prodded me. Mike Brito of the Dodgers had timed me over 60 yards, got me in 6.36, said they'd take me for sure. Fed me steaks downtown. First round for sure, probably, Mike said. Then Darryl Strawberry, Crenshaw High, was taken number one in the first round, the number one pick in all the United States, by the Mets. Then the rest of the first round passed. Then the second, the third, and fourth rounds went by. I went back to school. Coach Dickson shrugged it off. The first day ends with six rounds. I wasn't taken. Darryl, on the other hand, had already been in *Sports Illustrated*. Sometimes I think he wanted it so bad he just willed it to happen—but it was probably more a case of good advance pub. I was just . . . a guy. Really, at this point I thought they wouldn't take me at all, even though Straw hit .490 his senior year, while I hit .635. If you're true, real, bona fide big-league material, they can hardly get you out at all in high school, anyway.

I was at home when Larry Barton Jr. called and said the Reds had taken me on the eighth round. The lower the round, the less money you get as a signing bonus. I said "Okay," a little bit confused. I wanted to be happy and I *was* happy, but I was also ignorant about what I was getting myself into. He ended up coming by my house. Now Larry's walking back and forth, and Ham and Shirley are there on the couch, having been polite and offered the visitor something to drink, and now not knowing anything either. Cincinnati then offered $15,000 for their son's services as a ballplayer. Fifteen large was a bunch of money then. I thought, "Pepperdine wants me for basketball, a few schools in the Northwest, too. But fifteen thousand dollars!" I asked Ham and Shirley what they thought, and they told me it was my life. "Whatever decision you make, stick it out, and we'll back you one hundred percent," Ham said. "Do what's in your heart," said Shirley. All that talking must have got them up to 20,000. I thought I might not get a chance to make 20 grand in one whop again. That was about as much as Ham made at Boys in a year. I signed. "Nice handwriting," said Larry. I nodded in the direction of my mother, and she beamed.

It was a very big moment. It defined the rest of my life. That moment is the reason you're holding this book right now. I had never been happier, to tell you the truth, but looking back on it, I'd have to say I'd always been happy, there in South Central L.A. My parents and relatives were responsible for the security I felt, them as much as me being what Ham called a natural. It was the proudest moment of my life up to that time—having that pen in my hand, three adults watching, caring which way I'd go, two of them my parents. To have an occupation where one day I might be able to do something for them. To be graduating high school, and having my brother, Jim, playing college hoop up in Idaho. I was thinking, "Bean, he'll handle the basketball end from now on, in a professional sense, but I'll always be able to beat him." I was recalling wearing his orange-and-black college uniform to practice, atop the cardinal and gray of Fremont, wearing those old-school Dr. J Converse sneakers my brother sent me, and having an article in my pocket about how he had scored 27 points and was a tournament MVP up there. Now I had my own path, playing professional baseball with the Big Red Machine, the Cincinnati Reds. I was just . . . very proud.

Later, in what would have been my sophomore year in college, a freshman from North Carolina, Michael Jordan, hit a jump shot to win Dean Smith's first national championship at the Louisiana Superdome in the spring of '82. By then, I was in Cedar Rapids, Iowa, learning the craft the hard way. In those lean years, I watched as Byron Scott, Jay Humphries—all my home boys I'd played against—and Michael Jordan had stellar college careers, then went to the NBA. I could've been there with them, I felt, but I was lying on a funky, lumpy mattress in a fleabag hotel down in a small minor-league town, tossing up a tobacco tin, juggling the tin and two baseballs, wondering when I would get the call to the major leagues. Now that I'm older, seen the top end, those guys have been winnowed out of the NBA, and I don't think about it as much—not until I see Michael playing. I would've liked to have tried my luck against him. I would've liked to have competed.

My mother was about to open a restaurant in Long Beach. S & G Southern Kitchen. She'd cooked for so many for so long, she was in the habit. The two biggest mouths she had to feed were gone. She took an insurance settlement and opened a restaurant. Ham didn't like her going to work outside the home. They had argued about it, thinking I hadn't heard them, but I had.

My father said, "If you're gonna play, then play." I can't remember who took me to the airport the next day for the flight north, to my new life. My brother didn't take me. He was trying to get back home before I left, but we missed each other. Life had already changed up on me, without me fully realizing it yet. So I left L.A. for rookie ball in Eugene, Oregon, the very next day, after I signed the contract, in the spring of 1980. For the next four years, I'd be in the bushes. Eugene, Cedar Rapids, Wichita, Waterbury, Indianapolis. My brother never went back to Idaho.

I wish he had, now.

THREE / SPRING 1983

ADVERSITY/BLESSING

Apprentice

STRATEGY/LIFE LESSON

Pay Attention, Learn Patience

The spring of '83 was my first real spring with the big club, the Cincinnati Reds, the Big Red Machine, or what was left of it by then. Flew down to Tampa, down to Al Lopez Field, where big Klu, Ted Kluszewski, stood suited up and sleeveless, those guns of his folded across his chest. He wasn't blinking. I knew he knew who I was, or who I was supposed to be, and I knew he didn't care. He'd hit 49 bombs in one season in the '50s. Wasn't by accident. That's what he *did*, that was his level. Cincinnati had a model of what a home-run hitter looked like. Now here I come, six three, 165 pounds soaking wet, and supposed to be a bomber? No wonder some older coaches couldn't believe in me. Not that I thought of it that way then. I just thought nobody believed in me.

When I asked Ham for advice during my time in the minor leagues, he couldn't give me baseball answers. He couldn't say, "Son, Donnie Baylor was built like a man at age 19, and MVP of every minor league he played in, and it took four years for Baltimore to bring him up. Same with Bobby Grich. Usually, if he's gonna make it, a really big if, a guy will make it up between the ages of 23 and 25, as an everyday player. Pitchers can do it sooner." There are a lot of sons of ex-big leaguers in the major leagues, but I'm not one of them. Ham couldn't explain or help me with the politics and realities of baseball because he was not part of that world. What he had given me would have to be enough. So I come to work every day, play hard, go home, play with my girls after they were born. I learned the routine from Ham when growing up, but it got me in trouble. Baseball people thought I wasn't a "good guy," a bootlicker. I didn't understand the politics of it. The minors are to show you how the game is played. I didn't realize what I was going through. I thought I was unwanted.

Sherrie says I have a hard shell but a soft center. Even if it's true I wasn't admitting it in the spring of '83 when I checked my awe in Tampa to do what I had to do—make the big leagues after three years in the minors. Not just make it, but be a vital cog of a new Big Red Machine. Just to have an opportunity to put that major-league uniform on, being surrounded by Johnny Bench, Dan Driessen, Dave Concepcion, Mario Soto, Tom Hume, Tony Perez, Ken Griffey Sr. Just walking into that clubhouse. I'm a confident individual, but when you walked into that clubhouse for the first time, you were to be seen, not heard, and you knew that. Couldn't talk the way these kids do today. They would've had you in a basket. That's just how serious it was—your respect for what they had accomplished on the field. It had to be done on the field. Until you did something in the big leagues you were seen, not heard, and they made that statement quickly to you. Just watching these guys, the way they went about their business—it was all like a dream come true, for me.

When I grew up in L.A. in the '70s, the big leagues were all about the Dodgers and the Reds. When I was a teenager and in high school, it was the era of the Big Red Machine in the National League, and the Dodgers were in the National League, so L.A. was Dodgertown. But I always liked the Reds—don't know if it was that I liked them or I figured they were my destiny. Bobby Tolan could hit. He went to Fremont High. Played with the Reds. Bench, Perez, Morgan, Rose, Griffey, Driessen, Concepcion, Geronimo, Foster—man, what a squad! The Dodgers put in some work in the '70s, too, and the A's and Yankees, but the Reds were *the* powerhouse team, to me, back when I played against Straw for the city Little League championship at Baldwin Hills. The Reds were who I saw, who started scouting me in the tenth grade, who played me with their "winter league" team in southern California at age 15, who I wanted to prove myself with and be a part of.

After years of seeing those players, all of a sudden I'm in the same uniform. Overwhelming. I respected them. I respected the game, but mostly I respected them—the men, the ones who played. And I respected what they accomplished. That's why it was overwhelming. If I didn't respect them, it wouldn't have felt overwhelming physically. Physically I said, "I can do this. God gave me this."

They gave me number 55. I was doing the speed limit. On the back: DAVIS. Broad letters.

Felt good. I was in heaven. But I was also intimidated at first.

I'd gone up to Eugene, Oregon, in 1980, after I signed. It was a double dose of culture shock. Learned to put a pinch between my gum and my lip and put the tin cup of smokeless tobacco in my back pocket. I was young. It was something I could do to fit in. Tobacco was and still is a big part of baseball. Smoking or smokeless, it's out there. Everybody has experience with it of some kind or another, maybe because it's a time killer. Also a lung and lip killer, but it's still there, in the culture. Don't know why. But I felt that was one of the things I could do to fit in. So I did it.

It didn't help all that much, though. I still came within a

phone call of quitting in 1981 because they sent me to an extended spring, which meant I was going back to rookie league and manager Jim Hoff, who appeared to me to seriously hate my guts. I was playing shortstop at this time. Wore number 3, after wearing number 6 at Fremont. I'd broken my right hand my first year in big-league camp, just before spring training started in '83. The Reds had the "winter league" team in California. All youths in the Reds' organization played. Your body, no matter how athletic, has to be conditioned to playing baseball everyday, especially your hands and your eyes. Your hands have to be toughened up. Your eyes have to be conditioned to the speed of the ball off the bat, the speed of the pitches you are going to try to hit out of the ballpark. Your mind has to be conditioned, too. And any way you look at it, it can be dangerous out there. I had a cast on after breaking a bone in my hand, a spiral fracture. I went down to Florida that spring and ripped the cast off myself. Swore I wouldn't mess it up, wouldn't do anything.

My manager in extended spring was this Jim Hoff gentleman. He was a militant kind of guy, except his militancy was that he didn't like players from California. "Pretty boys from California," he'd say. The weather was too good, we had it too easy, he said. The weather *is* good in southern California, good for baseball year-round, so that is where the high draft picks come from. People envy that. Plus I'm black, sticking out in the boonies, 18 years old. I couldn't process all that stuff. So I just thought, "This man doesn't like me," and that was it, which was probably true and probably irrelevant. Take what the man has to show you and move on. I wasn't gonna be in rookie ball forever. Sometimes it seemed like forever then and patience is something I have more of only now.

Baseball is a game where farm boys, country boys, city guys, rich guys, poor guys, little guys, big guys, beggars, thieves all compete and are thrown together. But the minors are straight good ol' boy, occasionally flat-out redneck. The Reds sent me back to extended spring. I was playing shortstop in Florida and hitting about .440 at the time. I had seven or eight home runs in two weeks. I felt I was the best player down there. They say you keep going until you reach your level of competition. That's what I wanted to do. Straw was in the big leagues by the spring of '83.

I always compared myself not to Straw or my teammates but to the players who played my position on the other clubs. If we played against the Cardinal organization, I was going to be the best shortstop out there. And I'm just beating them all up. But no matter what I did, Hoff always criticized me. I hit a home run to left-center field off the Expos. I mean I crushed it. My blood was pumping and I rounded the sacks and the fellows high-fived me and this man came to me and told me, "That pitch was away; you shoudda taken it to right field." I'm sitting there, stunned, thinking, "I just crushed it 450 feet to left center for a tater and he's telling me I shoudda hit to right?" Stuff like that kept happening, and being young, I felt like giving up. I might steal second base, have it not even be close, not close to being close. And Hoff tells me I got a bad jump. "You got to work on your jumps." So I'm sitting there saying "Why is this dude tripping on me?" I'm 18, 19 years old and I have no perspective. I hadn't accomplished anything back then. But I was burning to do it, and when I did it, or felt I was doing it, it seemed as though I was knocked down. At the time, I was upset about a lot of stuff. Packed my gear, called Ham to tell him I was coming home. He talked me out of it.

Ham said, "Maybe he's trying to test your character. You know, trying to see if you're going to break." Ham turned it around for me, eventually made me see it was another test, like work. He said, "You don't know Hoff's agenda; don't take it that he doesn't like you. Take it as though he might be trying to see if you're strong mentally." But also there was not the same home to go back to. My parents had separated. My father might not have known baseball, but he knew it was the best thing I had. In the off-season, Ham and I were staying at 6606 Denver.

My mother had moved out to Orange County, so had my sister, and my brother spent a lot of time out there, too. My brother could cook almost as well as my mother, and he worked for her at the S&G Southern Kitchen. I stuck it out with my father. It happens. You don't want to choose, but you do. I stayed with Ham at 6606, my brother went back and forth, stayed in the streets a lot. The Hoover Crips were becoming a second family to him. My brother wasn't at home much anymore, out hanging with his boy Chris Tyaska, but also the Hoover Crips. Something was up in the streets, something called crack, or 'base, and my brother was out there in it, to get paid. Living a life he didn't have to live. My dad didn't know exactly what Jim was doing, just knew something was wrong. Looking back, my brother was as hurt by my parents' breakup as I was. We just handled it different. I took my frustrations out on a baseball. He'd already been down to the county lockup a couple of times by then. It had already started. Ham asked what was going on, could he help? My brother said he had gotten into it, and he would get out of it. Ham didn't mention this to me. I was making $600 a month in A ball. Didn't have money. When the meat man came through the neighborhood, it was a sizable investment for me and Ham to spend 20 dollars cash for 10 frozen steaks, T-bones—thin as shoe soles, but T-bones. We'd have 'em marked. Two for Wednesday, two for Sunday. A package might last three weeks that way. One day I came in from working out. I sniffed the air. The smell in the apartment made my mouth water, like only my mother or my brother made it smell. I went in the kitchen and Jim Bean is in there firing up steaks, and sitting there wolfing them down is . . . the Jackson 5?! Well, Randy Jackson, anyway, and his friend. My brother was the sort who could know you in five minutes. How he had met Randy Jackson, I don't know. I know Randy Jackson was sitting in my house eating my and Ham's steaks. I was excited—"You . . . say, you *are* Randy Jackson, you *are!*" But, at the same time, these were the only decent provisions my father and I had. Jim Bean could go out to Orange County, to S&G Southern Kitchen, where I wasn't going, and eat. He was taking food out of our mouths. Everything had been taken from us. Didn't he understand anything?

I got mad. "Bean, what you doing, man? Me and Ham gotta live off them steaks."

"Hey man, he was hungry."

"Bean, they the *Jackson Five*, man. They're rich." Jim Bean kept cooking, and the more he ignored me the madder I got, and suddenly, for the first and only times in our lives, Jim and I were fighting. I don't even remember Ham coming in, trying to get between us. He says he did anyway, but I didn't even feel him. We were in our early twenties now, Jim and I, strong, and Ham was in his forties, and tired from work. We were going at it hard until I heard my father say, "Look! Look here I say!" and we turned around with each other in a death grip and my father had his pistol out. That stopped us. "You boys are too big for me to be trying to fight," he said quietly. "Quit it!"

"But Ham, them was our steaks!" I said hotly.

"Yeah, they were," my father said.

"But you *know* you said if people were hungry and they came over to your house, it wasn't right not to feed them!" Jim Bean yelled.

"Yeah, I did say that," my father said.

You know the movie *Boyz N the Hood*, and the father, Furious Styles? Very realistic in terms of firearms being prevalent in the 'hood. You have to be able to defend your door when 911 won't answer. Jim and I weren't upset that Ham had pulled his gun. So that was the situation at home. And now I had to deal with this Jim Hoff telling me I couldn't play when I knew very well that I could.

"Everything good I do, he's got something bad to say about it, Ham."

"I know."

"I'm the best player on the team."

"I know. But don't quit now, Keith. It might just be they want to see if you'll quit."

"They're *about* to. I'll come home. I mean, this man is just constantly on me."

"So they make you quit, not 'cause you can't play, but because of what somebody says?"

"Make *me* quit?"

So, over the phone, Ham talked me out of quitting organized baseball. "Come home to what?" he asked. He told me to give it another couple of weeks. I said I could come home and still get a basketball scholarship. "All right," he said, sighing, "if that's what you want. Just give it a couple more weeks." He wasn't particular about me coming home. Hoff was still trying to get me released as far as I was concerned, and probably would have preferred if I was some big corn-fed guy who reminded him of himself. But you know, contrary to popular myth, baseball ain't all cornfields. I couldn't help who I was and where I came from. I didn't want to help it. I grew up *liking* who I was. The game is between the ball, the bat, and the glove; they don't care what kind or color hands are holding them, what part of town they came from. Some guys in the minors care. I can't tell you how many times a minor-league coach said that he would've made it if only for this guy, that guy; if it hadn't been for Morgan or Lou Whitaker, he would've made it. After I'd been a big leaguer 10 years, it dawned on me. Those coaches just didn't have big-league ability. If you have big-league ability, no player will keep you out of the majors, even if he has more ability than you. Because there's more than one job available at your position. Say you're an outfielder, the fifth best outfielder in the Cincinnati system, big leagues on down. There are a hundred other outfield jobs in the big leagues. You can play—just not in Cincinnati. If you can play, you can play; they'll find you. That's why they make trades. Some career coaches in the minor leagues pretend otherwise. Some of them accept it and are there to teach the game the best they know how to young guys who come with big-league ability. Those are the kind of coaches you want to have.

What I didn't understand then was the intricate pathway of making the big leagues. They don't just have VACANCY signs hanging out. For every job, there are several veterans already up there, or up and down, and bonus babies, and if a rookie comes up and makes it, that means death for somebody who is already a big leaguer. Usually what happens is a regular gets hurt, you're in position to come up and get some run, and then you play so well you can't be sent down again, or somebody else claims you, in time. Sometimes it's the politics, trades get made, seems like you'll never come up. I understand that's probably why Greg Riddock, now a coach with the Tampa Bay Devil Rays, my manager in Eugene, changed me to the outfield, back in '81. Playing the outfield meant a greater likelihood of injury, but there's only one shortstop per major league roster, plus a utility infielder who can play short. At the same time, there are four outfielders on each big-league roster—sometimes five. Riddock said the Reds were going to release me—said Hoff didn't think I could play. Greg told Hoff, "Don't release him. Send him to me and let's try him in the outfield."

I felt I'd shown I can play, but I went back to Eugene a second year. Riddock asked, "Ever play outfield before?" I said, "No." He said, "Okay," then he handed me a big outfielder's glove and said, "Let's see what you can do in the pasture." He put me in left. Anthony Walker was playing center. Second game of the season he blew out his hamstring. That's how it happens, how you get a shot. Riddock put me in center. Didn't take me long to figure out the angles, throws, backup plays, the way the ball comes off the bat from there. It's like playing big shortstop. For the rest of my career in the Cincinnati system, that's where I was, in center, when healthy. For a while, in the '80s, I didn't take a backseat to anybody as a center fielder. For that '81 season in A ball in Eugene, I got comfortable in the field, stole 40 bags in 60 games. (You play 60 games in rookie ball.) I had 39 ribbies, hit 11 homers, scored 67 runs—over one a game—and hit .322.

In 1982 I went to A ball in Cedar Rapids, Iowa. I hit 16 home runs. The playing was fine, but the downtime in Cedar Rapids was hard for me. I was making $700 a month, so it wasn't like I was going on pleasure excursions. I had gone to a wedding in L.A. during the winter of '82 and met a fine young lady, a well-raised young lady, and I felt like I was getting some rhythm from her even though she was playing hard to get. Her name was Sherrie. Sherrie Brewer. She was from L.A., too. Her parents had been born and raised in Arkansas. I thought she was all that and a bag of chips. Very much so. A lot of my $700 ended up at the phone company that season. One thing about being in Cedar Rapids—there wasn't anything to do but play ball and call Sherrie. Oh yeah, there was a slaughterhouse nearby. It gave the area a certain bouquet. There was a nice ballpark, voted the best minor league ballpark every year for years and years. The Annies who turned out there were not tempting, especially now that I'd met Sherrie and she was playing it kind of cool on me.

I had been named MVP in 1981 in Eugene, then was twice named Player of the Week while playing in Cedar Rapids in '82. That minor-league season I hit five triples, 20 doubles, and 15 home runs in 453 at-bats, limped in (for me) at .276, but stole 53 bases in 65 attempts, then 30 out of 32 in the Florida Instructional League. I was ready to do some serious damage in 1983.

Walking onto Al Lopez Field, I was scared, frankly. First to have the opportunity to put that major-league uniform on for the first time. Then being surrounded by big leaguers, and being all of 20 years old at the time. Johnny Bench. Dan Driessen. Dave Concepcion. Tony Perez wasn't there right then, but within the next couple of years he would be, as coach or manager. Watching these veteran Reds go about their business was like a dream come true to me. Showed me how to carry myself, how to approach the game. I studied their every twitch. I've always believed in myself, since my days playing with Jim and Ham, then with Straw and the high school athletes I competed with in L.A. It wasn't physically intimidating. I already could do what any everyday major leaguer could do, in a physical sense. I ran fast, I jumped high, I hit the ball hard, sometimes out of the ballpark. I was what they call a "five-tool player," a guy who could run, catch, throw, hit, and hit for power. But it was mentally intimidating to me. I'd just come out of AA ball. And these guys were messing with my head. Half of it is initiation. Half is probably fear. Fear of losing their jobs to a talented youngster like that number 55, that ghetto superstar. Whatever you want to see. I was at full height now, six three, but still weighed only about a buck sixty-five. Thin and hard as a rail.

That spring training I was the coffee boy, the coffee fetcher, the errand-runner, the butt of some jokes. Some guys get looked at and asked, "What are you doing here, worm?" Some guys, if their skills are borderline and their confidence is likewise, that's all it takes to get rid of them. Most guys gut it out. Most still don't make the major leagues, but most gut it out until somebody suggests they would be better off finding another line of work. I had skills. I could run. According to the vets, this meant I had to lead and win in every wind sprint. Couldn't lag behind. I didn't get hit with pranks as other guys did. Guess I had a look like I wasn't having too much of that but I was trying to keep the open-mouthed awe off my face. If they only knew. I was scared. Nobody put shaving cream in my shoes or gave me a Three-Man Lift. That's where a big strong veteran bets a rookie that he can pick up three guys. Nobody's that strong, the rookie thinks. So the rook is told he's the middle man, to make his body as rigid as possible. Two other guys (vets, which should make rookies suspicious) get on either side. "How much you weigh, rook?" "I weigh 205." "Good, then you and so-and-so and so-and-so are a combined 600 pounds. You get in the middle 'cause you're strong, bein' so young and all." The veteran sells the rookie the setup, then the other two guys hold him by the arms and ankles so he can't move. Gotta be rigid, so the veteran can pick up all three guys, see. Two guys hold him, then the veteran is joined by the other veterans and they pour anything they can get their hands on—shaving cream, beer, potato salad, baby powder—all over the rookie, who's being held by the other two veterans and can't get away.

Never had a Three-Man Lift done to me. Caught a few hot-foots, some bubble-gum beanie propellers, cut neckties, but not much worse. They missed me with a shaving-cream pie. Too quick.

I played well that spring in Tampa. I was 20 years old and feeling I was about to do something good. That was when Darryl went up to the Mets, and he and the Mets were the talk of ball. I'm thinking, "You're supposed to be up there, too." Now I'm not thinking that I won't make the big club. I'm thinking, "Who else besides me is going to make it, and can they help us beat the Dodgers, the Giants, and the Mets?" I hit a few bombs in spring training. When Pete Rose came back from playing in Montreal, he'd say, "Kid, if you keep your nose clean, you're gonna be good." This is *Pete Rose* telling me this. I was believing it. I kept playing well. Then Vern Rapp, the manager of the big club, called me in one day and said, "I'd like to send you out to Wichita. You're the best player we got right now. You're the best outfielder we got by far. Go down to Triple-A and get some games in, and if something happens, you're gonna be the first one we call."

I reported to the Triple-A camp the next day. The camps are close together. Triple-A camp is by the big-league camp, the way it was set up in Florida, so I didn't have that far to go. When I got over there, they didn't have my name on the Triple-A roster. Roy Hartsfield looked me over, blinked, and said, "You're not on my roster. You probably want to check the Double-A roster."

"The manager of the big club told me to report to Triple-A," I said.

"Well, like I say, you're not on my roster. So . . ."

It was like I had just showed up from one of the local high schools, asking for a tryout. It was like back at Fremont High when I first showed up at varsity practice and Coach Dickson turned up his nose at me and sent me down to the JV field. Pete Rose was telling me I could be great if I kept my nose clean, and Vern Rapp was telling me I was going to be the first one called to the big club if something happened, but Hartsfield, the Triple-A manager, acted like he didn't know who I was. That confused me. So I reported to the Double-A camp. The manager there was Jimmy Lett. The Double-A club played in Waterbury, Connecticut. The Triple-A was in Indianapolis, a short haul from Cincinnati, but still a universe away from Riverfront Stadium and the bigs, which is where I wanted to be, helping some of the great Reds as they aged, while they filled me up with knowledge of the major leagues. If I waited too long, they'd all be gone. Joe Morgan was gone already. Wait too long, and by the time I got there—*if* I ever got there—it would be all young guys like me and Paul O'Neill, Kal Daniels, Kurt Stillwell, Barry Larkin, Rob Dibble, the young, raw talent coming into the Cincinnati system. I hadn't learned that unless somebody got hurt or traded and you got in there and put up numbers, you weren't coming up until the brass was ready for you to come up. Didn't have anything to do with being ready. Might be a Triple-A spot was reserved for a guy who'd been in the minors a long time, couldn't "take" a demotion to Double-A. Maybe they needed a place to park me and some guys for a while. No need to explain anything to me.

I was about to be 21. They figured I was young and strong enough to take it. No one told me that players usually make it up between the ages of 23 and 25. My heart is beating faster because I need to know where I belong, or where I'm going, at least. So I go and ask Lett, What's going on? Where'm I supposed to be? The big-league skipper told me to report to Triple-A. The Triple-A skipper acted as if he never heard of me. Lett told me he didn't have me on his roster either. If they are trying to confuse me, it's working. It's not like I've been playing bad. I've been playing very well. Catching everything, hitting the ball hard, out of the ballpark. Somehow I got on the agenda of the big powwow that evening with all the managers. And Rapp said, "Okay, it's decided you're going to be on the Double-A roster." Sometimes you have to just say fine and take it from there. But I was 20, and had considerable pride, so I said,

"Can't I even compete for the Triple-A center-field job?"

"No. You're not ready yet."

So on to Waterbury, Connecticut. Eastern League. I hit lead-off for Lett. In 89 games I stole 39 bags, hit 15 HRs, 13 doubles, five triples, scored 56 runs, drove in 43, averaged .290. That just seems like a line of numbers, but to a ballplayer they represent a series of days, living the days just to get to your four ABs, trying not to be overanxious but also trying to knock the crap out of the ball, hitting good pitches, hitting mistakes, missing balls you should've hit, reading spin, learning to make throws automatically, learning situations, progression of play, pitching sequences, what pitchers want to do to you, what your adjustment pattern should be. Learning very slowly how to make the best gucss. I hit leadoff from then until '86, when I established myself in Cincinnati. I'm beating on the ball in Double-A, and catching everything in center. Middle of July, I've got the 15 home runs and I'm hitting about .295, and then I'm told we just got a call at the ballpark.

I think they're calling me in to send me to Triple-A, and I figure I'm in the big leagues by the time I'm 22, at the latest. Then I can get down to some serious business with Sherrie. I'm thinking about Sherrie a lot. Whatever she's doing, I'm liking it. I got called up to Triple-A by August 6. I figured I had 20 or so games to play in Triple-A. So I'm just killing them in Indianapolis. Laying them out on a slab, cold. I had big numbers, stole 20 bags in a little over three weeks. Drove in 19 runs in 19 games, with seven home runs and a .299 average, coming right off the bus. Skeeter Barnes was on that team. One day, at the end of August, just about the time of the September roster call-ups to the big leagues, I saw Skeeter get called into the manager's office, and then there were a few more guys who got called in. Skeeter and the other four guys came out of the office glowing like 29-year-old women getting married.

"I'm going to the Show! I just got the call, baby!" And I'm happy and excited. When they call me into the office, I'm thinking, "It's 1983, I'm 21, been in the system for my fourth season, been killing at Triple-A. There are guys who are not as talented as I am and they're getting that call. I've got to be going, too." I had a combined season average of .298 average, 22 home runs, 60 bags stolen, 70 ribbies, hitting leadoff, scored over a hundred runs. I'm going to the Show!

I went in there, and Roy Hartsfield said, "Young man, they want you . . . they want you to go . . . back to the Instructional League."

"What?" You talk about a quick drop, a hard fall. Man. What a big letdown. "Instructional League? For *what?*"

"They want you to go down there and work on bunting."

Ain't nobody making the major leagues because he can bunt. They won't pay me because I can bunt. I can't tell Sherrie, "Look, we can get married, because I can bunt." I ain't buntin'. I can hit the ball 450 feet on a line. They want me to chop down, look at me and just see a greyhound. Oh I can run, too. I'm going to steal bags regardless of bunting. Already proved that. But I can also hit the ball out of any ballpark. I don't want to be limited to stealing bags, not when I can hit the ball out of the ballpark. And Straw was already up, was Rookie of the Year with the Mets. Straw was in the big leagues producing and I was nowhere. Straw had seven homers that spring, and with all the hype he had in the New York media, they couldn't keep him down. They didn't want opening-day pressure on him, but before April was out, Straw was up. I felt if Straw did it by now, I should've been up there too, because he was my peer. Plus, I knew he wasn't better than me.

I came out of Roy Hartsfield's manager's office stunned. Everybody was asking me, "You going up?" I had to say, "Man . . . I'm going down to the Instructional League."

"*Instructional* League? You?" They offered to drown in rum with me. I obliged. Nobody can appreciate a stiff drink like a ballplayer being sent down. I felt wrecked. It was a combination of what was happening in baseball and a nagging feeling I could no longer go home, that I'd have to make a new home, that baseball was part of that, pivotal to that. I went down to the Instructional League, ended up doing nothing but bunting for a few weeks. Disappointed? Beyond disappointed. This was my third year in a row going down there. The Reds wouldn't let me go play winter ball in Puerto Rico. Scared somebody was going to see me, I guess. I just knew I was being called up. I had built my whole peace of mind around what I felt was that fact. So that was the only time I'd been built up to be let down. They didn't say I was getting called up when the rosters expanded, but everybody who went into the office in Indianapolis came out a big leaguer. It was a slap in the face. I'd outplayed 'em. Even today I see guys getting get called up and, brother, these guys would be getting released back then. With the numbers they're bringing up, .260, seven and 40? No way.

Ham gave me perspective, as much as he could, saying they saw me as a young hitter more than a good hitter. Time alone helped me through this period. Vern Rapp may never have seen a ballplayer built like me who could do what I could. He couldn't see the power. But it was there.

FOUR / SPRING 1997

Relocation

Choose Well, Adjust Fast, Produce

I came out of a premature, one-year retirement in 1996, after missing the '95 season with a neck injury and surgery to relieve a painful bulging disc. I had suffered the neck injury when I ran into the center-field wall in Fenway Park in Boston in a gray Detroit road uniform, chasing a drive off the bat of Hawk Dawson, for Sparky Anderson's Tigers, early in the '94 season. Pain haunted me, kept me from even turning my head much less playing effectively, but I did continue to play, up until the strike. I had a loss of zest for the game. There was a lot of water under the bridge.

I had wanted so *badly* to produce for Sparky—the architect of the Big Red Machine. It frustrated me when I couldn't. The surgery on my neck was my eighth major surgical procedure. No fun. So I retired. My body healed. I spent 1995 at home in L.A. By then, my brother was out of prison for the last time. He was doing better, working, coming by our house in Woodland Hills to wash his car and my car, getting to know my daughters, proudly showing me his first checkstub from the job. My father had a bout with prostate cancer. They caught it early, so things were okay. I returned to play in Cincinnati in '96, hit .287, 26 bombs, 83 RBI, 23 steals. The Reds thought the juice was squeezed out of the orange. Baltimore didn't. So I signed with the Orioles for '97.

Pat Gillick, the Orioles' general manager, was in Toronto when the Blue Jays won it all twice with Cito Gaston managing. Kevin Malone, the Baltimore assistant general manager, was working in Montreal when the Expos were in line to win the National League pennant in '94, the year of the strike. I thought it over. Then Davey Johnson, the Baltimore manager, called, and he was really upbeat and I could tell just from talking to him that he believed in my ability, and in case I missed the point, he told me.

"I know what you can do, E.D."

"Well all right, let's do it then," I said, then launched right into the logistics of relocating. Coming back in 1996 to play in Cincinnati had been easy in this way—it was familiar territory, I knew the lay of the land, Sherrie had gotten to liking it. But now the girls were older, in school in Woodland Hills. It wasn't like I had to be in a comfort zone in order for me to go to Baltimore. I can adapt to any situation. Whether the team is not a good team or a good team, a young team or a veteran team, all white or all black, I'm going to adapt. You produce, that blends you in. When I walked into the Fort Lauderdale clubhouse, I didn't have to introduce myself. We are all big leaguers. But it was important that Cal welcomed me because he has so much clout in Baltimore.

Starting with a new club is always different. You may find they don't expect that much of you. That's fairly easy. The only thing damaged is your pride. Then there's the situation of coming in as the Man, signing a big deal, making the Glue, the bank, the cheese. Then there's my situation in Baltimore in '97—a team that came close to going to the World Series brings me in, hoping I'm one of the final pieces of the puzzle. I look around and see all these top-end big leaguers. They've got a good team and I've got to come in here and just do what I do, then we'll be all right.

Actually it's tougher to go in under these circumstances. If the team had been terrible, and four or five newcomers had come in at the same time, okay, they're regrouping. But when you're as close as the Orioles had been in '96, and they bring in one player—*you*—to get them over the hump—that can be tough. But the Oriole players made it easy for me to come in and do what I do. I scouted them, looking for their preparation, to see how in tune with the game they were. Things they do over the course of a game. How they get ready. You want to see who is successful, how you can complement that. I saw, but also by then, the spring of '97, I knew what I was looking at.

I had played in a lot of celebrity games and All Star games with Cal Jr. by the spring of '97, so I knew he was a purist who appreciated players. He's often called "Iron Man," but that doesn't do him justice. Two-time AL MVP, he'd played in over 2,300 games at the time, 16 straight All Star games. Because his understanding of the game is so acute, his appreciation of the skills of players so pure, I thought he'd make a good manager, if that was something he wanted to do. B. J. Surhoff is a gamer, intense, sometimes too intense, wants to crank a three-run bomb every time up. B.J. was the most intense player on the ballclub and it wasn't close. Haven't run into anybody, outside of my old teammate with the Reds, Paul O'Neill, who wants to get a hit every time up as bad as Beej. If he doesn't get a hit every time, B.J. is offended.

I didn't know Robby Alomar was so good until the '97 season. I always knew he was good, he could hit, could field, could steal a bag, could throw, do it all, but you really don't appreciate all the plays he makes, all the plays he keeps in order, all the imagination for the game that he has, until you see him play the field every day. Robby make plays another second baseman won't—not that it would be an error on the other second baseman but after a while you find yourself thinking, "Bay-Bay would've made that play." I've seen him peg behind runners rounding first or second after they've gotten a potential RBI hit and there looks like there's a play at the plate and Robby whirls to throw home and the guy on the base just is a little relaxed and *bam*, whip throw, slap tag, out. Hard to do him justice in words. Highest fielding percentage in history. Six straight Gold Gloves. I have three. He has six straight. Nine straight All Star games. I've been in a couple of All Star games, was named NL Player of the Month five times, a record I share with Mike Schmidt. I have a World Series ring, while Robby has two. It felt good to be among peers in terms of ability and accomplishment. Not to mention playing with people like this gives you a chance to win.

I didn't have to look too long at Rafael Palmeiro. Consistent. Like clockwork. Picture-book swing. What you see is what you get. He's going to the post every day. He doesn't show a lot of emotion, and it might not look like he's going that hard, but that's his personality. Watching Mike Bordick day in, day out, I learned he's one of the steadiest shortstops I ever played with. I called him "Pac-Man." He wasn't missing too many ground balls. Brady Anderson was going to do what he has to do to be successful. Could be that hitting 50 homers in one season, 1996, was the worst thing that happened to him. When I got to Fort Lauderdale in the spring of '97, all they talked about was the 50. Sometimes you can have success and it creates a monster. When Brady hit 50 in '96, it created the wrong image of who he is as a player. It put undue pressure on him to be that kind of player instead of a 20-30-40 guy—20 homers, 30 steals, 40 doubles, as a left fielder.

The young outfielder from Teaneck, New Jersey, by way of Stanford—Jeffrey Hammonds. He reminded me of myself, coming up behind Dave Parker. When I first came up with Cincinnati in 1984. Hammer had heard of me and had watched me in the World Series in '90, but I'd never had a chance to see Hammer play. I knew he could play, but my thing to him was to show him the way to play the game: how to prepare yourself, the things that will be expected and demanded of you that might not be expected or demanded of others. He would not get much rope. He had to produce. You don't get compared to another player who is your contemporary. You get compared to the greatest ballplayers of all time. Whether you want to accept it or not, it's there. Your career is going to be based on that, being the next Willie Mays, the next whoever, so if you're not that—and who could be?—it's a letdown. You have nowhere to go but down if you don't hit 500 bombs. If I hit 300 career homers in the major leagues, I didn't fulfill my potential? If you think about it—it's a joke. You know the difference between a guy who hits 300 homers and a guy who hits 500? Circumstances. Anybody who hits 300 home runs in the Show, lifetime, is a Man.

What I stressed to Jeffrey—he was so hungry to know—was that until you hit 30 homers, you don't have the potential to hit 30, so don't let people put pressure on you. Once you hit 30, then you have the potential to do it again. Just be Jeffrey—don't be Eric, Brady, Willie, or anybody else. Jeffrey knows how Jeffrey plays. I told him to go back to when he was younger. What were you thinking about then? You weren't thinking about money, or pressure, you were playing. See it, hit it. Don't worry about the pitcher. Concentrate on what you need to do, and what you do well, and everything will take care of itself. Jeffrey hung on my every word—as I once hung on Parker's. In '97, despite nicks, Hammer had a good year—21 HRs, 19 doubles, 71 runs, 55 RBI in 118 games.

I saw this was not a hit-and-run team, or a stolen-base team. This was a *powerful* team. Since that's what it was, when you manage such a team, you've gotta know that, sit back and let your boys do what they do, and that's exactly what Davey Johnson did in the 1997 season and post-season. It's an awesome feeling when you play with guys and figure out their games and you add yours to the mix and everything clicks as it did for the Orioles in '97. It's an awesome feeling, but you recognize that feeling; if you've won it all before, you want your teammates to recognize early exactly why you have joined them. You want 'em to think, "Oh, man, this brother can carry us for a month at a time. He is the total package." But for the most part, I knew more about my teammates than they did about me. So I felt I had to show them the person I am. They kind of knew me as a ballplayer, but I wanted them to also know what I stand for on the field and off, and what my personal game is about. This happened in spring training that season, from playing the way I play, from my enthusiasm for the game, and being able to converse with anybody about anything pertaining to the game. Just being a professional ballplayer. Coming in and trying to blend in and do what I could do to help us win it, hustling, picking up little things to pass along.

I'd played in the AL parks in part of '93 and '94, with Detroit. Didn't get a chance to see all the pitchers because I got hurt, then there was the strike, and then I retired. I wasn't concerned about the umpiring. Never had been. Never had run-ins with umps. Only been thrown out of one game in life. Bruce Froemming threw me out for arguing balls and strikes. Later he apologized for doing it. I don't play the game worrying about obstacles. Don't worry much about managers either in the sense that it's something I can't control. I've had good ones, bad ones, great ones, creeps. Had all kinds. And sometimes you can get all those kinds I mentioned all wrapped up in one guy.

Well, you couldn't have written a better script for the beginning of the '97 season. Going to a new team, being an RBI man, a power hitter, I wanted to flex, concentrate, hit a few early, so my teammates could say, "Okay, this man can *play*." I'd played well in spring training. Had five home runs playing part time, hitting it all over the place, going deep to all fields. Making diving catches. Playing my total game. Didn't have any reason to feel I couldn't do it. My confidence was at an all-time high—seemed I'd never known more about the game, and still had the physical tools and reflexes to play well. Good feeling. The fun was showing this to my teammates. Davey had managed against me so many times in the National League, seen me do so many things. A couple of times I caught him watching the fellows' reactions after I jacked a dinger out the opposite way. That was fun. You can see highlights and hear what people say about a player, but when they saw me going from first to third on balls that don't call for a two-base advance, when they saw me launching 500-footers in b.p., the way God enabled me to hit, I saw the excitement in their eyes.

The first week or so in April, I swung good but didn't get a lot of hits. I had to rethink, like Pops taught me. In the American League, you have to almost think backward, one-eighty your adjustment pattern. In the National League you know at 2–0 you're going to get a fastball unless you're facing Greg Maddux or something. With Maddux, you guess, you'll guess wrong: if you say, 'I'm just gonna react,' you're *still* wrong. He can hit corners, has five pitches by my count—fastball, curve, a cutter, a change-up, a change-up *off* the change. In the National League, with a 2–0 count, you know what you're gonna get. Cheese. Heat. But Maddux is *wack*. At 2–0 Maddux may throw a change. Then on a 2–1 throw the change *off* the change. You might hit it, but you can only hit it to one particular field. If you don't accept that, you're going to make nothing but outs. If he runs a 2–2 pitch off the plate outside four inches and you give up on it and take it, then it backs up on you, and catches the black, you're shocked, then on your way back to the dugout, muttering "Gutless———!" There ain't a helluva lot you can do with Maddux but curse him under your breath, stay patient, professional, hope he catches too much plate, take him the other way, don't try to do too much. Not much of a living can be made there as a hitter. Eighty-five percent says that you're getting heat

2–0 in the National League. In the American League, only a 35 percent chance of a fastball at 2–0. I wasn't going to see 3–2 fastballs. I'd see 3-and-2 sliders, 3–2 changes. Not even at 3–1 did I get over 50 percent fastballs. In the National League they miss with the other pitches but get you out with the fastballs. Not in the American League.

I jammed my shoulder diving after the ball in the outfield, made the catch, but missed a few games. Came back April 22 against the White Sox at Camden Yards. Raffy and I hit back-to-back jacks off Danny Darwin; we beat the Sox 3–2 behind Mike Mussina, and were undefeated, 7–0 at Camden Yards, 12–4 on the year. For the next three or four weeks, I was red hot. I was clubbing. Didn't matter what they did, who was pitching, it just didn't matter, because—well, we know, as hitters, as athletes, you get into zones where no matter what you do it's going to come out right. You can feel it. No matter what they do, you know you're going to win. You know you're better. You hit a home run *before* you hit it—you don't know what's coming, but when you're hot, all your guesses are right. A hitter never knows what's coming. We think we do, when we're hot, but often it's straight guess. Baseball is a guessing game because you just don't know unless you steal a sign. But you've learned from the past, and know what might come. My idea was making sure my adjustment pattern was where it needed to be. When you're hot, the ump may as well not be there. Each at-bat, you're going to get a pitch to hit. The question is, are you ready for that pitch, or not? *Do you recognize that pitch excitedly, or do you recognize it relaxed?* The one who is most ready for that pitch, who is prepared, is the one who succeeds. I was succeeding. I felt like whenever I picked up the bat, no matter what the pitchers did, I was going to hit the ball hard.

The next night, April 23, we lost, but the guys embraced me. Cold night at Camden Yards, raining off and on, White Sox pasting us, 9–1. Down four when I came up in the seventh with the bases juiced. I launched a tracer into the seats in left for my ninth career grand slam, this off Jamie Navarro. Even though we lost, 11–9, Davey said, "It would have been a great win for us. As it was, a tough win for Chicago. They had it bagged until Eric stepped up . . . man, he's electric!"

Any *good* hitter will tell you at some point during a season he's going to go through two weeks where he's locked in. I'd locked in early. American League Player of the Week, April 21–27. I was hitting .395 with seven homers, 19 RBI in 21 games. On April 27 I took Steve Avery deep twice. I was 6-for-6 stealing bases. I knew I wouldn't run as much with this team, but I still had the highest stolen-base percentage in history for players with over 300 steals, at the time over .870—higher than Rickey Henderson, Lou Brock, Ty Cobb. I was asked what I thought of our lineup. "Frankly, it can be awesome," I said, thinking of Raffy, Robby, Cal, Bainesy, B.J., Hammer, and Brady more than me. "Pick your poison. A different guy can do it every night."

Even though the little nagging injuries that every player has were always there, I never felt better at the plate. Had a new lease on life. I had a little shoulder pain, and then caught a bug in Minneapolis, where we played the Twins at the end of April. Sherrie had come up. As soon as she got there I started not feeling well—cold sweats, symptoms of flu. Sherie was concerned, but I brushed it off. When you've been together for as long as we have, you get into a comfort zone. She knows me, and she knows a large part of my mind is involved in the everyday preparation for production in season. Healthy, I'd always hit a hard .290, but now I felt more powerful than I ever had before at the plate, deeper in my knowledge of the game, in my approach. I didn't know what my top end was as a hitter at this stage of my career, when I still had bat speed but knew more than I did at 25. A little virus wouldn't keep me out of the lineup, not now. Shake it off. *"If you're going to play, play."* By the second week of May, we were 21–9, best record in the league. I was hitting .388, leading the AL, slugging at a .710 clip after going 4-for-4 on May 6. Locked in.

What I didn't know was that I was having symptoms already. Symptoms of cancer.

At the time I didn't know they were symptoms. I thought I was getting tired too quick, long before the dog days of summer, because all of a sudden my bat got heavy. I was swinging a 32-ounce stick at the time. Swinging it pretty good, too, but didn't feel the quickness, the usual snap that's there in spring. We left and went on a West Coast road trip. I had strained my quadriceps muscle above the knee, missed two ball games. After the trip I was down to around .350. The symptoms were hitting me. There was gas in my stomach, cramps, queasiness, and I just thought I was keeping late hours, not eating right on the road. I'd never gotten stomach cramps or had such a problem with gas before, but it never occurred to me that something was wrong internally.

We beat the Angels, 3–0, May 8. I pulled my hamstring rounding first. Davey rested me a couple of days. By May, we'd opened up a four-and-a-half-game lead over the Yankees and Red Sox. The Yanks got to within a game-and-half May 15, but would never get any closer after that.

Thomas Boswell in the *Washington Post* wrote this during that time: "Cal Ripken hasn't missed a game in 15 years. Brady Anderson plays with a broken rib . . . In the past decade, Rafael Palmeiro has missed less than 40 games. Then, there is the . . . case of Eric Davis who—believe it or not—may be a better baseball player than any of them . . . when he's healthy . . . With him batting cleanup and playing right field, the Orioles are very close to the complete package. Without him, their lineup often seems a brick shy of a load." Boswell pointed out that I had averaged playing 135 game per season over my career due to numerous injuries. He also mentioned I played hard.

I'd never felt better when the season started. But now I was able to sleep only in fits and starts, and started slumping. Not leveling off, but just hitting bingo numbers all of a sudden. The swing was suddenly just . . . gone. I began to feel something in my right side. Not yet pain. Just . . . something. When we came back off that road trip I had lost six pounds even though I was eating regularly, doing the things I normally do; I was down to 196, and had started the season at 202. Usually, I drop weight over the season, but this was a season's worth of drop in a month. I didn't feel strong. Something was draining my strength. It just came out of the blue. No warning. I was never in better shape. I had the body of a 25-year-old. I'd taken the '95 season off so my internal system had readjusted six years after my kidney was split in Oakland during the '90 World Series. The Orioles' team doctor, Mike Jacobs, said physically he'd never seen a better-looking ballplayer. I had a 30-inch waist, 16-inch biceps; I was sleek, no settling in my middle yet, with negligible body fat. I'd dinged up my shoulder and quadriceps in the first six weeks of the season, typical stuff. I play through the typical stuff. I know my body. When I began having the stomach pain mid-May, it bothered me more mentally. I couldn't pinpoint it. Tried to ignore it—play through it.

I wondered if my teammates could tell something was wrong. Probably so. I was in the throes of a 5-for-43 slump that dropped me from .395 to .302. I was going from first to third in Cleveland. It was May 22, 1997. I was designated hitting. Halfway between second and third, it hit me like a hot knife through butter, in my abdomen. I doubled over once I was standing safely on third. No biggie. Just like being hit by a pitch in the side. Only nothing had hit me. I scored the run though I was in such discomfort I can't remember how. I went back into the tunnel leading from the dugout to the visiting clubhouse at the Jake. I lay down in the tunnel, trying to relieve the pain in my side. Didn't work. When I tried to get up, I couldn't. I thought about my kidney injury, then put it out of my mind. That was over. I had to strain to get up. Me, the natural. "Richie!" I called for Richie Bancells and said my stomach was bothering me badly. He felt it and pressed down on something inside me, something hard. "It's swollen on the right side, E.D." I could turn a little, so I took one more at-bat—a terrible AB—then I said, "This is killing me, Richie. I want to get it checked out."

They called in doctors. They checked me for hernias. Cancer was the farthest thing from my mind. They couldn't find anything particular, except that swelling, so I went back to the hotel and chugged Maalox. I tried to sleep and couldn't, tossing and turning because of this pain. It was becoming excruciating. I played the last day in Cleveland. Everybody asked how I felt. I wasn't feeling great, but I felt I could play, so I said, "I'm okay," and played. I was 1-for-5, didn't swing the bat well, no strength, but still played. I've learned to take pain for granted, it's part of a big leaguer's life. But this was different. Internal. The pain didn't subside, just settled into a throb.

We went to New York. Had a day game scheduled. When I got to Yankee Stadium, I saw Straw, spoke, but couldn't play. The pain was great. When I say I can't play at Yankee Stadium, something's wrong. After the game I went to the hotel and ordered room service. Soup. Fruit. But I could barely choke it down. By 10 P.M. I had a game on the tube but couldn't concentrate on it—it swam in front of me. Pain was so great I couldn't even lay on my right side. By 3 A.M. the pain was so heavy I had tears in my eyes. I called Richie: "I've got to see somebody. Something's wrong."

Richie made train reservations for the next morning, set up appointments for me at the University of Maryland Medical Center, adjacent to Oriole Park at Camden Yards. I rode the Amtrak Metroliner from New York to Baltimore. I'd never ridden on a train in my life. I couldn't enjoy it, though. There was no thought in mind of any cancer. I had started strong, playing in front of fans, teammates, and a manager who saw what I could do. I was just about to turn 35.

PART II
Summer

FIVE / SUMMER 1997

ADVERSITY/BLESSING
Cancer

STRATEGY/LIFE LESSON
Family, Prayer, Second Opinions, Treatment, Heart, and the Whole Tool Box

I was admitted into the University of Maryland Medical Center, close to Camden Yards, near Baltimore's downtown Inner Harbor. I called my mother and my wife, and told them where I was. I guess by the quiet way I sounded, Sherrie knew to come in right away. Shirley stayed on hold. I was told that I had an abscess. An abscess was something concrete, not just unidentified pain, and so I accepted that explanation. Tell me *something*. The physicians put me on a cycle of antibiotics, and the pain went away almost immediately, at least it did initially. I felt good about that—whatever it was seemed treatable. I had something to feel good about now after weeks of mysterious pain and dwindling production, baseball-wise. Don't know which hurt worse at first, although soon enough it was very clear that the pain in my stomach was more intense, hands down. I could produce later. Had to get my insides straightened out first. The doctors said it was an abscess, but my main thing was, where did it come from, what caused it? They couldn't really tell me.

At first they tried to approach it by draining it. They gave me an epidural and stuck a tube in my stomach while I watched the procedure on a video monitor. They drained it, drained the infected pus, thinking it was an abscess and not a tumor. Looking back, I realize that draining it could have caused cancer cells to spread through my body. Nobody knows it's a tumor at the time, so nobody knows its cells are cancerous. They drain it. I live. After that, the attending physicians said, "Okay, Eric, we're going to try and shrink it." And it went down a little bit from antibiotics. After that, for a couple of days, the doctors came in and felt my stomach and then left. I'm sitting in the hospital feeling fine, because I'm not in the same kind of pain anymore. But after the fourth day, I'm antsy. I want out of that hospital room. I sent for the head of the hospital and I talked to her, and I asked, "What's going on? You all have got to tell me something." But she couldn't.

Dr. William Goldiner, one of the Orioles' team physicians, discounted speculation I would need surgery to repair what they were calling "the condition" in the Orioles notes in the local newspapers. They said I fought the idea of exploratory surgery. The doctors had spoken about it, but it didn't seem as if they actually knew anything; it was more like, well, we could go in and see. That's not enough for surgery, not to me. I was against it then, simply because it meant missing six to weight weeks of the season, minimum, due to the abdominal incision that would be required. Just to see. Dr. Barbara Bass was evaluating me, along with Dr. Goldiner and others. If it was an abscess, I didn't want to be out for most of the season for something that some medication might clear up, like antibiotics, so why cut? Cancer? Nobody said anything to me about cancer, or a tumor.

Doctors at the University of Maryland ran more tests to determine why the mass formed. On May 29, Dr. Goldiner told the *Baltimore Sun*, "Our suspicions are this is of benign origin."

On June 1, he said, "There's good reason to be optimistic about a relatively quick recovery . . . The best thing that could happen is if we never find out what caused this and it just heals up . . . (the) abscess stemmed from a minute perforation of unknown cause in the bowel . . . I would say his chance of being operated on are less than 50-50. I wouldn't have said that three days ago."

Three days later, I was at Johns Hopkins.

What happened was this: I called Pat Gillick, the Orioles' general manager, and asked for a second opinion. Ramona Baines, a friend of ours in Washington, D.C., just down the road from Baltimore, had told me about the great reputation of Johns Hopkins. She said, "Well, Eric, if the doctors at Maryland can't make a diagnosis, you have to go where they can." I told Pat I wanted to go to Johns Hopkins for an evaluation. Feeling lethargic and limp, I went to Hopkins on Friday, June 6. I drove the streets of Baltimore, a quaint city, lots of black people living in poverty or just at the line. And in the middle of it all is this institution, and this hospital. It's deeper in Baltimore city than the University of Maryland Hospital Center right next to Camden Yards. You drive into Baltimore a little to get to Johns Hopkins, into the 'hoods that reminded me a little of the ones I knew from South Central, different in this way, they were row houses stacked together like lines of leaning dominoes instead of stucco houses with yards on the wide avenues of my hometown.

As I came into the building, I saw a banner strung across a far wall: VOTED NO. 1 CANCER TREATMENT HOSPITAL IN AMERICA BY U.S. NEWS & WORLD REPORT, 1991, 1992, 1993, 1995, 1996. I remember looking at that sign and stopping short to stare. That may have been when the idea first struck my mind, and just as quickly I forced it out. Big leaguers are mentally strong in terms of focusing on what they want to focus on. Right now I wanted to know where this abscess had come from. So I'd come to Johns Hopkins. I was now waiting over at the outpatient center with my stomach throbbing dully—the antibiotics were losing their grip.

It was a Friday afternoon. I arrived at Dr. Keith Lillemoe's office and he smiled and we shook hands. Later he told me that he'd been following the articles about my illness and had wondered what was wrong with me, and that he'd gotten a call from Dr. Goldiner. When I came in I didn't look sick to him, or acutely or chronically ill. He examined me briefly, I gave him my medical history and the history of this pain as I recalled it. At first he asked if I knew what appendicitis was. Big guy, looked me in the eye. Then he said, "Well, come in Monday. We'll run some tests. But first let's do a tactile exam, and I'll consult with Dr. Fishman about these pictures of yours."

He pressed on my abdomen, pressing on the mass. I winced. "Hmp. Feels like a baseball in there," Dr. Lillemoe said. I tried to force an ironic smile. Don't know if I made it, though.

"You're a tremendously fit person," he said. "Don't have a bit of fat on you. This wouldn't be that palpable in a bigger person. But I feel it, right here." I said it had actually gone down some in size. Dr. Lillemoe told me later that he tried with every patient not to give a reaction on a tactile examination, but it was all he could do not to say "Wow," when he felt that large abdominal mass. I had brought with me three CT scans, the X-ray picture of the abdominal wall section that was done over at the University of Maryland Hospital. I had an initial CT scan, and then others after they tried to drain the mass. Dr. Lillemoe took the pictures and excused himself. I looked at pictures myself— pictures of Dr. Lillemoe's children, I guessed. I looked out into the hallway at orderlies wheeling bottles of what I assumed were volatile chemicals silently through wide halls. I dropped my head and sighed. To go from fresh air, sunshine, playing the national pastime, playing it well, from hitting .388 on what looked like one of the best teams in baseball, to this anonymous nearly silent oncology ward at one of the nation's great hospitals in just a few days. In *hours*.

Meanwhile, Dr. Lillemoe was in radiology, placing the pictures over the fluorescent lighting of the display that takes up one wall. He scrutinized the CT scans, the light reflecting off his eyeglasses and those of his colleague, Dr. Elliot Fishman, professor of radiology and a friend of Dr. Lillemoe's and another big sports fan. He and Dr. Lillemoe had season tickets to the NBA Washington Wizards. And almost everybody in Baltimore city is an Orioles' fan. "So . . . Elliot Fishman, I'd like you to meet Eric Davis," Dr. Lillemoe said, showing him the scans of my GI area. "Nice to meet you, Eric," Dr. Fishman said, looking up at the fluorescent background shaded by the grays and black of the negatives. Quickly he grew serious. He stared at the picture.

Then Dr. Fishman said, "Keith . . . I think that's cancer."

Keith . . . I think that's cancer.

He might as well have been talking to me directly. Even though I was completely alone I felt a chill, up in Dr. Lillemoe's office. Dr. Lillemoe told me later that he consulted with Dr. Fishman all the time, and in his opinion, he was as good as anyone at looking at a CT scan and making a diagnosis. In the five-minute walk from radiology back to his office, Dr. Lillemoe wondered how to tell me I needed surgery immediately. He wasn't sure whether I came to him because I'd been told I needed an operation and didn't want to have it or whether I thought I needed one and they weren't doing it. What I liked was that, as he told me later, he wasn't going to compromise my care; the fact I was a ballplayer and that baseball was in season wasn't going to affect his care management in any way. He might have thought, "He's only 35, he's an athlete, it's baseball season, the O's need him, he *can't* have cancer"—things some team doctors often do, frankly.

I found out a little about him just by looking around his office later, at the pictures he had out and the credentials on the walls. Oh, so he's athletic, from South Dakota, had coached Little League, girls basketball, collects a little sports memorabilia on the side, average weekend spent at four or five soccer games, lacrosse, once operated on Ernie Tyler, one of the Orioles' clubhouse employees, saw Glenn Davis, the former Astro and Oriole, for a possible hernia. Chief Professor of Surgery. Athletically minded enough to know who I was right away. Professional, poised, and able, but not arrogant. Seemed to have a lot of Jimmy Key in him, which would do me just fine. Jimmy Key is a big-game pitcher. Dr. Lillemoe graduated from Johns Hopkins medical school in '78, finished training in surgery in '85, became a faculty member on staff the same year. The clinical delivery of surgical care; a general surgeon specializing in GI surgery, gastrointestinal surgery, surgery involving the colon, stomach, intestines, pancreas, gall bladder, and liver.

He walked back into the office, paused, and said, "Eric, there's something seriously wrong with your colon."

I was sitting on the examining table, fully dressed.

"This could be a tumor. This could be a cancerous tumor . . ."

I didn't hear the rest of what he said. ". . . of your colon. There's no way to ignore this. There's no way we can't radically treat it. I think you're going to need an operation."

". . . What?"

"I said, I think you need surgery immediately," Dr. Lillemoe repeated.

I was numb. ". . . When?"

"Right away. As soon as possible."

I stayed quiet, very quiet. I tried to rein in my emotions. I treated it like a critical at-bat against a formidable pitcher. Strike one, strike two. But you're still alive. You just have to make your adjustments. I didn't say, "Fine," and I didn't say, "That's terrible! I can't do that!" I didn't show Dr. Lillemoe—or myself—any emotion. But I do know I was scared. I could barely hear him talking now. He said something about another test he wanted to run before we did the surgery, and a new set of pictures. He hadn't really gotten the kind of pictures he wanted of the abdominal wall, showing the relationship and structures inside and outside the bowel, and the fine lining of the intestine. They needed to do a barium enema and a colonoscopy. What he didn't tell me was that in the back of his mind he was concerned there might have been a perforation of the bowel. He knew from talking to Dr. Goldiner that there had been an elevation in my white blood cell count. So there were some signs of infection and he was concerned that the tumor itself may have perforated, dispersing cancer cells. If I had a perforation and they did the wrong tests, it could cause a more serious problem. I clearly wasn't acutely sick when I came to see him, and he wanted to be careful not to make me sick. He scheduled me to come in Monday, June 9, for a barium enema and a colonoscopy, to be performed at the Johns Hopkins outpatient center by Dr. Bob Gaylor. Now, I can't lie and tell you it was all so pleasant. It was rather unpleasant. But the procedures were done with the utmost care and positive bedside manner and professionalism. They had given me virtual chalk to drink, and I couldn't eat after a certain time on Sunday. A half hour after the tests, Dr. Lillemoe came in. "Eric, it's not an abscess. It's a tumor." He showed me the X-ray. "That's the tumor—it's the size of an orange. It's confirmed. We've got to go get it."

"When? When are you going to get it? You say it's got to come out. I'm trusting you. You say it's got to come out, then it's got to come out. We've got to do what we've got to do."

I'm scared down to my ankles, but not so scared I don't want to battle back. Okay, cancer, me and you. Head-up. Me and my people against you and your cells. Sometimes it helps, having to grow up tough and competitive, always playing against older and tougher and stronger boys, and always looking for a higher level at which to compete. The idea that I had a cancerous tumor scared me. My mind was dazed. I was confused. I drove for hours around the streets of Baltimore and D.C., listening to music without hearing it. To tell you the truth, I don't know exactly what my movements were between the time I got Dr. Lillemoe's diagnosis and the time I checked in for the surgery on Friday, June 13. I know I prayed. I know I spoke to my loved ones over the phone. But other than that—blank. Hard to think straight when you're given this diagnosis. Hard to know how to feel, other than know you need help. It's an emotional, physical, and spiritual earthquake, when you get the knowledge that you aren't in control anymore. I don't care how tough you are, you feel this. I had suspended all other feelings and I went through the motions of living. I called my mother. Sherrie had gone back home, but Shirley and Sherrie were coming to Baltimore later in the week, as soon as they could make arrangements. Next thing I knew I was getting dressed Monday, June 9, at the outpatient center. Dr. Lillemoe was going over pictures with Dr. Gaylor.

"Eric, I'm now concerned that you have a cancerous tumor in your colon and there's no doubt you need surgery," Dr. Lillemoe said calmly and slowly. "I know you want to get on with this as soon as possible. We need to do some preparation for the surgery. The bowel has to be cleaned out. We'll admit you on Wednesday, clean out the bowel, do the surgery on Thursday."

Dr. Lillemoe said he wanted to schedule the surgery for Thursday, June 12, but I told him I wanted my family to have enough time to get back to Baltimore first. Sherrie would have to make arrangements for the girls. Shirley would come in first. I said, "Let's do it on Friday."

"You know that's Friday the 13th," said Dr. Lillemoe.

"We have to wait until Friday," I said. "When my mother and my wife are here." Erica was graduating from elementary school on Thursday. Shirley was taking the red-eye in from L.A., if possible. "Friday is the 13th, Eric," Dr. Lillemoe repeated.

"That's okay, Doc. I'm not superstitious."

Dr. Lillemoe said the delay of one day was insignificant.

I came in on Thursday, under an alias I'd been given: Dave Stewart.

I was put on what they called a VIP floor, where patients have a little more privacy. So I came in and got prepped and the nurses, orderlies, technicians, and aides were all swell and great to me. I took all the chalky and the bitter liquids they gave me to sort of wash my system clean of fecal material, and also some antibiotics to prep for the surgery. Sherrie and Shirley were coming in and I was happy about that, but subdued. My mother'd be praying. Sherrie would be a comfort to her. When I woke up from the surgery I would know what kind of life I had left to resume, and I was calmed by the fact that my wife and mother would be with me when I came out of surgery.

I have a great family who really knows me through and through. Sherrie often says that when other people first meet me, or more likely, when they see me from afar, the first impression is the wrong impression; she knows I never put on a show for anybody, that if you push me, okay, but if you push too much—trouble. She knows often when there's trouble, not everything registers right away with me. I just keep on going, quiet, laid-back, until I get to know you, then I get more comfortable, and people can see I'm a good storyteller, good-humored gentleman, a typical man, respectful, restless. She always says that about me, that I'm well raised. She says I'm realistic, too, and I know what the Lord is capable of. That I'm trustworthy, that I care about people. That I'm going to make sure I see everybody who comes to see me. That I don't leave anybody out. I'm my own man, but Sherrie knows she's Mama, that our girls are everything to me. My wife and I are very much alike. We are both very observant. I thought a lot about my family that week. How would the girls make out? I didn't like to think of the girls out in the world without the idea of their father being there if they needed him. Funny, the stuff that runs through your mind. You're trying not think of having cancer, but the thought is there, so you suppress it with other thoughts.

It was helpful to have Angela Hunt, my public relations rep in Baltimore, to help with the arrangements to get my mother and my wife over to the hospital once they arrived. Without all my family's help, I would've felt lost, powerless, overwhelmed.

Part of me had just switched off, and I was going through the motions of living. More than anything, it was my mother's strength, faith, belief, attitude, and mere presence that reminded me that I was still firmly rooted in the land of the living and in the palm of the hand of God. Shirley reminded me of who was really in charge, and that it wasn't me (not that I didn't know), and it wasn't Dr. Lillemoe, and it wasn't her, it was God. My mother reminded me again of what I already knew—it was God's game to manage.

I knew she'd be there when I woke up. So I submitted first to the nurse who gave me the shot to dry my saliva glands. The last thing I remember was being wheeled into the operating bay.

Dr. Lillemoe began the procedure expecting the worst. He was concerned about this mass, about the size of it, then if it had perforated, or whether the mass had invaded the abdominal wall, into another part of my intestine, or my kidney or liver. He was concerned about the magnitude of the surgery. There was no way to tell how difficult or long it would be without going in. He was afraid that this was going to be a long, maybe an ugly, operation, so he set aside a whole half day. Frankly, he was expecting the worst, because this was a big mass. He kept these fears to himself at the time, which was probably the best thing to do. I had enough on my mind. When he got in, he was surprised to find that the mass was entirely confined to the ascending colon. It hadn't perforated, thank God, and it hadn't grown into any adjacent structures. It was freely there—part of the colon. He could actually pick the mass up and move it, along with the colon, which he said was to him a great sign. There was no sign of spread, no metastases he could see. Before I had signed the consent forms for the surgery, he told me there was a possibility that if they found the wrong set of circumstances in there, I could end up with a permanent colostomy bag for bowel movements. But now there might be a better outcome. He took a segment of the colon out and surgically cut away the tumor— **Mountain, get out of my way!**—then removed about one third of the right side of the colon (the right colon is the ascending side). He was able to put the ends back together. *The Lord is my shepherd, I shall not want . . .* The surgery went better than Dr. Lillemoe could've hoped. He later said there was little difficulty. The operation took about two hours, done through a six-inch incision. The tumor, the size of a baseball, was sent to pathology, and they confirmed it as cancer by the time I came out from under the anesthetic in the recovery room. In fact, I believe Dr. Lillemoe was told what it was and what stage it was in before he had sewn me up. He didn't know beyond what he'd seen with his naked eye about the depth of invasion, or the actual stage of the tumor. He didn't know from that about lymph node invasion, but felt confident that a lot of bad things that could've been there didn't exist, thank God. He came down to the recovery room to talk to me and my family. Dr. Lillemoe gave my mother the news before I woke up. He said he knew who she was before she told him. My mother is the kind of woman who, if you're talking about her children, requires the truth. If you avoid it she'll sense it. They were in the private consultation area. That's where he met Shirley, and Angela. He told Shirley the diagnosis: I had cancer, but that the operation went very well. My mother might have been sober or reflective for maybe one second. Or maybe two. That's it. After that, she was just all positive. She looked at the doctor and said calmly, "Did you get it all?" He was surprised by her calm, and said, "Yes."

Then she asked him, "When can I see him? When can I see my child?"

So I'm in recovery, slowly coming out of the anesthesia, in and out, and I see my mother's face swimming in front of me. She was smiling at me, a bit of a forced smile but I'm glad to be there to see it, and beside her is Angela, and she's smiling, too. I feel my mother's hands squeezing mine. I can also tell Dr. Lillemoe is there. He says something to me.

"Eric, it was a tumor—it was a cancerous tumor. A malignant tumor, but . . ."

When the news registered with me after the surgery that it was cancer, when I was in my room, coming out from under the anesthesia, I cried, I just broke down and cried, and my mother comforted me. Then my mother said, "Yes, cry now, get it all out, because after this there will be no more crying or negativity, no more questioning, nothing but smiles and encouragement." And that began in the next instant. I didn't have time to think, "I've got cancer, it's malignant, and that means it's going to spread all over my body and I'm going to die." God didn't leave me much time for all that, for which I'm grateful. Later Dr. Lillemoe said they got it all, and so I asked him what was the next step. His recommendation was follow-up chemotherapy.

Over the next few days until I left the hospital in a wheelchair on June 17, I spoke to Dr. Lillemoe several times. He had brought in Dr. Ross Donahower, who was to be my oncologist, another very professional doctor. After Dr. Lillemoe explained to me that it was specifically colon cancer and told me some things about the disease, and why the surgery and now the adjuvant chemotherapy were recommended, I did a little reading up on the subject. I picked up a pamphlet from some of the literature at the hospital ... *Every year, colon cancer kills more Americans than breast cancer and prostate cancer combined ... over 50,000 lives lost each and every year ... the second most virulent form ...* I closed that particular pamphlet and never picked it up again.

Positive thinking techniques. I relied on them heavily.

Dr. Lillemoe explained that a tumor at stage zero hasn't invaded anywhere else at all. The tumor stage A is confined to the level of the bowel wall, at a superficial level. Tumor stage B is confined to the wall, but not superficially. Tumor stage C has lymph node involvement. Tumor stage D has spread throughout the body. If it's a tumor stage zero and they operate, it's gone; if there's no evidence of invasion, you've got a good shot; you become a member of another kind of big league—the Field of Cancer Survivors. The tumor stage A is cured in 90 percent of people who have surgery. Tumor stage B survival rate comes down to 60 or 70 percent. The doctors also said we know that from following a group of people, say a thousand, with tumor stage B, follow them the rest of their lives, a certain percentage, maybe a third, the tumor will come back. My tumor was stage B, and Dr. Lillemoe felt he'd gotten it all, but explained to me that studies show the tumor at that stage can come back. That's why he and the Baltimore oncologist, Dr. Donahower, and later Dr. Isakoff in L.A., recommended chemo. If you have an inoperable tumor, it doesn't have a lot of effect. But if you have cancerous cells, so small as to be invisible to the naked eye or tiny tumors that are so small the doctors can't detect them, the chemo is designed to kill those cells and tiny tumors, either to delay their surfacing or eradicate them totally. I liked that word: "Eradicate."

So I agreed to have adjuvant chemotherapy to eradicate any latent cancer cells or tumors. ("Adjuvant" means it's in addition to the primary treatment, which was the surgery.)

After the surgery, I didn't have much to say. I was going back in my mind through my whole life. I wasn't emotional. I wasn't upset. I was just going back over it all. Each day I did better, mentally. I didn't need a colostomy bag for long because the surgery was quick and not as radical as some procedures can get. Dr. Lillemoe had said it can get ugly, and he would know, he's one of the best in the business of surgery in the gastrointestinal area. He had given me as small a scar as possible, knowing how important it was to me to be able to turn at the waist swinging a bat. The incision was six inches, from a little bit below my navel and up toward my breastbone. I had the surgery on Friday, June 13, and by the next Monday started on a liquid diet, and my bowels moved almost right away. This relieved the doctors (and me). They had to wait and see if I could do what we take for granted in our lower GI. They can't let you out of the hospital until you can show you can urinate freely, move your bowels, and pass gas. They were relieved when I finally passed gas. So was I. Amazing, the things you take for granted. When you take out a section of bowel and put it back together, it's not like plumbing, where you just turn the water back on and see if it flows right. You wait a few days to make sure that it heals up first.

The recovery was fast because the surgery went smoothly, because of the expertise of Dr. Lillemoe and his team and then the technicians, nurses, and attendants at Johns Hopkins, all big leaguers at what they do, and because I was in great physical condition. Mostly, I think, because of the prayers sent up by my mother, my family, everybody I knew. The doctors called my recovery from surgery "phenomenally quick," and for a little while I was the talk of the cancer ward: *He just had colon cancer surgery on Friday and he's going home Wednesday morning!*"

Other patients were wheeled by to see me, the "Miracle Man," and I smiled and spoke to them, and even felt strong enough to get up and go down to the nurses' stations and crack jokes with them. One of them pressed my hand and said I was doing the other patients on the ward a lot more good than a whole tanker truck full of chemicals. On Tuesday, June 17, they got the final pathology results back and they confirmed what we knew: it was cancer, stage B, and there were no lymph node metastases. That night, the Orioles held a press conference to announce it.

Dr. Lillemoe asked me, "What do you want me to say?"

"Tell 'em what you feel like they need to know, Doc."

"Eric, one thing I'm not going to do now and I'll never do is given them percentages, or rates of survival. I'm not going to say Eric Davis has a 50-50 chance or a 60-40 chance or a 90-10 chance. Statistics don't reflect individual patients, and they can be deceiving, just like in baseball."

"Then just forget the stats, Doc. Just tell 'em the truth."

*   *   *

Two days after I had the surgery, the day before I was released and wheeled out of Johns Hopkins University Hospital, Mr. Peter Angelos came to visit me, unannounced. My family had left the hospital for the day. I was just lying there feeling sore, and now wondering about this chemotherapy program. Honestly, in my mind I was already beginning to think about what I could do, to show my appreciation to God for saving my life yet again. What can I do to serve you, God? And then there was Mr. Angelos and the baseball world again, standing in the doorway.

Before he said a word, I knew this was meaningful to me. The Orioles had the division lead, thanks in some small part to my early play, had a chance at the World Series. He could've moved on. It had happened to me before. I'd been treated as a disposable part. Although I wanted the Orioles to do well, I wasn't thinking about coming back to play, though the team had my support emotionally. Sherrie wasn't surprised when Reds' team owner Marge Schott didn't visit me in Oakland when I lacerated my kidney on the field during the '90 World Series. As Sherrie said, "That was Marge." Though I was hurt and disappointed at the time, by now I'd learned to separate my problems and the business of baseball. I was lying there thinking about my girls, mostly. They wouldn't be losing Dad so quick after all. Erica had found out the specifics about my illness at school. She came home sniffling. Sherrie asked her what was wrong. She said, "People at my school say Daddy has cancer." So then Mommy had to be straight with Erica, and she handled it. I was thinking about Erica and Sacha, whether or not I had done the best job I could in providing for them. I could sleep feeling I had. This had been instilled in me by example as a child. So it was only after I looked up from my thoughts and saw Peter Angelos that I thought about baseball. You have to realize, I have been in life-threatening situations before during baseball season, like in '90, when I lacerated my kidney in Game Four of the World Series, went into intensive care in an Oakland hospital, and my team, the Cincinnati Reds, won the World Series later that day, and hardly anybody came to visit me. So this time, I had no real expectations. No one called me to say Mr. Angelos was coming around. There was just this knock at my hospital door, so soft I thought I imagined it. It came again.

"Yes?"

I tried to get up, but—your stomach muscles control movement you don't even think about until you're laid up. I sat up in bed and I saw him, all suited up. He was sharp, and I'm known to appreciate a sharp dresser. "Is that . . . Mr. . . . . Angelos?"

"May I come in?"

"Come on. Come on in."

He smiled. He was alone. That really got me. That he had come by himself. I'd mostly seen him from a distance, never alone, and here he was by himself. He came in and asked, "How're you feeling, Eric?" and just sat down like it was the most normal thing in the world, like we visited this way all the time, like I was one of his guys, or he was one of mine. He told me how much he admired me, not just because of what I was going through now. He asked how I felt, and I said, "Fine, considering." He said, "No, please tell me, how are you *really* feeling?" I tried to tell him everything that happened. Mr. Angelos sat there, nodding and conversing politely, and I could sense a genuine concern on his part. It was important to me, being able to tell somebody. I could tell he was interested. His eyes didn't glaze over as I talked to him. Look, it's a cold business. There's no getting around it. Peter Angelos coming to see me had been the farthest thing from my mind. But now, I felt good about it. That was when, in the back of my mind, I started thinking I'd try and come back to try to help get to and win a World Series. That's the inner confidence you have to have to make it and make it big, and become a Man in the major leagues. I believed then that if I could somehow get back, the '97 Orioles would have a better chance to win. I'd already helped a team get to a World Series on one leg, for a team owner I didn't respect half as much as I respected this man who had taken the time out to come see a grunt like me in my time of trouble.

People have asked me how I was able to handle this change in my life—from being a strong professional athlete one minute to being a cancer patient totally at the mercy of medicine and the whims of fate the next. Well, in the first place, I didn't feel I was ever completely at the disease's mercy. It's true I didn't have a choice about what happens to me, the way someone who drinks and drives or someone who just gives up and kills himself does. It was not hard to deal with and overcome when you believe in something. You know going in that there are things that are out of your control, whether you believe in something or not. But if you believe in something, you know there is a place you can go for relief and comfort. If you're driving drunk and crash, you were in control of that car, that situation. You had a choice. If things are going badly in your life, and you decide to take a gun and put it to your head and pull the trigger—you had a choice. You didn't have to do it. You took what was the easy way out. I didn't have a choice about what happened to me. I couldn't spend any time worrying about whether or not I could control it. Why does tragedy have to hit someone else? I have been asked if I was afraid of dying. I look at it as wanting to live, loving life rather than being afraid to die. I'm afraid of what might happen to the people I love, my daughters, if I were to die prematurely. I'd told people from time to time, "As sure as we were born, we are going to die. It's just a matter of when, where, how."

But for some reason, I never felt this was the time or the place or the way for me. I never sat in the hospital and said, "I'm dying." But there were times when I'd say, "Lord, thank You so much for allowing me to live. Thank You for allowing me to be an example of Your power."

That happened in my quiet time, or when I would take a

shower and looked down at my abdomen, at the scar, at where that tumor had been cut out of me. I realized it was just me and God then, and I marveled, and the tears would come. It had been inside me. Now it was gone. So many people die every year from this form of cancer. What also helped me was thinking about my brother. We talked a few times as soon as I got out of the hospital. I also talked to my crazy (in a good way) sister, Rochea, and she basically demanded good health of me. But I was gratified to talk to my brother, although I could tell he was hurting for me. "Wrong one got sick," he said.

"Don't say that, Jim Bean. Man, I can get sick. I'm human."

"Naw. Wrong one got sick, brother. You know it," he said quietly.

"That's bull—and if you say it again I'm kickin' your ass."

"You have to get out of that hospital to do that, so . . . bring it on," he said.

I went back to L.A. to race rehab and chemotherapy, back home to Woodland Hills, where my girls, my wife, and my mother could look out for me. The incision healed very quickly. Dr. Lillemoe had been precise. He and I had agreed to try and keep the diagnosis quiet, but the press had figured it out. The *Sun* had had a medical writer call and he had asked Dr. Lillemoe a bunch of questions. Dr. Lillemoe had done a nice tap dance, and tried to maintain privacy, but the medical writer surmised that it was cancer, even though Doc didn't violate my confidence.

Two days later, Dr. Meyer Heyman, an Orioles' team doctor, told the *Sun*, "It's hard to imagine from the size of that thing that he had the symptoms for only two weeks." But the size of the tumor had Dr. Goldiner thinking "Disaster." The *Sun* noted it was "doubtful" that I would play again that season. My eyes narrowed when I heard that, and I wanted to thank them for the frank assessment. Doubt and belief working hand in hand moving in the right direction are great motivational tools for anybody—well, I know they are great motivational tools for me.

Fans at Camden Yards were already holding up signs, GET WELL ERIC! ERIC, WE LOVE YOU.

Dr. Goldiner had been quoted as saying, "I see no reason why he could not play again."

Eventually I prepared a statement and was allowed to make it on videotape by the Orioles: "I am feeling well and looking forward to making a full recovery. I would like to thank my family, all of the fans, my teammates, my friends, the Orioles' organization, and the staff at Johns Hopkins for all the support they gave me. I have been following the team very closely, and I am excited to see we are doing so well. I hope to be back on the playing field as soon as I can. Thank you all."

"We were hopeful he could return this season, but I would not say that is probable," general manager Pat Gillick said to the press. Now, down in the clubhouse, I knew all the fellows were with me, even though I'd barely been able to get in six weeks with 'em. But they were a *good* six weeks, and they had ended with us comfortably in first place. "You have to get close to Eric to know the kind of person he is," said Lenny Webster, the catcher. "He's a very giving person, always there for you. If you know Eric, you know you can count on him to do whatever it takes to get back."

We, the Orioles, had a chance to get to the World Series. I knew I could be a part of that. I already was a part of it. We had a six-and-a-half-game lead when I went on the DL with the "abscess" on May 27; now my teammates had taken to wearing my number 24 decals on their batting helmets, shoes, and uniforms. We had become a fairly close-knit team, but you have to always keep a little of yourself in reserve, because it is a cold business, and people get blamed, fingers get pointed. But with Mr. Angelos coming around and being so nice, putting my face up on the Jumbotron at Camden Yards so I could say those few words of thanks to the Baltimore fans and my teammates and those in the organization who had supported me, it made me want to get back in uniform. Soon.

* * *

I've been asked, "Why did you get colon cancer?" I didn't have a family predisposition. My father had prostate cancer, which Dr. Lillemoe told me was unrelated. In looking at my tumor microscopically, it did have a "genetic distinction," according to doctors, but oddly enough that didn't mean there was anything in my family that could've predicted this, necessarily. But there was probably a reason, something that happened in my system had led to this. What are guidelines to prevent it? Diet would be the number one thing. Omega-3 oils, found in certain fish, mono-unsaturated fats, olives, beans, avocado, getting your roughage and fiber, drinking your water. You've got to eat right.

Now, my initial oncologist, Dr. Donahower, felt that the kind of tumor that I had responded well to the chemo he put me on, but I also wanted to get back to playing baseball, and he knew it. But at the same time, I debated myself about the adjuvant chemotherapy. It's not something you jump into without thought. It is a shock to the system; it can make you ill, cause changes, depression. I'd also be rehabbing to get back into a semblance of game condition in time for playoffs. The stats Dr. Lillemoe gave me stayed with me. My daughters' faces would not let me refuse chemo.

Dr. Lillemoe called a friend of his at UCLA and arranged for me to see Dr. Bill Isakoff. He worked in concert with Dr. Donahower so that I could take the treatments in Baltimore or in Los Angeles once—*if*—I was able to get back onto the active roster, assuming I would be able to rehab, in September. I would be barely a month into chemo at that point. Dr. Lillemoe told me that from the surgery-recovery perspective, I could be back playing in a couple of months, which would be August 13 or thereabouts. But the big unknown was what effect the chemo would have on my strength, vision, depth perception, any number of things we take for granted in everyday life that are bread and butter for a ballplayer. Things happen fast on the diamond. It can be dangerous.

The playoffs and World Series would be over by the end of October, but the chemo program I was on wouldn't finish until February of 1998. They sent Dr. Isakoff every record they had on me, and soon it was unanimous. Everybody in medicine that I saw said the same thing: *"You're young, chemotherapy will not have that big of an effect on you in terms of side effects."*

They admitted that it was possible it might throw off my timetable to play baseball in the '97 season. "You're not taking chemo for this baseball season, you're doing it for you daughters and for your future. The best chance is to get it. Nothing is 100 percent." It was basically unanimous. Dr. Lillemoe agreed. "Eric, these are the experts, and they think you should do it. I think you should do it." I talked to Sherrie and she said, "You know you have to do it." So right around the Fourth of July, I was back at UCLA. It wasn't an easy decision. Even Joe Average doesn't make that decision too lightly. Most people don't just walk in and say, "Oh yeah, think I'll have some of that chemo." Most people have to think about it some.

The decision not only affected my family, people in the Orioles' organization, but also it was a matter of staying busy. And I also had to get back in there and not just to help the team get to the World Series and see what I could do, but to show the brass what I could do because the next season was an option year at $2.5 million. Who picks up the option of a cancer survivor? Feel sorry for him, sure. But depend on him, no.

I had concerns not only about my future but also the financial future of my family. Dr. Lillemoe was aware of it; he'd had those kinds of conversations with his patients from all walks of life, and all economic classes. I didn't assume Mr. Angelos and the Orioles would even pick up my option. I knew he didn't have to, but I got a good feeling from him coming to see me, so that took some of that pressure away. The only pressure I felt to return was not really pressure at all. It was pure desire, a desire to help contribute to the team, be passionate about the game, be able to participate in what I loved, in what I thought was an excellent year, maybe even a World Series year, 1997.

People have also asked me where I got the strength to endure. when I say I got a lot of it from how I was raised, from my parents, from Jimmy Sr. and Shirley, and the beliefs they instilled in me, some people won't let it rest. They ask, "Well then, where did *they* get it from?" Good question.

SIX / SUMMER 1972

ADVERSITY/BLESSING
Remembering Things Past

LIFE LESSON/STRATEGY
Translating Things to Come

I used to dream I could fly. I clearly remember those dreams. I could just take a few steps, one two three, spring! into the air, above the rooftops and trees. I may have first had that dream while sleeping in the backseat of the car, sleeping to the tune of tires humming on asphalt as we went back, back, all the way back to Natchez, Mississippi, my parents' hometown. We would drive back there from L.A. every summer when I was young, until around age 14 or so; me, Jim, my mother, and my sister, or my aunt and her children, or different combinations, with my dad often driving my mother's car, her yellow Ford Torino, gliding across flat and endless Texas.

I don't know how many African American families did the same—driving across Texas on Interstate 10, I-20, or I-40, through Amarillo and Oklahoma. When asked where we were "from," my brother and sister and I would tell you "I'm from L.A.," and would've scoffed if you'd said we were from Natchez—but that's where the people who brought us up were from. The home we grew up in was run by a man and a woman from Natchez, and those people had a greater influence on me than I realized at the time. It was an annual thing to go back every summer, and I dreaded it, because it was hot, and a different kind of hot than L.A., a sticky, alarming heat, plus it took forever to get there just to be hot. We always drove. We didn't fly. Maybe that's why I flew in my dreams. We loaded the Ford for the overland haul. Mom spent days preparing food—potato salad, cold chicken, sandwiches, cakes, bottles of soda pop, and the five us would fire up the Ford and we'd ride.

Texas took "three days" to cross. That's what we used to call it—*three days.* "Is it three days yet?" Seemed like it took three days to get across it, but it was more like a full 24-hour day, three cycles of sunrise, sunset, sunrise. Three days to a child. Three Days seemed like it would never end, but it always did. I remember the signs off the interstate, finally, after what seemed like a week in that Ford. We turned off onto the local state highways in Louisiana. VIDALIA/FERRIDAY 6 MILES; NATCHEZ 10 MILES . . . we slept, and I dreamed that I could fly, and then we would be there, through Texas, in Louisiana, then in Natchez, in Mississippi, and everybody would be smiling at us, like we were ambassadors from some great place that was powerful, far away, and better.

Natchez is situated on a bluff, like a big wedge of devil's food cake above the Mississippi River, 160 miles upstream from Baton Rouge, Louisiana, where the mouth of the Mississippi used to be, long before the white man, black man, or red man were around. The mouth of the river is 200 miles below Baton Rouge now; over time the river created its own landfill, and on that landfill, halfway between Baton Rouge and the Gulf of Mexico, sits New Orleans. For planter society, Natchez was to New Orleans what a place like Martha's Vineyard is to New York, or what Monterey and Carmel are to L.A. Back when we used to go there in the summers, the population was around 19,000, no more than 20,000 there today, and of that total, half would be black people, and they would be poor.

There are signs telling a visitor about the Natchez Trace, the old road from Natchez to Nashville, 300 miles north by northeast, gateway to the eastern United States back in the time of the War of 1812, Andrew Jackson, and slavery. (That's the one word that describes it best for the relatives on both sides of my family.) Natchez is in Adams County, in the far southwest corner of Mississippi. Antebellum mansions made from cotton money and the profits of slave labor stand there today. People come to see them, go in, look around, sit on the porches. But if anybody is doing any reminiscing about those good old days, it isn't the local black American population.

Another Natchez tourist spot is the Grand Village of the Natchez. Indian burial mounds. I believed they were my people, too. My mother has red undertones in her skin, this kind of glow. So did her mother, Lesscena Bennett Springs. It's almost stereotypical for black people to claim Native American ancestry, but in many cases, including this one, it's so obviously true. Look in the Reds press guides of the '80s if you don't believe me. Natchez was named for a tribe of Native Americans who lived there, along with other Gulf tribes, the Chickasaw, Choctaw, Cherokee. But the Natchez tribe was on that bluff over the river, and they were athletic. They fought the French at Fort Rosalie back in the early 1800s. All the old folks around there talked about "the Natchez," meaning the original people, not the town. They said there were three classes of Natchez warriors, Great Suns, Suns, and Honorable Men. The tribe is now considered extinct, although some of them are rumored to have moved. The town is still named for them. The Natchez. Proud people.

A little brother can find fun anywhere as long as his older brother and sister are along. My parents said our lives in Los

Angeles were different from how they grew up in Natchez. Among other things, they'd seen a lot of prejudice and bigotry against blacks like us down there. My father would say, "It was just one of them Southern towns," and sort of shrug. My mother would say it was a good place to grow up, but maybe not the best of places to be grown, which was why they left. So on the one hand, there wasn't a lot of racism—or I didn't see a lot of it—growing up in L.A. Going to Natchez was like a historical educational experience. My dad would constantly tell us, "Boys, when we get there, you can't do this, you can't do that, don't go here, don't go there, don't make this kind of noise, don't whistle at girls 'cause it's not good home training for one, and you don't know who all everybody is, and if you're going somewhere, let me know where first . . ."

My brother and I might as well have been immortal in those days, no matter where we were. Nobody could outrun or out-play us anywhere, and what else is there to a boy and his older brother? We were young when we went down to Natchez in the summers. Once we got there, we saw our cousins, close and distant, seemed almost everybody we met was a relative of ours.

My father was an only child, raised by his grandmother. He had lots of aunts and uncles, my great-aunts and -uncles, only my parents were so young when they had us, they were like regular aunts and uncles. Ham's mother was a nurse at a retirement home, still working when we went back to visit. Sometimes she would get us ice cream, and would occasionally give us a quarter to have in our pockets. Now no grandmother wants to be out-quartered; we knew it and made sure they knew. My great-grandmother on my father's side was named Alzine Davis, the thoroughbred of a woman who raised him. She was a hardy black woman, granddaughter of slaves, had never been out of Adams County. My father says that these days somebody would call the police on his grandmother for child abuse for the way she laid it on him. His eyes and voice go soft when he says this. He loved her. She was rawhide tough and did not spare the rod raising my father. She taught him chores. Respect everybody. Do your job. My father's mother was named Frances Reed Davis.

Ham said his entire clan was from right there, in that little town. Mom's too.

When we went to Natchez, I was glad mostly to see my grandmother Lesscena. She was so warm, loving, like Shirley, and she had a restaurant, too, the Monte Carlo. Actually it was sort of a glorified jook joint. Jim and I would go there and eat and listen to the jukebox play "Try a Little Tenderness" by Otis Redding, and hear the stories of the truck drivers, hauling loads of lumber and hardwood. Sometimes my grandmother would let us run the cash register and act like we were a couple of big shots from out of town, which probably amused the truckers. We got to pocket the occasional coin or dollar bill that my grandmother sent our way. She had long ago divorced my mother's father. These are things you don't really think about when you are eight years old, visiting your roots, not particularly caring about them that much, and not even later, when the things that happened before begin to happen again. You think your own misery is the first misery the world has ever known. But usually it isn't. Usually there's some kind of precedent for it.

After being careful to tell us where we could and could not go, and what we were to say and not to say to people, in particular any white people we might come across, my father let us go. No doubt in every black parent's mind in those days, whenever they came back home to the South, was what happened to Emmett Till in 1955 in Mississippi, when he came down from Chicago and supposedly whistled at some white female.

We would just go play whatever was being played. A lot of baseball. There was this high school right across the street, wasn't even a block long. Sadie V. Thompson. One building, a little-bitty play area, little cement playground, little softball field, and we used to play on them, and when I would hit, the other boys down there learned to back up across the street. I used to beat up those houses down there. Because I would hit the ball so far. I would knock over flower pots on the old ladies' porches, and if the old ladies were out there, they'd be ducking. Even down in Natchez, it seemed I could hit. I didn't think anything of it, but my brother would shake his head. He was a good athlete; we were nearly the same size, but it seemed I just was a little taller, a little quicker, and I just generally had kept that edge. The great thing about my brother was that he never stopped trying to beat me whenever we played, and he never held a grudge when he couldn't.

My mom grew up in Natchez, in a little house at 121 East Franklin Street. To her, Natchez was a fun little city. She loved the seafood there, and she loved to cook, and she learned to do it there. She had gone to St. Francis High and graduated in 1959. Her parents stressed education to her. Her mother, my grandmother, had struggled to put my mother and her sisters through Catholic school, and she told them not to even think about flunking, and if they did just to pass right on by on their way out of town, don't even stop. That's where my mother learned to get on me about schoolwork. And they didn't lock their doors down there. There weren't any bars on the windows. Everybody knew everybody. Things moved slower, but steadier. We'd walk along, and people would say, "Jimmy Davis's boys! Jimmy must be home. Hey boys, how y'all doin'?" We never got over the shock of being recognized by people we did not know. But they knew us. They knew our faces, walks, mannerisms. We have extended family in Natchez and the area around Natchez. At one point it seemed like that in every town I went to on the road in the National or American Leagues, somebody would show up saying they were a cousin. I'd run the name past my mother and she'd say, "Oh, yesss! So-and-so's sister's child." Oh. My aunts are all over. I have relatives in New Orleans, a gang of 'em there.

"That's one just like his daddy!" "I see a lot of his mama in that one there!"

My mother's parents are still alive down in Natchez—

Grandfather David is around 84, my grandmother Lesscena is 76. Back when we would go down there in the early '70s, they were in the mature prime of their lives, fiftyish, wise, and still mobile. They had done factory work all their lives, at Blue Bell garment factory, at a cardboard box factory, went to Mt. Sinai Baptist Church on St. Catherine Street, where the Reverend Boss Man Williams called down thunder and glory, where my grandfather was a deacon. After my mother's parents divorced, my grandmother married a man named Willie Cage. Then she opened the Monte Carlo. She was a good cook, which is where my mother's talents come from, and which is where my brother and then I inherited it from. Her restaurant opened in 1964, not long after my parents left for California. Eventually my parents divorced too, and my mother opened S & G Southern Kitchen in Long Beach. She remarried too.

In his prime, Grandpa was a hunter, fisherman, great out-doorsman. He had suggested that my parents leave Natchez. A good place to grow up, but not the best place to be grown, he said, just as my mother said later.

My mother's parents helped bring the vote to Natchez for black people. Her grandmother, Hattie Bennett, Lesscena's mother, helped raise them over at number Six O'Brien Street. Something about that kind of living seems to slow down the metabolism. People seemed to last longer. There always seemed to be many more old people than young whenever we went there, which was one reason why, as the years went by, we were less interested in going. We never made any lasting friendships with children our own age. There just weren't that many down there. But we bonded with our forebears. That's in me too, I guess. My mother comes from a large family. We would spend those three weeks down there every summer, roaming, exploring when we weren't playing, working, or eating. We learned who we were without knowing that's what we were doing.

SEVEN / SUMMER 1986

ADVERSITY/BLESSING
Hitting the Big Time

LIFE LESSON/STRATEGY
Don't Rush It, Let It Come

Pete Rose took over the helm as the Reds' manager in 1984. I started out in Wichita, Kansas, that year. If it hadn't been for Sherrie, I'd have been out of my mind, to still be down in the bushes after four long years. I hadn't been in a big-league game yet and Straw was already elected Rookie of the Year in the National League, and supposedly headed for sophomore jinx. On May 29, I turned 22, and I felt old, like a failure who time had passed by. With four years in, I was on schedule, actually, but I didn't see it that way. I asked Sherrie to come see me in Wichita, and she came. I want to thank her parents for letting her come to Wichita and keep me sane. We weren't putting anything over on them.

Double-A pitching wasn't a problem to me. I was hitting .314 with 14 homers, 34 RBI, 42 runs scored in 194 at-bats when I got the call. Meet them in St. Louis. Them? Who? The big club? When the day finally came, it caught me off guard, by surprise. Catch a plane at 10 A.M. Get a cab. Go to Busch Stadium. I was tingling as I got dressed in the visiting clubhouse. Pete sent me up to pinch-hit during the game. I didn't have a number. I didn't even have my name on the back of my game jersey. I had on a blank gray Reds' road jersey. Dave Parker smiled and said, "Don't wanna hear what you did in Wichita. Up here, that don't count, and we don't care."

In my mind, Parker challenged me. I'd show 'em. I went up to the plate facing a big-league crowd for the first time, and a big-league arm, Joaquin Andujar, in my first major-league at-bat. I was a skinny 165-pounder, six foot three, standing in against one of the hardest-throwing right-handers in the National League, who was known as the self-proclaimed "one tough Dominican," one of the best pitchers from that country since Juan Marichal. Walking Underwear, the commentators often mispronounced his name. He came in on me and almost sawed my bat off but I was quick and hit a hopper deep to the hole at short. I bolted out of the box and flew down the first-base line, looking for my first big-league hit. I forgot who was playing short-stop. Ozzie Smith. Ozzola. The Wizard. Just before my foot hit the first-base bag I heard the pop of the baseball in the first-baseman's mitt, and Blue pulled the string on the outboard and called me out. I shook my head in disbelief and trotted back to the dugout. This was going to be tougher than I thought. The veteran outfielders—Parker, Eddie Milner, Gary Redus—chortled at the lesson. Although that may be a hit down in Wichita, in St. Louis, up here in the big leagues, against the likes of Ozzie Smith, it was just a routine out.

I was the regular center fielder for much of the rest of the season, but playing on the artificial turf took a toll, just as a general grind. Center field is a defensive position, and so are second base, shortstop, and catcher. Strong up the middle defensively. On the corners, in right and left field, at third and first base, you have to bring more offense to the party. My average—.224, in 174 at-bats—wasn't anything to call home to Shirley or Sherrie about, but the vets said to give 'em the hitter who figured out big-league pitching a little at a time, rather than the guy who comes up with a big splash and then after the pitchers figure out where his hole is, he sinks without a trace.

I remember the first trip into L.A., to Dodger Stadium in Chavez Ravine. I was so proud to be able to leave tickets for my father, my brother. I looked for them once the game started. My father was there. He seemed happily stunned by it all. It was a day game, so he left before it was over. Had to pull a shift at Boys. Later I went over home, and Jim stopped by, and we had dinner. Steaks. As we ate, I noticed Jim was packing. He had his piece in his coat as he was leaving.

"Where are going, man?" I asked.

"Got things to handle, brother. You don't need to know."

"I can go with you, if you want."

Jim Bean looked at me. "You can't go with me, brother. Keith man, you're Eric Davis!"

Then he left. I went back to the team hotel.

Already I was dinged from playing on artificial turf—bone chips on the outside of my right knee. My first surgery came that off-season, on my right knee. Not before I put on a little display. In September of '84, I hit five home runs in one four-game stretch, making me the first Red to hit a home run in four straight games since George Foster did it in 1978, the year he hit 52. I fell a game short of Johnny Bench's team record of homering in five straight. My rookie year and I was threatening Reds records accumulated by the members of the Big Red Machine. That helped my confidence. Confidence is everything in baseball. Pete had a rep of being a player's manager. He was an other-side-of-the-tracks guy who had hung out with the black players when he was young because the white vets had shunned the young "Charlie Hustle"—it was supposed to be a derogatory nickname at first. I have to let you know that I'm partial when it comes to Pete Rose. Pete gave me a chance to play in the big leagues. He told me not to worry about expectations, just go out there and have fun and play my game. Coming from the legend, to have him tell me, that was *big.* Somebody in the Cincinnati organization believed in *me,* the way I believed in Ham and the sun coming over the mountains in the morning. I thought, "If I can gain this man's respect with my performance, then there is no other respect in baseball I need to gain." To have him put his job on the line for me, that was more than any young player could ask for.

Dave Parker was the teammate who was most important, my instructor and mentor on all things peculiar and particular to the big leagues, my guide and benefactor, my model and the one who showed me by example what the Man is supposed to do on a team. Not everybody has the capability of carrying a team. Parker had that capability, even though he was getting older by then and had come to the Reds from the Pirates a few seasons after they won the World Series in 1979. Parker had won his two National League batting titles while throwing runners out at the plate in All Star games and hitting 39 bombs in a season and driving in 100 like clockwork and just being that finger-waving, Cadillac-king, home-run-trotting dude—"The Thang," he called his home-run trot. I can recall him pulling into the players' parking lot down in Tampa, getting out of his Porsche. I introduced myself, my eyes on that Porsche all the while. "Mr. Parker, my name is Eric Davis and I . . . uh." He broke into a grin, working over a wad of gum. "Nyah. I know who you are, little dude," he said, using an out-of-the-side-of-his-mouth gangster movie voice. "Nyah. Oh you a bad little boy. Nyah. Oh I know who are you. Nyah. You know who I am? Well, you better know."

From then on, he took care of me. I was his son. He said so. He made sure I hit in his hitting group during pre-game batting practice. Dave had been the Man with the Pirates for years, but he was getting along now. Maybe one day I could be a top-end big leaguer. Took me under his wing. Even offered me pairs of his spikes, but he wore 12s and I wore 9s, so shoes were out. But he let me drive that Porsche. He only let me drive from one field to another, to the hotel and back to the ballpark. He would let *nobody* drive his car, but he let me. He schooled me on all facets of the game, on how good I could be if I did this, why I would fail if I didn't do that. He just gave me a trust I couldn't have imagined. Hey, here's somebody else that's rooting for me? I never asked him why because it wasn't that important. Either it was personal and he liked what he saw in me or it was professional and he wanted to help his ball club. Either way, it was good for me. Even though Parker's best years were with Pittsburgh. When I see him now, I still call him "Pops." He was my Ham in baseball. He went through trials and tribulations but didn't let it break him. Finally the Reds traded him to Oakland for the pitcher Jose Rijo in the proverbial Trade That Helps Both Teams; the A's won the World Series with Dave in '89. We did okay with Rijo too, in '90. When I broke the Reds' rookie record for homers, Parker had a bottle of Dom in my locker. I appreciated having him around. He made it easier for me. I came with so much hype, yet didn't know much, never having been through a lot in baseball.

Of course I picked him up, too, as much as I could. His knees were in terrible shape. He was a big man, and playing all those years on artificial turf in Pittsburgh took its toll. When I was in center and he would be in right and a ball would be hit into the right-center-field gap, as I flew after it I could hear him yelling, "Go get it, son!" I can still hear him now: *"Go get it, son!"* He'd point and I'd run it down and if—*when*—I caught it, he'd smile and shake his head and say, "Boy, you are gonna make a *whole* lotta money one day." The reason I started winning Gold Gloves and kept on winning them was because I had Parker and his bad knees on one side and Kal Daniels on the other. Kal could hit, he could really hit, but he had bad knees and a cast-iron glove. Clank.

Parker had an outstanding rollicking sense of humor as well.

I wish every player could have had the opportunity of being in the clubhouse with that man. He didn't allow you to be nervous. You were too busy laughing hard. I don't care what the situation was, if you were desperately trying to make a big-league club for the first time in spring training, or if it was a dog-day game, or a gut-grinder in the middle of a September pennant race, Dave was fun-*nay*. He just wouldn't allow you to be nervous, or jaded, or less than your best. Dave Parker was going to walk in the clubhouse and talk about everybody in there. He had a nickname for everybody. Mine was "My Son." He told Eddie Milner, a fellow outfielder, "Eddie, you can go in the woods and be anything you want to be—squirrel, bear, moose, snake. I don't care. You top 'em all, boy. You one strange-looking soldier!" He used to call Pete Rose "Barney Rubble." Even after he got to Oakland, he was naming people. Called Dennis Eckersley "Denise," because of his hair. I think the Reds got rid of Dave because some people were intimidated by him. I was sorry to see him go. He lost patience with me for being sorry. "This is the way it *is*, son," he said. "This is the way it'll be for *you*, one day. Use all that game you got. That's what you do." Dave Parker helped me make it.

I wish I could have learned more from Pete Rose about hitting. If Pete had had a seminar on hitting, everybody would have been there. But he never really talked about hitting. Didn't want to step on the toes of Billy DeMars, the hitting instructor. Vern Rapp had been on me; supposedly I didn't want to work with Billy DeMars. I didn't have a problem working with Billy, it's just that I wasn't following him around everywhere. Then Tony Perez became hitting instructor. Tony was the kind of guy who didn't care who you got advice from as long as it worked. He wasn't one of those "I can turn this kid around" types, though there were those types in the Reds' organization in my early years in the minor leagues. I never stopped to think that if I was always going in the right direction, always heading up, why should I turn around? Tony wasn't like that. Sometimes in

Florida, I would sit there and listen to Tony Perez and Dave Parker, and if you think I didn't learn about the difficulties and strategies necessary to driving in runs in the big leagues, you'd be *real* wrong. Tony would throw his philosophies out there and Dave would throw his out there. As a young hitter, I tried to grasp it all, tried to incorporate what they said into what could work for me. Pete never talked about his approach to hitting, what he looked for, how he set up pitchers, that kind of stuff. But Tony Perez did. Concepcion did. Parker did. Buddy Bell, Bo Diaz, Cesar Geronimo—they all tried to help out the skinny kid from South Central L.A.

Dave Parker clued me in on the entire history of the Cincinnati Reds, way back to when a guy named Powel Crosley owned the team. The ballpark on the West End was named after him—Crosley Field. Pops was from Cincinnati. He educated me on women who hung around, salesmen who hung around selling jewelry, clothes, anything they can think of to get between a ballplayer and his Glue. Pops was death on me about drugs, which made me smile to myself. That made *him* think I was dissing him, but really, I was smiling because he was coming through for me, trying to protect me, like Jim Bean. Jim Bean was like that, too. Pops had been through this big scandal at the time in Pittsburgh, going back to when he played there and was the Man for the Pirates. I hear him telling me so clear, "Son, if you ever deal with that stuff . . . I'll kill you." And I think he was surprised at me when I smiled, but that was because I'd heard it before, from Jim Bean. A lot of hanger-on guys in those days, they thought being your friend meant offering you some dope. But I always took that to mean a guy really wasn't my friend. He was trying to bring me down.

In a way, Pops was like a second father to me. I still love him dearly. He educated me, and he didn't have to, but he saw something in me that made him feel like he wanted—or had to—share knowledge with me. He said Willie Stargell had done the same for him, although he didn't always listen, so he was halfway expecting me not to. Said he'd called Stargell "Pops," just like I called him, and one day some young ballplayer I was schooling would call me Pops, because that's the way it is. He felt if he didn't pass it along, it would stop. He told me that, in just those terms.

Parker bought me my first big-league suit of clothes. We had to wear suits on the road—no facial hair in Cincinnati—and I wasn't making but forty-two-five, $42,500, the league minimum, which could keep me in razor blades, but I didn't have what you might call business suits to travel in. By the end of the '86 season, Sherrie was pregnant with Erica and I was sending money home to Ham, who was still living at 6606 Denver. Jim Bean was in and out of jail. Parker and veterans like Ed Milner and Gary Redus would tell me, "You ain't paying for nothing, boy. You ain't done nothing in this league yet, so your money don't spend. Here, get these shoes, get this suit." Parker did that for me, and Milner and Redus followed suit, you might say. When I got older and Lenny Harris and Barry Larkin came up behind me, I did the same for them. I tried to instill in them what Dave Parker instilled in me. And until this day, Barry Larkin does that in Cincinnati, takes young guys under his wing. What I instilled in him hopefully he's instilled in others. When it's drilled into you, respect for and knowledge of the game, the whole history and not just the TV history or the Hall of Fame history, then hopefully that will keep young players going, and keep 'em from going off on a tangent, so they will know they weren't the first to go through things, and the sacrifices that the Jackie Robinsons, Larry Dobys, and Curt Floods made won't be lost, or die.

In 1985 I opened the season with the Reds but soon found myself in Denver, where I hit 15 home runs, stole 35 bags in 40 tries

in 207 at-bats, and hit .275. The managers in the American Association graded me as the league's fastest base runner, best defensive outfielder, outfielder with the best arm. I didn't like going
back down that year, but I was determined and starting to figure
it out. Talking to Parker helped. He explained to me that it was
not uncommon to be yo-yoed up and down until you eased
yourself into a starting job or a role with the big club. I made up
in my mind that once I went back, it would be hard to get me
out of there again. September call-up brought me back. I went
13 for 32, hit three homers in the last four games. Pete told me,
"You're my centerfielder." That off-season I tried to avoid
walking under ladders. Pops said I was can't-miss. Sherrie was
pregnant with Erica, and that was the final piece of the puzzle
for me.

Talk about motivation. Talk about responsibility. For a long
time I had felt rootless, which is unnatural for me, coming up in
the way I did. But with my mom going off to a new life, my father sitting there in that apartment basically by himself, and my
brother in and out of penal institutions and that gang life—I
needed something. And really, I'm forever grateful Sherrie came
along.

In '86 I was really focused on the job at hand, and Pete Rose
believed in me and put me in there. I had Parker playing right
field. I moved into the starting lineup for good on June 15, 1986.
I'll never forget it. It was my job now. In the remaining 93
games, I hit 23 home runs with 63 stolen bases, 60 RBI, 78 runs
scored, and a .297 average and what Pops Parker called "All-
World D." "Don't *nothing* get by My Son," he'd say proudly.
I'd have to say our pitchers liked me. Helped their collective
ERA with my catches. For the season I ended up with 80 stolen
bags, second in the National League, one short of Joe Morgan's
club record. That made Rickey Henderson and me the only two
players in the history of the big leagues to hit 20 homers and
steal 80 bases in the same season. I scored 97 runs that year, third

best in the National League, and hit 27 home runs, which, believe it or not, was good for fifth-best in the league that year.

This was preexpansion baseball, and pitching was at a premium in the National League, maybe not quite as tough as it was back in the '60s and '70s, as Pops Parker pointed out to me time and again in that agitated honeybee voice, "Little 'un, I'm tellin' ya, you used to go in against the Phillies, that Carlton with that slider, go oh-for-the-Mets, Seaver, Nolie, Matlack, Koosman."

I didn't have to point out that you could still go 0-for-Mets, them pitching Sid Fernandez, Doc Gooden, Ron Darling, David Cone, but Pops never missed a beat filling me up with historical details, and wasn't the kind you interrupt with something as meaningless as your rookie opinion. "Even the Cubbies had Sutter, with the original split-finger dropping off the table. But when the leaves turned brown, I wore the crown, son." He meant the batting crown. He'd won two.

That season, in July, in the first month after I'd finally won a starting job in the big leagues, I won the first of those five National League Player of the Month awards, this one for July of 1986, when I hit .381, six homers, 16 RBI and 25 steals and 26 attempts, and tied club records with five runs scored in one game, four steals in another game, and three home runs in yet another.

I didn't have time to be happy about being in Cincinnati itself, finally living in a big city as opposed to a minor-league town, because I couldn't really do the things I really wanted to do on a level that I felt they needed to be done. I really wanted to get involved with the community, in my own way, and be like Earl Brown, O. J. Knighten, Sam Watson, a good community guy with the young people, particularly the athletic boys. The guy with the van who went and got people and didn't just talk. But I did try to open doors for the young black players. I did the first commercial with Provident Bank. Did it for one dollar. The reason I did it for a dollar is because first of all it was hard for a black athlete to get a commercial in Cincinnati. But I was confident in my ability. I said, "Give me a dollar, that's all. If the commercial is a success, we can do another and we'll see you on the back end and you can help me in the city." It was the number one commercial in the area for two years, and the relationship I developed went far beyond them paying me. They sponsored the Eric Davis Outfield Club, helping less privileged children come out to games at Riverfront and enjoy themselves. When Kroger, the grocery store chain, saw that, I started doing commercials with Kroger. Later, after Larkin came up, he started doing commercials, and for the first time they saw athletes who weren't looking only at the money they were being paid but at the opportunity to open avenues. I did the spots with a smile and they said, "Whatever you need us to do, we're doing," and as the team got better as the '80s drew to a close, a lot of people were being helped.

We went down to the Salvation Army on one Christmas with a vice president from Provident Bank. We went on a shopping spree, bought all these toys and food and handed it out, and I can't really say whose face was shining more—the children's or the bank vice president's. Then there was this one man in Indiana who had a son who needed a bone marrow transplant. He wrote me a letter and wanted me to send him a ball or a bat or even some spikes because they were having an auction at their church to help defray the costs of finding a donor and having the transplant done.

The boy was five years old.

I'm sitting there thinking, "What can he get for this ball? Two hundred dollars? What can he get for this bat? Three hundred?" So I wrote a check for five grand and sent it. Because if a man, in the first place, thinks enough of me to name his child after me, this may be the least I can do.

*　*　*

Pete didn't care who you were or where you were from, and he definitely didn't care what you looked like. He didn't care, brother. He gave a lot of young guys the opportunity. He's the kind of guy who only cared about whether you could play: he didn't care how old you were, how fat or thin. If you could play, you could play. He wanted to win. Period. That's how Pete looked at it. Pete broke in with five rooks in '87: Kal Daniels, Tracy Jones, Kurt Stillwell, Barry Larkin, Paul O'Neill. Yep. And even though I wasn't technically a rookie (I was a rookie in 1984), I was still young in the game, wet behind the ears, learning how things were done in the big leagues. Pete looked at these guys, and Pete's not the kind to keep 12 pitchers at the expense of everyday ballplayers who can hit because even though pitching is everything, Pete's still Pete, the National League is still the National League. So in '87, we broke spring camp with *eight* outfielders. You heard me right. Eight! That left 17 spots for pitchers, catchers, and infielders. Stillwell was a shortstop. They drafted shortstops back to back, Stillwell and Larkin, brought them along fast. They wanted Stillwell at short and wanted to move Larkin to second base. I told Barry, "Don't let 'em move you if you can help it. You don't want to end up in the outfield with the rest of us. Once you're out of your domain, it's easier to rotate you somewhere else. Then you are more likely to become what's called a utility man. Look at Pops's knees." I didn't have to tell Barry Larkin that but once. Stillwell was later traded. We finished second in the NL West in '87, and finished in second for four of my first five seasons, from '84 through '89. But it was in the second half of 1986 when I began to play every day, and that's when I began to really light it up in the Show.

EIGHT / SUMMER 1987

ADVERSITY/BLESSING
Overnight Sensation

LIFE LESSON/STRATEGY
Study Your Success

In 1987 I became a top-end big leaguer. Superstar. Dave Parker and Pete Rose had told me that it was in me, which was different from me saying it to myself. I had told myself I could do it many times, when I was down there in the bushes, but that meant nothing. Talk is cheap, even talking to yourself. Getting the chance was the first order of business. Pete gave me that. Having some idea of what I was trying to do was the second thing, and Pops Parker and all the guys who on their long slow way out gave me a helping hand, they get a lot of credit. The rest was between me and God and the pitchers, hitters, fielders, and managers of the National League.

For four out of five years, from 1984 until 1989, the Cincinnati Reds finished in second place in the NL West. Then, in 1990, the Cincinnati Reds did *not* finish second. This was top-end big-league baseball in a nice five-year block, and I was right there—it was me, Barry Larkin, Paul O'Neill, Randy Myers, Rob Dibble, Jack Armstrong, Tommy Browning, Danny Jackson, Hal Morris, Chris Sabo, and, in time, Mariano Duncan, and Billy Hatcher—we were top-end major leaguers. There are always levels of the game even in the big leagues. You have guys who are good enough to make it, and that's their goal, at least at first; just to make it up, just to do the job, get it done, get in enough time for the pension; anything else is gravy. I wanted to come up and be a great player, a top-end big leaguer. That was the level of game I strove for. Still do. I got there in '87.

It was more than a notion to do, I'll tell you that. It was not easy. Our club fit in the history of baseball this way: the Baltimore Orioles won the World Series in 1983—the last time they'd won it, come to think of it, as of the 1998 season. Sparky Anderson's Detroit Tigers won in 1984. Kansas City won in 1985 with Bret Saberhagen, George Brett, and Frank White beating St. Louis, with Ozzie Smith, Jack Clark, Willie McGee, and all the others. The Mets won in '86, over the Red Sox. The Dodgers won in '88, somehow beating first the Mets in the playoffs and then the Oakland A's in the World Series. "Somehow" had a name: Orel Hersheiser. Bulldog. His pitching was how the Dodgers got by us in the 162-game grind in 1988 in the first place and how they somehow beat the Mets in the National League Championship Series and how they beat the mighty Oakland A's in the World Series. Without Bulldog they could've never outfought us over the grind in the first place. Outside of Orel and Kirk Gibson, the Dodgers were like a B split-squad compared to us. But we were young, coming, and they were nothing if not veteran. It's competitive at the top end of the big leagues. Always was. Still is. The Pirates of that time, late '80s, had a strong club; Barry Bonds, Jimmy Leyland managing, and he runs a game just about as well as I've seen games run in the big leagues. Atlanta Braves were just gearing up for about a 10-year run of good ball. Then there was us—the Reds. But the dominant team for that five-year period from 1984 through 1989 was probably the Mets. Call them what you want—cocky, arrogant, bats, corkers, airheads, burning it at both ends—but *goood*. Now some might disagree with me there and say the dominant team of the era was the Oakland A's, with Rickey Henderson,

Jose Canseco, Mark McGwire, Dave Stewart, and Dennis Eckersley. But I think the Mets. Both teams won one World Series, the Mets in '86 and the A's in '89. The A's were in three World Series in a row, from '88 to '90. The Mets had as many stars, and Davey Johnson, and a little more pitching. I mean, Jesse Orosco was a key reliever on that team, and he was still getting guys out for the Orioles in '98, so you know he was wicked back in the '80s.

Our competition with the Mets was often bitter. I think they could feel us coming and knew we were right behind them experience-wise and with them talent-wise, or at least not far behind, and that we'd surpass them one day, if nothing else but by the law of averages. There was history there, too—Pete Rose versus Buddy Harrelson, among others. The Mets were good. We were, too—too good to finish second forever. In '87, in a game at Riverfront, in one of those periods when I was so hot it didn't look like anybody could get me, I was rolling into third. I'd stolen 80 bags the year before, 53 in the second half alone. In the first half of the '87 season I'd found my level—a level I've aspired to from then on. This was what I was capable of, when healthy. I hit .293 with 37 home runs, 97 runs scored, 50 steals, and 100 RBI in 129 games, 474 at-bats. That, to me, became my norm. If you work up those numbers over a 600-at-bat season, they'd be interesting, but as my career went on I had to accept that 600-at-bat seasons were unrealistic for what I asked my body to do in the field, on the bases. In '87 I won the first of three straight Gold Gloves for defense and was on the Silver Slugger team for offense. I was Player of the Month in consecutive months, April and May. First time that had happened since '79, when Michael Jack Schmidt did it. So those numbers aren't unrealistic when I'm healthy. Those numbers, that pace—that's what I feel I can and should do.

So one day in Cincy I steal second base, then third, beat the ball and the tag to the bag and suddenly the Mets' third baseman Ray Knight started swinging at me with his fists. I popped up, but for some reason I didn't swing back on him, just lifted him up. God held me back, that's my only conclusion. Where I was raised, it's automatic, if a guy starts swinging at you, then you swing back, quick and hard, and discourage him. But I didn't swing back, and then umpire Eric Gregg had me in a bear hug, and as big as Eric Gregg is, *bear* hug is about right. I still don't know why Knight got mad and started punching. I've been told since that Jackie Robinson had a similar scene with a third baseman of the New York Giants, Alvin Dark, way back in the '50s, after Jackie had made an aggressive play, basically run over a Giants second baseman on a bunt play. So when Jackie rolled into third, Dark was waiting, and they had a little duster. Nothing serious. Serious is dead. Dark was nearly as good an athlete as Jackie, an All-American running back at LSU. But he had certain "ideas" about black ballplayers. Jackie was an All-American running back, a track man *and* a basketball player at UCLA, an army lieutenant, intelligent, articulate, proud guy. There were probably personal feelings between them. You can nearly always add race to this list if that's what you want to do, pretty easy then and now to fall back on somebody else's ignorance, or your own, but to me bottom line is that the Giants and Dodgers were bitterly competitive rivals, and in the end I think that's really behind a lot of bad blood. The Mets and Reds were the bitterest rivals in the '70s and '80s. There was bad blood between the teams then. And that was the bottom line.

So I figure maybe Ray and the Mets felt us coming in the '87 season, really starting with the second half of 1986, when I became a full-time, top-end, big-league starting center fielder. Dealing with the Reds meant dealing with Eric Davis. That's what I had always wanted it to mean ever since I signed on in '80. I just always felt like I belonged there. We were heirs to the Big Red Machine. That was something I could do, a challenge to the gifts God gave me. Talent alone is not enough, you have to hone and harness and apply it—you have to work, and work hard. Took me four years, but now the world champion Mets were feeling me. In '88, the Mets were playing great, playing scared—scared of our talent. The Mets were having a great year in '88, but we were coming. We'd get there. They could feel us. There was a game in early May at Riverfront that got so tense that our manager, Pete, got thrown out of the game by Dave Pallone, a replacement umpire, then later suspended for 30 days and fined $10,000 by commissioner Bart Giamatti for shoving Pallone.

So it wasn't like it was just me and Ray Knight.

In '88, we finished second for the fourth straight year, and the Dodgers played the Mets in the NL playoffs and beat 'em. In '89 we finished second to the Giants, adjusting to losing Pete. This time his penalty was more than being suspended for 30 days. He was ostracized, banned from being elected to the Hall of Fame for betting on games. I loved Pete as a manager because he put me out there and tried to win. In '89 the A's avenged their loss, beat the San Francisco Giants in the World Series. They were dominant—as dominant as the Mets were in the mid-'80s—maybe more dominant. It's all in how you want to look at it. That led to 1990. Funny how it works. Your average big leaguer remembers a season by the numbers he got, the anecdotes of that season. But the top-end player remembers how he won or just missed winning it all. That's what separates top-enders from average big leaguers.

In the middle season of this period, in 1987, I found my level in the bigs. I established myself as a top-end player, which was just what I wanted to do and where I wanted to be. The 1987 season defined me, in terms of what I expected of myself, when healthy. I was 25 at the time. I was still susceptible to the strike-out, but hey, aren't we all? Reginald Martinez Jackson struck out more times than anybody in history, but that ain't what I remember about him. How about you? Well, in May of '87, in the Astrodome, I struck out nine straight times. The Astros threw Mike Scott and Nolan Ryan at us, and they punched me out nine straight times.

I took Nolan into the yellow seat in Riverfront once and when I got to home plate he was standing there. He had watched me all the way around. When I got to home plate he was already there, glowering. I'd heard stories from the vets. You don't bunt on Nolan. After I took him deep I went in and gave everybody high-five and sat down. The next time up, he walked around the mound, storming. It was like he was saying, "I'm tired of this young dude." I still haven't seen the next pitch he threw me. The only thing I did was hear it. Like a *boom* in the catcher's mitt. If he had been throwing at me, he would've killed me, because I didn't see it. That was the hardest thing I ever didn't see in my life. Now, they got me in Houston, nine times in a row, in May of '87. Scott, then Nolan. They got me eight times in a row. Mike got me four times the first game, Nolan got me four times in the second game, then Danny Darwin got me in extra innings. Then we got the hell out of the 'Dome, and was I glad of it.

I have faced people before and since who threw hard. But nobody that threw harder than Nolan Ryan. Doc Gooden came close. Roger Clemens came close. I never faced J. R. Richard. Doc Gooden was a legitimate Hitter's Nightmare, too. Doc struck out 300 big-league batters with straight cheese. Doc's ball would start down low, you'd swing and it would be up high. Vida Blue threw hard. Joe Morgan always talked about Vida. I guess with Joe Morgan being a left-handed batter, Vida was nasty to him. I knew by then to keep my head up. We went to Philly from Houston. In four games at the Vet, I went 10-for-14, with five home runs, including two grannies, in a weekend. Can't keep a good brother down. Always did eat Philadelphia Phillies' pitching alive; left dents all over the Vet in Philly, and also in Candlestick in San Francisco. The next weekend I was on the cover of *Sports Illustrated*, with a photo catching my swing at the moment of impact. The headline read SMASH HIT. Parker, Pete, and Willie Mays and Hank Aaron said a lot of nice things about me, but the thing I always remembered was Mays saying, "It's an honor to be compared to Eric Davis. I hope Eric is

124 / ERIC DAVIS

honored. In the end, all they'll do is compare numbers on paper. And that's not always the game."

By mid-August of '87, I had 37 home runs, 100 RBI, 124 runs scored, and 53 stolen bases. I was hitting .297, and there were still 35 games left in the season. Only one in the league keeping pace was Andre Dawson, who wound up hitting 49 home runs and being elected National League MVP. We were playing the Cubs in Chicago. John Franco was on the mound. We might have been a game or two behind the Dodgers. Two men were on, two outs, and some guy—I think it was Ryne Sandberg—hit a bullet to right center off of Franco. *"Go get it, son!"* Boom, I'm off. I'm thinking, "Oh, I can catch this." I mean I'm wide open. Flat out. In my mind I'm thinking the ball seems to slow down for me to catch it; but as I do, I plaster myself to the right-center-field, ivy-covered wall at Wrigley Field. They have to peel me off that wall, even though I made the catch and we won. But I had ended my season that day. Bruised my shoulder, fractured a rib, and ended up missing the last five weeks of the year, basically. So I played in 135 games that season and still put up substantial numbers, was about to be a 40-40 man (40 home runs, 40 stolen bases), on my way to scoring 150 runs, hitting 50 home runs or so. And in my mind I can still go back to that time, when I was playing at my level, and Parker was sitting on the bench and I was sitting beside him, picking up that informal knowledge, holding a 31-ounce club in both hands, waggling it, not being able to wait to get back up there, Pops's voice a buzz: "Look here, young blood. This is what you need to do right here. Be relaxed. Not excited. Nyah. See?"

I would be nodding. You think you can play ball, and all of a sudden you're out there facing the Orels, or the Dwight Goodens, or the Nolan Ryans, and it's then you realize you don't know what's going on in terms of the progression, the ritual, the knowledge of the game, and learning from Pops, and learning that all experience in hitting leads up to this: The whole thing is recognizing the pitch fast, and do you recognize that pitch excitedly, or do you recognize that pitch relaxed? If you recognize that pitch excitedly, you're not going to hit it square very often. Not often enough. If you recognize it relaxed, you've got a better chance of crushing it often. And when you don't play continually, you can't recognize that pitch relaxed because you ain't seen it. Well, in '87, I started seeing and recognizing the pitches, but I was still young and aggressive, still striking out, and I always will, but by then beginning to understand and relax. This was where I belonged, finally, and no matter what else happens, I always will belong there. Maybe that's why I wanted to get there so bad in the first place. That was my place in the game. Dave Parker taught me a lot about what it was to come to the post every day in the big leagues as well. He was like Ham in that way, only he was that way in baseball. I had seen Ham put in work like that, but not in baseball. When you're every bit of six five and 260 pounds, having both knees drained and you're playing right field on hard turf under that Lamp—that's tenacity, right there. I watched Parker get 32 cc's of bloody fluid drawn out of both knees at 5 P.M., be in the lineup playing at 7:30 that evening, take people out at second base to break up a double play at 8:45 that night.

I learned to like Cincinnati. I moved into Amberly Village, an affluent area. Parker, a Cincinnati native, lived there, in the northeast part of town—not the Wyoming district, and not Indian Hill, where Marge Schott and the head of Proctor and Gamble, Carl Lender, lived, but nice, and still close enough to the people in places like Kennedy Heights and the West End, where Crosley Field used to be, where I liked to hang out. Avondale was in the central city. It was mostly a black neighborhood. I showed my face there too because I wanted to represent all the citizens of all seven hills of Cincinnati—hard to do because though it's a baseball town, it's very conservative, and that's why I stood out even more, plus with my style—it wasn't all that flamboyant for L.A., but it was *way* out there for Cincinnati, especially when I was younger with my white Mercedes-Benz and my leather suits. Hickey-Freeman suits and Bruno Magli shoes never did it for me

WLW, the big radio giant in Cincinnati, gave me a hard time, had a history of talking about and often bashing Eric Davis for whatever reason, his dress and style probably being an unspoken part of the criticism. I always had an earring, too. But now, I was a local hero in Cincinnati and I was visible. The radio shows often talked about me, and I didn't listen mostly, but then one day I went on with them, let them rip me. "Eric Davis, you're a good ballplayer, but you're always hurt."

"Let me ask you," I replied. "What would happen if you got hurt on your job? I know it's a stretch, because what can you hurt sitting in a chair and talking to a mike? Let's just say the chair breaks and you fall and hurt your back. Should they fire you? Get rid of you? I've never been out fighting in any bars. I've never gone around beating up women. I've never been DUI. Everything I've ever done to get hurt has been diving for balls, running into walls, going over walls—getting hurt trying to do the best job of playing baseball I could do. If your boss walked in tomorrow and told you, 'We've got to let you go because you keep getting hurt trying to do your job . . .' "

They weren't hearing it. Then one guy called in, and he was emotional. "You guys don't know Eric Davis; you don't know the type of man he is." He skipped over the baseball part and told a story. He had written to me hoping to get a couple of cracked bats and scuffed balls to raise money for a young kid that had AIDS, loved Eric Davis, and had the same name. I remembered now. There was suddenly deadpan silence on the radio, after beating me up for 20 minutes. Then the host of the show came on and said, "Well he should let us know about stuff like that."

But that would kill it for me, running around blowing a horn every time I did something for somebody. That would change it. There ain't no bandwagon following kindness. But this was the story behind that call: I often volunteered to sign autographs and memorabilia with the proceeds going to the Salvation Army so they could buy Christmas gifts for the underprivileged. Once we were in the Florence Mall, and a girl was waiting patiently. A lot of people in the line were loud and boisterous, having fun and arguing, so in that kind of environment, the silent one stands out. A young teenaged girl was there. I noticed her because she was so quiet. She slowly came up through the line. When she got to me finally, she said she wanted an autograph for her brother.

"Mr. Davis, he's the biggest Eric Davis fan in the world," she said.

"Well, why didn't he come on down here?" I asked.

"He couldn't come."

"No? Why not?"

"He has AIDS . . . he's in junior high . . . Mr. Davis, I know everybody asks you to do things for them, but could you please just call him?" My friend Wayne "Box" Miller was there with me, and he said I could sign but that I couldn't be calling everybody, and I let him talk. And then later we got in the car and were driving across the river. I thought about it. "Stop the car," I said.

"What?"

"I said stop the car."

I got out, called the boy. I didn't tell anybody I called him. I didn't want anybody to know about it but me and him, and whoever he wanted to tell. I remember that vibrancy in his voice after I asked for him and said Eric Davis was calling and he got on the line breathless. (I heard two other extensions pick up.) I told him to never give up the fight and that the next home run I hit had his name on it, and I felt like for one moment in that young man's life, the world was his, and by putting it the way I did, I was in no danger of letting him down. I didn't say I'd hit a homer in the next game. I said the next homer was his, knowing for sure the next homer would come. It just happened to come in the next game.

I was often in everybody's conversation around Cincinnati because (1) that's the nature of baseball; (2) it's a long grind during the summer and people talk; (3) then there's the "Hot Stove League" over the winter, when ballplayers and teams and trades and prospects are discussed by the general population and everybody thinks they're experts; and (4) Cincinnati is a baseball town with the history of the Big Red Machine. But I was also often discussed because of my stand-up ways and never shirking away from anything. Being in that clubhouse with me, you couldn't tell if I was 4-for-5 or 0-for-5, because I was the same way with my teammates and the press. I was the Man at an early age and I tried to be a stand-up Man. People often were looking for me to make excuses so they could bash me more, it seems: "He's making excuses." I learned very early in Cincinnati not to do that. Whether anybody there wanted to admit it or not, the Cincinnati Reds really needed me. They thrived on me being there, in almost every sense. Even if we didn't win the game, I gave them a story. I gave the fans something to be amazed by. I helped give us a chance to win every game that we went into. I never shirked responsibility, I never hid from the press in the training room, I never put a moratorium on speaking to the media, except once. Eric Davis was going to give 'em something to talk about either way. It was frustrating not to be at least appreciated for that. It really didn't bother me then, but in a sense it did, because the people in the Cincinnati organization, the hierarchy, even to a degree the fan base, until this day, have never focused on the things I accomplished in a Reds' uniform. They were spoiled by all the great players on the Big Red Machine giving them a great decade in the '70s. We gave them a good decade in the '80s, and then we gave them 1990, the great team season. Individually, Rickey Henderson and I were the only players in history to steal 80 bases and hit 20 homers in the same season. I won the five NL Player of the Month awards. Only

Mike Schmidt and I did it. Barry Bonds and I were the only ones to hit 30 homers and steal 50 bases in a season. Since I left Cincinnati, I don't think they've had a player drive in 100 runs. I had three straight Gold Gloves patrolling the outfield in Cincinnati. So many memories of so many things. So many things I did in that uniform. I loved that uniform. I loved playing there.

During the off-seasons in the late '80s, I kept busy in L.A. Straw and I started the Program in '81, before either of us was in the big leagues. By the winter of '87, the year after Straw and the Mets won the World Series beating Boston, the Program was at its height. It lasted 10 years, through 1991. We could have held it at one of those nice college campuses, UCLA, USC, or Long Beach State, or one of the Cal-Poly system campuses, but we stayed in town, held it at Harvard Park, with Crips territory on one side and Bloods turf on the other, us on neutral ground. If you were a prospective ballplayer, you could go there with no trouble and work together. If anything, those gang members were proud, too, asking us for autographs. Everybody's a baseball fan, deep down. On a hard-scrabble field with no grass, at Harvard Park, at 62nd and Denker, me in my red Reds' gear, not being bothered, Straw in his blue Mets' gear, the same, even though we all knew you didn't wear red unless you were a Blood, and you didn't wear blue unless you were a Crip.

By 1988 we had 100 young people out there, and big leaguers like Shane Mack, Frank Thomas, Shawon Dunston, and Barry Larkin helped. In keeping with my wish to work with youth, we helped high schoolers, college players, even minor leaguers with ability, people who would grow, if not as players, as coaches or in other positions. Dijon Watson, Johnny "Guitar" Watson's son, came through the Program and is now a scout for the Reds. Kenny Williams now works in a front office with the Chicago White Sox. Royce Clayton, the shortstop who has played with the Giants, the Cardinals, and the Rangers—I remember when his father first brought him out to Harvard Park from St. Bernard's High, where he was a shy 18-year-old, back in '87. We had clinics, took BP with the pitchers' standing behind plastic garbage bins instead of screens because we didn't have screens. There was no charge for enrollment in the Program. We tried to share what we knew.

I got married that winter, in December of '87, at Mt. Moriah Baptist. We had an informal bachelor party over at the Paradise Club in Santa Monica after one of the workouts with the Program. We went over in a kind of caravan. Larkin is riding with me. We've earned the expensive cars we're in by playing in the major leagues. Out in the parking lot, some guys started getting into it over some ladies. Soon police arrived, and people were getting handcuffed, including me. They asked me to get on my knees. As long as it isn't in an oil slick, I said, I'll comply. Then the helicopters came around, shining their lights down. Then we got lucky. An African American police captain shows up and says, "Isn't that . . . Eric Davis?! And that over there, isn't that . . . Darryl Strawberry?! What are you guys doing out here in this?" We'd caught a couple of rookies who thought since we were in expensive cars, we had to be dealing dope, and the dispute had to be over that, and they had a great collar. It happens in L.A., in Cincinnati. I just . . . happens. You can let it give you high blood pressure or not. First off, my brother's life was ruined in the streets. His life was ruined behind dope. I *saw* it happen. Jim had grabbed me many a time and said, "You don't want to be out here, brother. You *don't.*"

When we got back to my place after getting rousted on the way to my informal bachelor party, Larkin called his mother back in Cincinnati and talked for 45 minutes, and promised her that he was coming home soon. I haven't seen Barry in Los Angeles hanging out with me ever since. I'm kidding. I always see Barry, he's one of the better friends I've made through baseball, and was one of the most dependable teammates, too.

PART III
Fall

NINE / FALL 1997

Loss

When One Door Closes . . .

On August 31, 1997, I was traveling with the team, and we were playing the Marlins down in Miami. I was anxious to get off the DL by mid–September and help my teammates and Davey Johnson and all the personnel and fans get to the Series. That was the job description I signed on for, and I also considered myself in a challenge to get back from cancer surgery and chemo, get back in, run a few balls down on defense, put good wood on the ball. We were in first place by six games in the AL East. The Yankees wouldn't catch us. Had to get back, get sharp, help the club.

Then . . . Sherrie called. "Eric." Her tone was serious, protective. Something was wrong. I sat up. She broke it to me clean. My brother . . . dead? Found . . . outside a church?

Jim Bean? Dead? At first, the breath rushed out of me.

"No. Nooooo!" But it was true. Nothing can ever change it.

I don't even remember hanging up the phone. I wanted to burst through the door, help him.

But there was nowhere for me to run. So my only brother, Jimmy Davis Jr., Li'l Jim, Jim Bean, my model, my protector, my competitor, died on August 31, 1997. He was 36—one year older than me. I'd begun taking chemotherapy just before he died. I'd been talking to him regularly. He'd called me every day since I was diagnosed with cancer. Every single day. He had gotten out of prison for the last time, and was working and had a new girlfriend and was doing better. Usually, you call your older brother for advice, for strength, but with all the things he and I'd been through, it was like I'd become the older brother. Sometimes he would call me just to tell me he'd had a good day.

Earlier on, his life had gone wrong, he'd sold dope, he'd been in gangs. But I'm not ashamed of my brother. He did do those things. But I remembered him before all of that. I know he knew God, he was smart, he was intelligent. But he got caught up. My brother was in and out of prison for 10 or 12 years— may have spent more time in prison than he did on the street, on drug-related offenses, recidivism, caught up in the system, minor things. He wasn't a bad person, but he was one of those who could not leave the streets alone. He had friends in the streets, and that became his workplace. He had made certain choices in establishing a particular way of life. His friends were important to him. His image out there was important to him. His relationship to gang members, to his fellow former Crips, even after he got older and a lot of 'em ended up dead or in prison, those relationships remained important because that had been his life. It was hard to accept that much of his life had been wasted. He wanted those people to have been worth what he had sacrificed.

The Crips. That gang became important to him when I was in the minor leagues. The Crips were, in essence, his Cincinnati Reds. What people don't understand when they talk about gangs, crime, and so forth is what they are talking about are real people—they can have good senses of humor, they can do things to help you, protect you, make you feel wanted, needed. This is particularly meaningful for those young people with home lives that have broken down, if they ever existed for them in the first place. So they end up feeling indebted to the gang. The gang becomes family. Everybody is not going to have a good, stable home environment, just like not everybody is going to go to college. Everybody is not going to be a professional ballplayer. How you grow up is out of your hands, but how you survive is more on you. Jim Bean made his choice. I wasn't proud of it, my parents weren't proud of it, but that was the life he chose. That's what became important to him, and for a very long time I didn't and couldn't understand it. But then again, often I wasn't there.

Prior to his death and my becoming ill, I had stayed distant from him, yet was constantly preaching to him over the phone about independence from the gangbangers and dope slingers. I told him, "The Reds were all I knew, and I was traded away from them, and did okay. So you can break out. You can be your own man, do your own thing, you don't need them, stay out of those situations." He did listen. When he was incarcerated, he said his family became his best friend. But when he was out, the streets became his best friend again. I think he felt distant from me. Before his death, it was dawning on him that he could change. He was giving a valiant effort to changing, and he did change a lot. My daughters saw it. I'd gotten him a job, he was working, he was doing a lot of positive things, and so that's why the news of his sudden death was so shocking to me.

"Wrong one got sick, brother."

He was working inventory control at a warehouse. He was really enjoying the independence of working, and I was enjoying being a brother who was blessed to be able to help. I wouldn't just give to my brother. I'd help, but my thing was, if you help yourself, I'll bend over backwards for you. I'm not going to give you anything just to be giving it to you, because you won't keep it. You won't appreciate it. If you help yourself, then I'm there for you. If it's helping you with a down payment on an apartment you need to be close to your job—I'm there. I had just bought him a Cadillac. He loved Cadillacs. And he was just at that point where he seemed to be crossing that road, coming on over to the good side. And I guess it was time for the Lord to bring him home.

I don't really know the circumstances of his death. Nobody killed him. That was important to me, that nobody killed him. Had somebody shot him or done something else to him, it would have been important to me to find out who that was and why it happened. Because my brother would've done that for me. I know vengeance is God's, not mine. My brother had a lot of notoriety on the streets. He knew everybody. Everybody knew him. So I didn't really worry about anything but him maybe relapsing. And maybe that's what happened. My mother told me my brother had a heart attack and ran toward a church. That's where he died, trying to get inside a church. Until this day, I've not seen the autopsy report. Something was bothering him . . . he went in the streets to try and forget. Made sense to me that he'd try to get to a church at the end. He had a seizure, 911 was called, paramedics came. He was pronounced dead at Martin Luther King Hospital.

Sherrie was the one who told me my brother was dead because I'm sure my mother and my sister just couldn't do it. I knew they wouldn't tell me if something happened to Jim Bean. They would tell my wife, and have her tell me, because they couldn't take telling me, giving me another burden. When Sherrie told me, it was like my whole body went numb. I watched him survive the incarceration, gangs—now, when he finally starts changing his life around for the better, this. If only a few people realize how dangerous drugs can be from learning about my brother's story, then hopefully something good will come of explaining my brother's situation. His situation always bothered me—not to a point where I was in a constant mental struggle, but I *was* often in a constant state of worry. When he died, I came home and cried, because I love my brother. I cried and I did all the things people do when they lose a loved one. But in some ways it was like a relief to me, because I worried about him constantly. I used to tell him how much I worried about him whenever he called me. He had been calling a lot since I had been diagnosed with colon cancer and had the surgery. I was not in the habit of calling him. In fact, I would almost never call him because I didn't think of him as that . . . being available. That was how our relationship evolved.

I didn't want to see my brother behind bars. So I never went to visit him when he was in Chino or one of the other prisons. He would call me, and if he called, then I would talk to him all day long if he wanted me to, but I never called, and I never went to see him because I didn't know what his situation might be. Since the bogus drug accusations thrown at me on the front page of the *Cincinnati Enquirer* back in 1988, I didn't want to get caught up, be close to a situation that could be used against me, no matter what my motives might have been. I never wrote Jim Bean because I knew he wouldn't answer. He was where he was. He didn't have to be there. He chose to be there. Not calling, not visiting, and not writing were also my way of letting him know I was disappointed. Because of the relationship we had, I've always relied on him, being my big brother, opening doors and avenues for me as I grew up, teaching me—then, to see the one I looked up to go the way he went, being behind bars, doing stuff he didn't need to do . . . it was disappointing.

After I got sick, he was working and trying to stay away from the life that was basically just outside the front door. During the prior off-season, before I came to Baltimore, I talked to him every day then, and sometimes three and four times a day. At this point my way of covering him was to say, "If there's the slightest thought in your mind about doing something you know is wrong, you call me, and we'll talk about it." He called me when he didn't feel right, or if there was anger or confusion in his heart, whether it was something he did or his girlfriend did, or whatever life brought to him that made him want to slip back into that street life.

I did not do enough for my brother because I wanted so

badly for him to do for himself. That's the way we were raised, to do things for ourselves. I design my own clothes, I cook—not as good as my mother and Jim Bean could cook, but I know my way around the kitchen. If we're having company, Sherrie will ask, What are you cooking? It makes me smile. I don't ride in limos. I like to drive myself. And I wanted Jim to experience things I've experienced—being down, fighting and winning against odds—succeeding for myself, Sherrie, the girls, my mother, and my father. I wanted Jim to feel what I felt when I made it to the big leagues, after I didn't think I would get there. I overcame my own doubts. And that's what you have to do. I wanted him to feel what I felt when I bought my first car. It doesn't seem like a big deal, does it? But when you get your own, when it's not given to you, and you earn it out for yourself, there's a feeling of accomplishment in that. "That's mine. I did that." I wanted my brother to feel that. That's why I would help him, but only at the last minute, in trying to coerce him into doing for himself, to experience his own success. Success breeds success. Doesn't matter the level of success—to me, success doesn't have levels. I wanted him to turn his life around, get his own check that *he* earned, do what *he* could do.

Before the '97 season, he called me up and proudly said, "Got my paycheck, brother. It's only a little, though, compared to you." Then I said, "Yeah, Jim Bean, but it's *yours,* brother. Open an account. Deposit it. Get a checkbook, write a check."

You feel good when you do things like that.

Those are the things I wanted to convey to him, and those were the last things we talked about. Our relationship was deep, but not for other people to see. *"Wrong one got sick."* That's what he was feeling when I was diagnosed with cancer. He never said, "It should have been me." I know that's what he was saying. He'd say, "Brother, you don't deserve this. Not you. Not you." I know that's how he felt. He was saying, this isn't right. He knew everything there was to know about me. I was his little brother. He helped make me the person I am.

Because of his struggles and battles, he kept me on the straight and narrow path. And he'd say, "Brother, you don't want anything that's out there. I'm out there, and I know—these streets ain't nothing to play with. Just keep on doing what you're doing. You don't want nothing in these streets. These streets is real."

"Hey Keith man—you're Eric Davis!"

Physically, my brother wasn't as big as me, not as tall as me, but you would never know it by his heart and how friendly he was with people. Believe it nor not, my brother was a speaking friend of Jerry Buss, the Lakers' owner. He was just like that. Could come right up to you and start talking to you. Just weak in having a plan for his life. I've always had to have my own plan. To make up for it. My brother wasn't as athletic as me but you would never know it by his heart. And I know that with his friends and fellows in the streets, even though he had tried to square up his life, he had so much respect that if someone had killed my brother, it would have been on. But they told us it was a heart attack—cardiac arrest. It wasn't a bullet that ended his life. I never asked if it was drug-related. But in the back of my mind, I programmed myself to believe it was drug-related. Because you just don't go into cardiac arrest like that. So even though much of his life he was wrong, in the end, I try to look at it from the perspective of how it helped me. His being on the path he was on helped me. It educated me to stay on the path I needed to stay on. It's hard, now, thinking about him, talking about him. You have people who are paid to critique this and that about athletes and their lives, but how is my life so different from anybody else who grew up in the places and situations I did? How is my life so different from yours? Until you've walked in a guy's shoes, you don't know what he has to deal with. You have no idea how hard it is, not to play the game—the game is the easy part—but when you step out of that clubhouse, to know your brother is dead, after running to try to get to a church, and you were not able to help.

I've had people tell me "I'd give an arm and a leg to be in your situation."

You would? Suppose you found out that being there wasn't enough? I gave a kidney to my situation. I gave a third of my colon to my situation. I gave my knees to my situation. I gave up my brother to be in my situation. I thought of this all through a sleepless night, and all the next morning, September 1, in the cabin on the flight back to L.A., going back to bury my big brother.

My father took it harder than my mother. My brother was a junior. Jimmy Davis Jr. My father couldn't even be around the house in Woodland Hills for very long. He'd just shake his head, and wince, and wince, and shake his head, and return to his house, which was not too far away. He stayed at his house. He'd come by for 15 or 20 minutes when I first came back. But he pretty much stayed at home and that was his quiet time, for him to do whatever he did.

My mom actually handled it pretty well. She's strong spiritually and a take-charge sort of woman, anyway. She had just been through the cancer diagnosis and surgery and recovery and chemotherapy with me. She came back to Baltimore for me, when I was diagnosed, and was in the room with me when I came to from the anesthesia. She wouldn't let me sulk or be depressed for very long. Some people fall to pieces in situations like that. My mother is not one of them. She broke down in her quiet time after my brother died so unexpectedly, but for the most part, she surprised me with the calm way she handled it. She had always been the one to write to my brother and visit him in prison. My father, too. They did that. I didn't do that. It's never easy when you lose a loved one, but to lose a brother is not the same thing as losing a son. It's not the same. That's your child; that came out of you. It's part of you, as a brother. Brotherly love is strong, but there's nothing like parental love. Totally different chapter of the book. So I know it was harder for them.

But my mom handled it. She is the most incredibly strong person I know, really.

Jim Bean was his nickname. That's why, when I came back with the Orioles in September, I wrote J.B. on my cap. Jim Bean. That was for my brother. Those were trying times. There's no path, no book that I could pick up that tells you how to deal with losing a loved one that all along you hoped—knew—would be saved, because he was part of *you*, and *you* had always been saved. It is still hard for me until this day. Even now, I see people that don't know, but know us, and they'll ask, "How's your brother?" Damn, man. My brother passed. "What?" A constant reminder because he knew many people. He knew so many people. "How's your brother?" Me knowing in my heart it was drug-related, and people asking, "What happened?" You don't get the feeling you want to go into detail with them, I can tell you that. There's only so many details I know about it myself. Only so many details I even want to know. The important thing is that he's not here, and in the end, what else is there to know? I know nobody killed him. That's what I needed to know.

My father never sat down and asked if there was anything I knew or could tell him about my brother's death. We would just sit in the quiet. I think Jim Bean's death brought my father and me closer together. I am the only son he has left. He has no grandsons. I have my two daughters, and he has a daughter, my sister. I'm the son he has left. He lives only six minutes away from us in Woodland Hills, and comes by every day when I'm home, just to say hi, spend a little quality time. We never had been able to do much of that before because when I was growing up he was always working in the grocery store warehouse, and even though he still works, he slowed down once I was in the big leagues and on the road. The quality time we spent together was back when I was a boy, when it was mostly just me and him and my brother, playing ball together, him cutting us no slack. By the time I started playing sports competitively, I knew how to play. When I could play with Ham, kids my own age were no problem. Seems like I have twice as much feeling for Dad now that Jim is gone. More than before. Seeing him hurt—it hurt me. Seeing him not be able to see or talk to someone he brought into the world, seeing the pain on his face created pain for me.

I think only fondly of my brother now. He took me with him everywhere—reluctantly, but he took me. You know how big brothers are: "I don't want you tagging along." Might have wanted to try to do things he didn't want me to know about. But my mother always said, "If you're going, you're taking your li'l brother with you." And he would.

So my brother, Jim Bean, Jimmy Davis Jr., fulfilled all that a brother could ever ask an older brother for, outside of leaving me at only 36 years of age. He left me only in sight, because he'll always be in my heart. *For we walk by faith, not by sight.* I was not one of the pallbearers at his funeral. Those were his boys, one was his best friend. Chris Tyaska. We always called Chris "Julio" because he looked Latino. They'd lived the fast life together, but Julio got out of it, and Jim Bean was getting out. Just couldn't turn that final corner. Chris was like me, the opposite of my brother, and if my brother could not find me and talk to me sometimes, Chris was the one he would call. Chris helped him as much as I did, probably more. They grew up together, too.

What really got to me was my younger daughter's reaction. Sacha went up to see my brother as he lay in the coffin. She came back and told Sherrie, "Mommy, they had makeup on his face!" Sacha's the one who would notice this kind of thing. Erica was quieter, as usual. I hated that they had to learn about mortality in this way. "Mommy, he taught me to ride a bike," Sacha said. Yes, I cried then. I cried hard. Jim Bean—the only brother I ever knew, had, or needed. The best brother I could've ever had. *"Keith, man—you're Eric Davis!"*

* * *

I had a week at home before my first game back, September 15. The only way I knew to glorify my brother's name was through my own actions, to do the things I knew how to do best. Raise my girls that he loved dearly, raise them right, love my wife even more, grow closer to my—our—sister, mother, and father, and to God. Second to that, play ball. Baseball was like an out for me.

The funeral was on Saturday, September 6. I left for the East Coast on Monday, September 8. The Orioles were starting a 12-game home stand, trying to wrap up the division title, and during that home stand I would be put back on the active roster. I couldn't let animosity or sadness take control. I had to say, "It's not a sad time. On earth we have problems. He's in a better place. Ain't ever going to be sick no more. Never want for food, crave a hit; he will never have any of those earthly concerns. We are the ones who have to deal now. So what am I going to do, fold up like some cardboard box? That wouldn't be me.

"Keith, man—you are Eric Davis!"

I came back officially on September 15. The Cleveland Indians were in town. Dr. Lillemoe was at the first game I played when I came back. Doc had gone to the Sunday-night game. We had talked. He had come down to Camden Yards to see me and his handiwork, and to visit Boog Powell, who had also been diagnosed with colon cancer. Dr. Lillemoe had just operated on Boog within the last two weeks. I'd gone down to Johns Hopkins to see Boog. I had everybody on the floor laughing. I saw Dr. Lillemoe turn the corner with a frown, because usually it's quiet. He saw me and understood why all the nurses and patients were smiling. I had come to see Boog and it seemed to hit me that I could make the people there brighten up. I held court, joked, signed autographs and hats, hugged nurses. Tears were flowing, tears of joy. I warmed it up in there that day, and we were all sincere. These people helped save my life, among many others. I thought back to when I was in Johns Hopkins for five days surrounding surgery. In all that time, nobody asked me for an autograph. Nobody did anything but treat me professionally.

Now I'd come back. If I could've taken 'em all—doctors, nurses, technicians, patients—back to the ballpark, I would've done it.

Back in the clubhouse, I was in my element. I was subdued, because of Jim Bean. But the visit to Boog had brought me out of sad thoughts. Our careers hadn't overlapped. After Brooks Robinson and Cal Ripken and Jim Palmer, Boog is, probably, the fourth most popular player in Oriole history. Baltimore is his life and the city loves Boog. Dr. Lillemoe was sitting up in the press box when I came to the plate against Brian Anderson. The crowd gave me a long standing O, and I took off my batting helmet and held it aloft, looking around. I thought this was nice of them, to treat me this way. Baltimore is truly a baseball town. You can see it when you come to the games: there's not too many who come to Oriole Park without something orange and black on, whether it's a cap, a shirt, socks, something. I saw all this orange and black swimming in front of me now as I kept my batting helmet held up high, acknowledging the emotion and sincerity I felt from the cheers. I glanced at my teammates. They were applauding. Hammer. Cal. Bainesy, Tractor Man, Bay-Bay, Pac-Man, Raffy, Beej. All the brothers. I was a long way from home now. And at the same time, I was completely *at* home. It was September 15, in just another ballgame, this time against the Cleveland Indians. I could've come back on the road but didn't want to. I wanted to come back in Baltimore because I thought the fans deserved to see that I *could* do it, especially for the way they and the organization had treated me. Peter Angelos had come to see me at the hospital after the surgery in June. I'd been surprised, not because of him, I hadn't known him until that day. I was surprised because of the way I'd always known big-league owners to be. When he left my room, I knew he was the type of man I wouldn't mind running into a wall for.

So I found myself back, standing in the batter's box on September 15 in Oriole Park at Camden Yards. I doffed my cap with "J.B." written on it and waved it to them all—to my family;

to the people at Johns Hopkins University Hospital, doctors, technicians, staff, and patients; my teammates; the Oriole fans who treated me so well; all the baseball fans who cheered; all the cancer patients I'd seen; and also Peter Angelos. I was thanking them all.

I still made an out on that at-bat . . . but I was going for it. It was an out, but it was a loud out. I was trying to touch 'em all. For everybody. Brian Anderson was pitching for Cleveland—lefty, good running fastball, good slider, good change-up. Three-pitch pitcher. I took him out to deep right field, but I got under it a little, a half inch or so. Just a loud out to right field, to Manny Ramirez. Hammer was on second and he advanced a base to third on the play. The fans cheered me like I just touched off a ninth-inning grand slam. I waved to them on my way back to the dugout, feeling like I'd gotten a World Series hit. Out in the field, I guess I was like a puppy again. Made four putouts in right field, made 'em eagerly. Hammer was in center, and I nearly ran him over to catch one drive in the gap by Matt Williams. We sort of gingerly ran into each other, and I know it's always the center fielder's call out there, but I'm a center fielder at heart. Hammer understood.

We won, 5–4. I was happy. I started 0-for-6, making me 0-for-my-last-24, counting the slump during May, before the cancer was diagnosed. I wasn't worried. I knew I was swinging the bat well. I felt a presence. Saturday, September 20, against the Tigers, next to last home game of the season, I came up as part of a nine-run third. I'd ended the home half of the first by grounding out hard to third on the first pitch from Scott Sanders. This made me 0-for-10 since coming back. I came up again in the third. This was after Harold Baines had hit a sac fly, Chris Hoiles had hit a bomb, then Mike Bordick had hit another. Then B.A. had singled to right. Robby had doubled hard off the right-field scoreboard. Now I was up again, runners on second and third. One of my old teammates with the Reds, Buddy Bell, was managing the Tigers. There were two men on. Buddy has a good memory. He brought in right-hander Kevin Jarvis. He busted me inside. No thank you. Then he tried to go away, and—flick, like a rattler's tongue—I hit it up the gap in right center. Two-run double. Slid in, popped up, stood in the sun. The fans cheered. Later, Davey pulled me. As I left the field the fans and my teammates gave me a standing O. I pushed up the roof, signaling to the fans to do the "big up" and doffed my cap again and disappeared from their view into the shade of the dugout.

Slept good that night, dog.

When we went on the road after that game, I was overwhelmed by how much love the fans showed me. Other than by God and my family it was the most loved and cheered that I've ever been and experienced in my life. It humbled me. Didn't matter where I went, the fans and people who weren't even fans were kind, offering congratulations, saying they hoped I felt all right, telling stories of their battles or their loved ones' battles with cancer. Telling me of their feelings. Like I was giving them hope. They said they had gotten renewed strength from what they saw as my strength. In Toronto, the fans cheered me. On September 25, we clinched the division title against the Blue Jays. I went 0-for-5, with four strikeouts, but I was happy. We'd won the division. Of the six teams in the history of organized ball to go wire to wire, be in first place from the first day of the season to the last, I had been on two of them—the '90 Reds and the '97 Orioles.

When I came back my incision was tight, because of the scar tissue. I knew it was there when I swung, but it didn't hinder my swing. I wasn't as strong as before the surgery, but I didn't have swing restrictions, wasn't checking up. I didn't have the same fluidity and pop I had before. But the incision didn't trouble me. I could swing the bat.

Milwaukee was next, to wind up the season. I had a chemotherapy treatment set up at the Marquette Hospital there. The first part of the chemo wasn't that bad, I was prepared, I had the herbal teas and my movie tapes. I knew we were facing pitcher

Jeff D'Amico in Milwaukee, and that I would be in there. But first I had to take this other chemotherapy treatment. I took it because I was scheduled to, but I also knew that I had to show Davey I could swing the bat, so he'd have no qualms about getting me in there in the playoffs. We had Geronimo "Chief" Berroa, picked up on the roster after I went down. He was a designated hitter, a guy who is death on some left-handed pitching, but even Chief would tell you he's a liability in the field, whereas I'd like to think I'm not.

With two games left in the season, I was hitting .281. I took the treatment. Afterward I had an appetite anyway, and ate a big breakfast. Jeff D'Amico was the best starter Milwaukee had that year, a big right-hander. My first time up, I got a base hit to right on a slider away. Second at-bat, I got a fastball and banged it up the middle for another base hit. Third at-bat, I got something in my power zone, something I could drive. *Stay back, stay back . . . Bomb Contact!* I knew it. I didn't have to look at it. The ball went deep into the stands in left center for a home run. My teammates were all over me in the dugout. They knew what it meant. I was on again. I was back.

Fourth at-bat, I got another base hit, this one to left. My teammates mobbed me when I returned to the dugout. I finished the year batting .304. The home run I had hit was the first one I'd had since May 6, which is Willie Mays's birthday. We ended up winning the game 5–4 when Robby hit a three-run homer in the ninth. Now, the playoffs were on, and I was in it, and of it.

It was incredible. I had come back and contributed. I had finished the season strong. It felt so good. And in Milwaukee, Toronto, no matter where I went, people were giving me nothing but love. "Hey Eric, how you feeling?" "Hey Eric, attaway!" "Hey Eric, you're looking great!" "Congratulations!" "Hope you're feeling all right!" "Eric, my uncle has it. He's watching you!" "My father died from that disease. I'm rooting for you with all my heart. God bless you."

The fact that I was in that uniform, out there competing, it made the fans see another side of me and allowed them to learn something about recovering from cancer that maybe they thought they'd never see or learn. They embraced a lot of things about my recovery that were there in them too—that a man or a woman can come back from cancer and not just exist, but produce at the same level—at a higher level. To me, it doesn't matter which team you're rooting for anymore. As long as you're a baseball fan, you're all right with me. It was the fans out there who made me feel this way. When I came back from cancer surgery and chemo, came back from my brother dying, it was the love from those fans to whom I'd dedicated the performance of my professional life that made me feel warm. Rivalries in baseball are important, but the game itself is most important. That's what you love. The fans showed me a side of them that's not always all about the home team. They were fans of baseball. It's about respect, love, sacrifice, years in, appreciation.

So I'd have to take it from here, and do what I had to do. Not only on Jim Bean's behalf, not just on my family's behalf, but on behalf of everybody who has ever looked up to a major leaguer, anybody who has ever been touched by cancer, or the tragic death of a loved one. This one's for all of you. Because if they see me crying, everybody else is going to cry. If they see me quitting, then everybody else is going to give up because they'll think that it's an all right thing to do. You've got to keep on living. Struggling. Producing. Living out your destiny. And for me, that means . . .

"Play ball!"

Kingdome. Seattle. Game One of the first postseason round, 1997. The winner of this series plays either the Indians or the Yankees for the American League pennant and a chance to go on to play in the World Series. Now it was just over a month after Jim Bean died, there I was in the Kingdome, standing in against Randy Johnson. It wasn't difficult. What did I have to lose? My brother had lost his life. I had cancer removed from my body. All I can do is what I do. If it's good enough, praise God, I'm happy it was. If it's not good enough, I did all I could. I walk to the plate for the third time in the game, against the Big Unit. Runners on second and third, one out. Orioles lead 2–1. Randy got me swinging first time up. He's throwing 100 m.p.h. I've got to do something. Davey put me in there. I've got to do something.

Putting it mildly, the Big Unit is intimidating. At six ten he looks like he's handing the ball to Seattle catcher Dan Wilson. When he's got his fastball controlled, coming in for strikes, there's not much you can do. He's not throwing his slider like he was before, because he's not always putting the fastball where he wants it. See, everything spins off the fast ball. If Randy's not throwing that blue heater for strikes, then he can't throw his breaking ball out of the strike zone for balls and get you to bite. When he's got to try to throw his breaking ball for strikes, it gives you a little chance, something to swing at. If he gets the breaking ball up, I can hurt him—but when he's throwing his fastball for strikes you've got to cheat. You've got to get that bat head moving or it'll be too late. If the fastball isn't getting over, then you're not swinging at that breaking ball that looks like it's in the strike zone then isn't. We've beaten him before. Chris Hoiles hits him pretty good, and so does utility infielder Jeff Reboulet. A dominant fastball pitcher often will have trouble with a guy they think is an easy out. For Unit, it's Reboulet. Moose's knuckle curve has been dancing. But we've got to score more runs. We've got to score. Two more runs, the game's out of reach, the way Mussina is throwing. I'd already been up twice with runners in scoring position and both times Randy struck me out, second time looking at a 100-m.p.h. heater on the outside black on 3-and-2. Wilson called time and they had a mound conference before that pitch.

Now I foul off two. Can't quite catch up with it. In the hole, 0-and-2. He comes high and tight, trying to get me off the plate. I foul off another one. He tried to come in again, but it's not far enough in. My arms collapse a little but I get some of it—just enough to chop a hit over Mike Blowers's head at third. Two runs score. I clap hard once as I round first and come back to the bag. I can see my teammates yelling. I hear the first-base coach, John Stearns, saying, "Attaway, E.D.!" as he slaps my hands and pounds my back. And the rout, as they say, is on. We win, beat Seattle three out of four games, and the Indians beat the Yankees, so now we play the Indians in the American League Championship Series for the right to go on to the 1997 World Series.

Game Five. A.L.C.S., at the Jake, Jacobs Field, in Cleveland. The Indians' relievers had been the difference. They were up three games to one. It was tense in our dugout. But if we can just get them back in Baltimore for the final two games, get to wear the white uniforms again . . .

Top of the ninth. We're leading 2–0. But the way the Indians had been rallying in the postseason, first against the Yankees, then against us, a 2–0 lead wasn't anything to write home about.

"Eric! Get ready." Davey didn't hesitate when they brought in lefty Paul Assenmacher to face Harold Baines. Davey sent me to pinch hit for H.B. I wasn't surprised to be pinch-hitting for one of the best hitters in the game, because that was the way Davey managed. Chief, Harold, and I were interchangeable late-inning pinch hitters. I'd pinch-hit against Assenmacher the night before and I'd just missed one. Crushed it, but straight up. Now I knew he wouldn't throw me any more cheese, because he knew I'd just missed getting him the night before. He knew I was on him.

It was a clear evening, a bite in the air. Everybody was at

Eric Keith Davis, age 10, 1972. Even then a sense of style—and a 'Fro, too.

Can you guess which one I am? I'm in the middle with my friends, Sean to my right and Anthony to my left, 1973. Ms. Marshall is taking me to Westwood to practice tennis with Arthur Ashe. No big physical difference between the three of us. I was of medium build. But I was a natural.

Not the Jackson 5. *(Left to right):* Darnell, Sean, me, Gary, and Anthony, at our sixth-grade graduation, 1974.

Swinging hard in Instructional League. Professional minor league ball—a different world.

Going to the hole for Fremont High Pathfinders against Gardena High, spring 1980.

Coach William Dickson *(left)*, who died in 1997, and my father *(middle)* standing with me at a ceremony to retire my baseball shirt, number 6, with the Fremont High Pathfinders baseball club, 1990s.

Confirmation of superstardom—a *Sports Illustrated* cover.

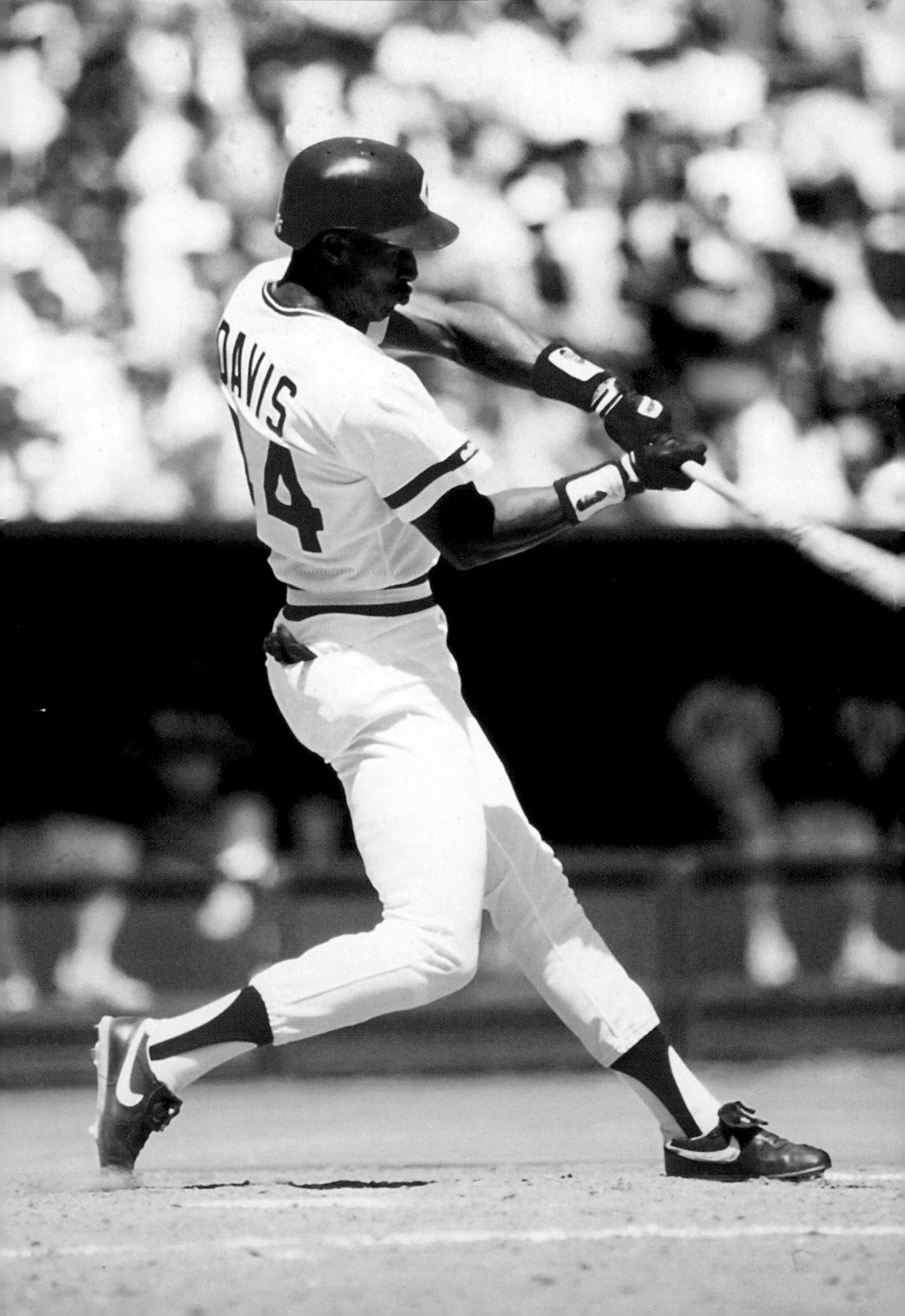

My brother Jim *(right)* and me, at my wedding to Sherrie at Mt. Moriah Baptist Church, located at the corner of 43rd and Figueroa, South-Central Los Angeles, 1987.

My mother Shirley with Jim, at my wedding, 1987.

Me *(in white)* at my wedding with my wedding party.

Erica and me with our game faces on, Family Day, 1991.

Family Day was always one of my favorites. Here I am in Cincinnati with four beautiful women.

The Dodger outfield in 1992—Straw, Brett Butler, and me. All three of us were later to be diagnosed with forms of cancer.

Sacha's graduation from preschool, 1995.

The women in my life *(left to right):* Sherrie in a gorgeous do; Rochea; and my mother, 1994.

(Left to right): Shirley, Rochea's husband Richard Miles, and Sherrie, Thanksgiving, 1991. We always try to celebrate Thanksgiving at my sister's, Christmas at my place, and New Year's at my mother's.

Sherrie and me, like a well-oiled machine.

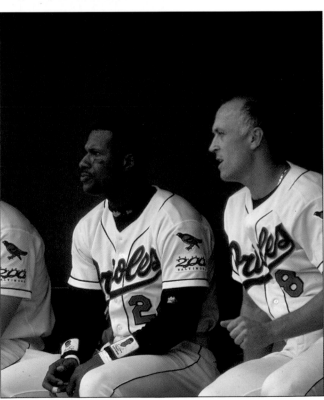

Cal and I drew inspiration from each other. We remain brothers.

home watching—Sherrie and the girls in Woodland Hills, my dad and his wife at his house, mom and her husband at their house. Everybody was watching. After throwing me three sliders and embarrassing me with 'em, he'd come back with another. Maybe. It's always just your best guess. When you're hot, you can react. I stepped out and breathed deep, and heard Dave Parker's voice, and Jim Hoff's, and Ham's, and Jim Bean's, and Sparky's, and Davey's telling me to get ready, to get a bat, that I was hitting for Bainesy. I stepped in. Assenmacher dealt. And it just so happened he got it up, just a hair, just the tiniest bit . . . *let's see it again . . . one more . . .*

I got a piece of it. Hit it out of the ballpark, into the crowd in the bleachers above the wall in left center field. A fan with an Indians' jersey or jacket caught the ball, then held up both arms. I didn't watch after that. I looked over at the dugout and watched my teammates, watched *them* watch it, smiles and the light coming to their faces.

Dr. Lillemoe was at the American College of Surgeons meeting in Chicago. After dinner, the docs retired to a Hilton Hotel bar and watched the game, not comfortable with that 2–0 lead. One asked, "What about your boy?" Dr. Lillemoe said, "Well, he is recovering from major cancer surgery, and he is on chemotherapy." "Yeah, but where is he?" Then I came up, and God was with me, and I hit the ball out of the park, and Dr. Lillemoe began high-fiving everybody who wasn't a Cleveland fan. People yelled, "Your man did it!"

At home in Woodland Hills, my daughters and my wife were hugging, hopping up and down.

My dad, he just sat there, alone, ruminating. Finally he made a fist.

My mom . . . she just said, "I knew you would do it." Moms are like that, aren't they?

I trotted around the sacks almost numb. When I got back to the dugout, Davey was there with both hands out, to take mine, smiling all over the place. Cal Jr., Bainesy, Brady, Robby, B.J., Jeff—they all came over to give me love. That crazy Tony Tarasco, who wasn't active, gave me one of them long handshakes, took at least 30 seconds. Later, when they asked him about it, he said, "I'd say 80 percent of the team knows it. It's a shake—and some fries."

When I'd touched home plate, and saw the looks and the excitement on my teammates' faces, I said, not directly to the Indians catcher, Sandy Alomar, but loud enough for him to hear: "One too many."

I meant Sandy called for one slider too many. If Assenmacher throws me a fastball, then he probably gets me out right there, because I'm not looking fastball. I'm sitting on the breaking ball, sitting slider because he'd thrown three in a row. When I crossed the plate and said, "One too many," Sandy knew what I meant. "Eric didn't hit a bad pitch," Assenmacher said later. He was right. I went down and got it from off my ankles. That home run started a mini-rally, gave us a 4–0 lead going into the bottom of the ninth inning. We needed it because Cleveland scored two runs. That homer was the winning run, and sent the series for the pennant back to Baltimore for Game Six.

"It made a lot of us happy over here, with what he's been through," Davey Johnson told the press later. "Harold Baines is a great hitter, and I know a lot of people were questioning [the decision for me to pinch-hit for Baines]. But I have a lot of faith in Eric."

Raffy kept telling the press, "He's my hero," embarrassing me. I just wanted to earn my keep.

Getting the hit against the Unit, hitting the homer against the Indians, made me feel proud. I felt like part of the team's quest. I knew then I would come back, be ready for spring in '98, though at the time I was thinking of Game Six against Cleveland. But I also knew, once I got the chemo behind me, it would be like I never was sick, like I never had cancer. Now there was no limit.

* * *

Davey came to me before the start of Game Six and said he was going to go with Chief in right field and with the left-handed bats. I was disappointed, very—but I told Davey to do what he believed he had to do. We'd both have to live by his decision. If it was me, I would've had me in there. But . . . after that, from the bench, it was the strangest game. Charlie Nagy gave up 10 hits, we got the leadoff runner on five times but couldn't push one run across. Our left-handed hitters weren't being patient and taking their walks; we had some runners, and Raffy and B.J. and H.B. are competitors and wanted to drive them in. Nagy preyed on that. He stayed just off the plate.

Moose Mussina was throwing just beautifully, but as we kept letting this chance after that chance get away, you get an uneasy feeling. Then Tony Fernandez yanked a weak slider or fork ball from Armando Benitez out of the ballpark, and suddenly it was the bottom of the eighth and I was up there again, as a pinch hitter, facing Brian Anderson, the same pitcher I'd faced in my first at-bat back in the lineup September 15. I worked it to a 3–1 count . . . *bring me the cheese . . .*

Anderson threw a straight change. I swung and missed. Early. I stepped out. Good pitch.

He took a deep breath, wound, dealt, a slider, I swung, it dove—dove better than I thought.

I went down, and I went down swinging, and all the air went out of the park, and probably out of Davey. I would've liked to have had four cracks at it, four ABs. But Chief had gotten a couple of singles, but not to drive in a run, and obviously he didn't score because we lost, 1–0. If I'd gotten on base, well. . . . Later, as the Indians raced onto the field to celebrate after Robby Alomar was called out on a pitch everybody in our dugout thought was ball four, I sat in the dugout. Long after the others went to the clubhouse bitterly disappointed, I sat on the bench and looked out at the field. You know, Camden Yards really is a beautiful place . . .

After all the things that I had gone through, I realized I was blessed: coming back, closing out the season strong, going 10-for-19, finishing at .304, back in that Orioles' uniform, and having another chance to contribute to the team and to the city of Baltimore, out there competing again, facing Randy Johnson, Paul Assenmacher, Brian Anderson. God had shined His Light on me. I was raised that way. Keep the faith. Save the day. Believe. People ask me what got me though. Well, besides the medical staff at Johns Hopkins and others across the country—in Milwaukee, at UCLA—besides my family, faith got me through. Believing I was going to be all right. You can't spend a lot of time worrying over things you can't control. I can't dictate life to life, or to God. The only thing I can do is run the plays out, go as hard as I can go, take three good cuts every AB. All I can do is pray, and keep on hoping for the best. If you give me bad news what can I do? Get up, fight, keep playing, do like I've been doing all my life. Don't have time to moan. Takes so much energy to be negative, to be sad. My mother taught me that. So now, for me, it takes no energy to smile, think pleasant thoughts. To laugh. You don't have to go out of your way to be happy, like you do to be unhappy. It's less stressful. It all comes down to love—and how you express it.

Now I'm full of joy every day. I'll never take putting on that uniform for granted. I enjoy it. Do anything for a long period of time, it becomes monotonous. But it's part of you. Whether it's a business, baseball, or whatever it is, it becomes another part. This is what life is for me. Baseball.

This is what I do. And love.

My love of the game is displayed between the lines.

It's not lip-service love. I left my love and my blood out there, on the field.

I knew then that the next spring training for me, in 1998, would be one of joy. If my teammates saw me down, then they'd be down. I didn't want them to look at me and see anything that would make them hesitate about me, or see me as a former cancer patient, or as someone who just had chemotherapy and is defeating all odds. I want them to know me as a player, that I'm here to have fun and do the same things I was doing before I was stricken with cancer. I'm hoping to hear their sincere laughter again, not out of sympathy, but because my teammates see this man loves being here, loves the game—he's enjoying himself and he's having fun, and hey, so am I!

In the off-season, the chemo was worse, because I had nothing to look forward to. The last two weeks of the treatment, I wanted so bad *not* to go . . . so bad. There were times I'd be driving on the freeway toward Westwood and the Medical Center and I would think, "Man, it would be *so* easy for me to turn around and go home." I never did. Never missed an appointment. I had a trick. I would visualize in my mind all the other cancer patients I had seen, young and old, rich and poor, black and brown and white and yellow, and that was what kept me driving to the hospital, all of their smiles, their enthusiasm, their effort, and I couldn't turn around, even though it was hard, but I couldn't turn around and go home. I had to do it not only for myself but also for the others in this battle with me who were looking up to me. I'm at my best when not doing something for myself. I didn't want to go, but I did, out of obligation to my family, to other cancer patients around the country I'd seen, or who'd written to me, or who'd just been diagnosed.

Once, right when I was having bad thoughts before taking a treatment, thinking maybe it wasn't working, a little girl said to me, "Why would you think it's not working?" So my thoughts then changed to, "It *is* working, so let me go ahead and finish this." Everywhere I went, including Milwaukee, I was in constant communication with other cancer patients. I got so many letters and cards from parents of patients, people talking about their children having it, or their parents, fathers, brothers, sisters, even twins—some said they were still living; some said they were doing great, some not so great; some had lost loved ones but didn't want me to give up the fight. Others said it's been in remission for 20 years. It was always uplifting to me, to hear from these people. They helped motivate me, no doubt about it. People talked about me being courageous—I couldn't have done it alone. I didn't do anything any other self-respecting human being wouldn't do, and that was fight for life. I didn't do anything different than what you would have done. Now I look forward to living. When you're here, you can do so much. When you're not here, you can't do a damned thing, and right now it's not important to me to be remembered. I want to do things while I am here on earth, if they are helpful things. I've never taken life for granted, but now I have a different perspective. Not just being able to put on the uniform. That's not that important. Being able to go out and enjoy life, and to provide a good life for my wife and daughters—that's *important*. If I die tomorrow, I won't have anything to be ashamed of. I have no regrets. Coming out of South Central L.A., I know nothing's promised to *any* of us. The only thing that's out there for you to have is the opportunity to live well. I've been blessed. Honestly, I couldn't even tell you just how blessed I am. But I know there *is* no limitation in life . . . not even for a cancer survivor.

TEN / FALL 1990

Winning It All, Copping the Rings

Be Careful Not to Lose More Important Things

The 1990 Cincinnati Reds were incredible—to me, one of the overlooked great big-league ball clubs of all time. We won our first nine that season, 25 of the first 34, and we were never headed in a division with the Dodgers, who'd won the World Series in '88; the Giants, who'd gone to the World Series in '89; and the Braves, who were starting to make the noise they'd make throughout the '90s, winning seven division titles in one decade. Even in this heat we won our first nine and finished 91–71, in a division where *everybody* could play. We won the division by five games over L.A., and we were never out of first, only the second National League team in history to do that—even the Big Red Machine hadn't done it. Then, in the 1990 National League Championship Series, we faced the Pittsburgh Pirates. Barry Bonds was the Man, Jim Leyland managed. How good were they? You tell me. Bonds, Bobby Bonilla, Jose Lind, Andy Van Slyke, Jeff King, Jay Bell, Jim Leyland. Even if we won, waiting were the mighty Oakland A's of Mark McGwire, Jose

Canseco, Rickey Henderson, Dave Stewart, Dennis Eckersley, Tony LaRussa.

And in the end, it wasn't even close.

That deal Marge Schott had signed me to the year before, the three-year, $9 million deal, it made her wring her hands, it stuck in her craw, to pay a ballplayer like me that much glue. You were not in the lap of luxury over at Riverfront in the first place. You were a ballplayer. That was supposed to be enough. It had to be. Wasn't much else. There were weights, but no weight room to speak of. The family lounge discouraged lounging. Marge could put a hammerlock on a buck.

"Now . . . are you promising me a World Series?" she asked as I signed the deal in '89. I couldn't do that alone, although I promised to try. But it has to be all 25 men. Fortunately, it all came together in '90, personnel-wise, by the luck of the draw, or the law of averages, blind faith, or skill. For some reason God smiled on us that year. I'd come up with Bill Bergesh as general manager, then Murray Cook, then Bob Quinn. There was also an administrative assistant who'd just come in, a young guy named Jim Bowden. He got his start with Syd Thrift, at the time the architect of the Pittsburgh club. All I know is somehow we got outfielder Billy Hatcher in April from Pittsburgh, and that was a key, getting another quality big-league outfielder. I was the Man for us—the one the batting order wheels around, who could carry the club a month at a time, who hit 300 or more bombs, lifetime, in the big leagues, who, if you're lucky, can help you win with his legs, his glove, his arm, especially his bat. That was me. That was Barry Bonds. I had a little more time in than Barry, although it wouldn't have mattered if the Pirates had had the pitching we had that year.

In '90, I did my usual thing, played well—got hurt—played less than great while hurt, but played on, played through it. I only played in 127 games due to two serious injuries. I sprained my right knee on April 24 stealing a base, caught between running and sliding between second and third base, in Philadelphia.

Out for a month, right off the bat. When I came back, sooner than I should have, in five weeks, wearing this big bulky knee brace, Lou Piniella took one look at my knee brace, knew it would limit my mobility, and moved me from my true Gold Glove position in center over to left. Your wheels have to be right to play center in the big leagues. Now Hatcher could play center, and a good thing he could. I went back into center in mid-June but was only hitting a buck seventy-eight on June 15. Then I got hot, and was named NL Player of the Week, June 18–24, for hitting .476. We trailed Montreal on July 16, 3–0. I came up with their bases loaded. Zane Smith tried to blow heat by me, make me chase high, only it wasn't high enough and I hit it out for my fifth career granny. Hit .351 from August 22 until the end of the regular season to jack up my average to .260, near my *injured* career average. My *healthy* career average, .290.

Then I ran into a wall. Missed five late-season games after running into the left corner wall, bruising my left shoulder and hip making a catch on September 27. I stole 21 bases in 24 tries in spite of the injuries, somehow, led the team in RBIs for the fourth straight year with 86, and was second in homers with 24 in spite of the missed time and short at-bats—only 453. Scored 84 runs on the bad jet. Larkin, my protégé, scored 85 runs in 614 at-bats; Chris Sabo scored 95 runs in 567 at-bats, hitting second. O'Neill scored 59 in 503 at-bats, often hitting behind me. Those four young players were the heart and soul of our team among the everyday players. And three of us are still ballin', still championship-caliber, top-end big leaguers today, in 1999, nine seasons later. In '90 we were younger, and in a championship sense unproven. I had more time in than the others, and the mantle of leader fell to me, which was pretty much what I wanted and expected. O'Neill played in right. He'd been drafted the year after me, in 1981, and had made it up in '86, when Pete called for that jailbreak from the minors. Paul was a serious guy, a moody guy who hated to make outs and brooded when he did. Even when you're going good—and he was pretty good that year, hit .270 with 28 doubles, 16 home runs, 74 RBI—you are still going to make outs. Our "A" lineup had me in left (or center), with the bad wheel, Hatcher in center (or left), and O'Neill in right. We also had Glenn Braggs over from Milwaukee. Braggs was cut, *swole,* six four, 220, and my age, from Bakersfield. Lou had always liked him. Hit .299 for us in 72 games, drove in and scored a combined 50 runs, with six homers. Good fill-in. We brought in Herm Winningham, a defensive outfielder, to hold the fort until I came back.

Pete said my wide-open game, especially on defense, would lead to breaks and sprains, wear and tear. He was right. The average amount of ABs that I had in that four-year period, from '87 to '90, was 465. That's not many ABs to be driving in that many runs, putting up big numbers. But in '90, I had more help. On the infield, Hal Morris played a lot at first base. Hal's still getting his hits for the Kansas City Royals in 1999. A good lefty bat, sprayed line drives around. He started 1990 as a reserve, didn't hit right away, got sent down to Nashville, came back up June 18 and hit .351, finishing at .340 for the year. Hal could hit. He split time with Todd Benzinger at first base. At second we had Mariano Duncan, who we got from the Dodgers for Kal Daniels and Lenny Harris. Mariano hit .306 for us, 33 extra-base hits, 55 RBI, 67 runs scored. He was a winner. Showed up on several playoff teams in his career, the last time with the Yankees in 1996. Backing him up we had the Billys—Doran, who used to play with the Houston Astros and was a Cincinnati native, and Bates, who played with the Cincinnati Reds but was a Houston native. Bates was a career minor leaguer, basically, but later that year, in the World Series, he'd come up with a big knock for us.

Barry Larkin came into his own that year at shortstop. He was the Reds' number one draft choice in 1985, but went to the University of Michigan, was named Big Ten MVP twice. In 1990 he was our MVP, you could see he had the grace, the quickness, the reflexes, and now the experience to take over from Ozzie as best in the league. He hit .301, 185 hits, stole 30 bags, drove in 67 runs. At third we had Chris Sabo, Spuds MacKenzie, Pocket Pete, who made himself into the image of Rose, or tried, and gave a good imitation that year—he hit 25 homers to lead the team, scored 95 runs from the two-hole to lead the team, drove in 71, hit .270. So we had no one single guy that you could say, "Don't let this guy beat you," hold him in check, and win the game. On the '90s Reds, anybody could beat you, and not only that, anybody could beat you in a variety of ways. We led the NL in team batting average (.265) and team fielding (.983) that season. Joe Oliver was a good defensive catcher who would get the big hit for you at times. He had been the top fielding catcher in all of the minor leagues for five years running before reaching the majors in '89. Hit a deceptive .231 in '90—deceptive because he drove in 52 runs on eight homers and 23 doubles in 364 ABs. He was backstop for our team's secret weapon—the monster pitching flamethrowers out in the bullpen. They were called "Nasty Boys": Norm Charlton, Randy Myers, Rob Dibble. I called 'em Hard, Harder, and Hardest, respectively. The first two of 'em are still getting outs in the big leagues today, and Dibble, when he bowed his neck, threw hardest of all.

We had a team that could peck you to death, hit and run and steal, that could hit bombs, that could sling leather on defense, take hits away, had great team speed, any player could steal a base at any time, and except for me and O'Neill, it was a team of contact hitters that manufactured runs on that Riverfront rug. But in the end, it was the pitching, as usual, that defined us. First we had excellent starting pitchers. Jack Armstrong (12–9); Tom Browning, the tough nut to crack and a guy I respected a lot, went 15–9 and anchored the staff, even though as it turned out, stuff-wise, he was our number four starter—behind Jose Rijo and Danny Jackson, and Jack Armstrong. Yet Brownie teamed with Randy Myers for three shutouts; twice he pitched nine full shutout innings without getting a decision. I always liked Brownie. He was from Wyoming. Danny Jackson, a big lefty, had ungodly stuff. Sometimes I would be standing out in center field doubled over laughing at the way he would make kindling out of hitters' bats. He broke six or seven bats every game. Even so, Jose Rijo was our horse that year. We got him from Oakland for Dave Parker in '88, after the A's had gotten Rijo from the Yanks a few years earlier for Rickey Henderson. Rijo found himself in the second half of '90, and once he did—lights out, dude. From September 12 to 26 he was 3–0 with a 1.00 ERA and 40 strikeouts in four starts. The opposition hit only .212 off Rijo all year, second best in the NL. He finished 14–8, with a 2.70 ERA, seven complete games, 197 innings pitched.

And in the bullpen, it was tail-out awesome: led the NL with a 2.93 ERA during the regular season, and then in the play-offs they really turned it up with an 0.29 ERA, a 2–1 record, five saves, and 33 K's in the N.L.C.S., and in the World Series a flat-line ERA, 0.00, in 13 innings. If you were behind after the sixth inning against the '90 Reds, you were pretty much history. Myers—"Sick Boy," I sometimes called him—appeared in 66 games, allowed three of 32 inherited runners to score, and the league hit only .193 off him. Struck out the first six he faced September 6 at Dodger Stadium, tying the league record. Norm Charlton, another lefty, got his first big-league save May 6 at St. Louis. By the end of June, he was 6–1, with two saves. He worked in and out of bullpen, could spot start. Rob Dibble, the Wild Bull of Connecticut, was six four, 230, a big bucking horse. He appeared in 68 games, had an 8–3 record, 1.74 ERA, and 136 strikeouts in 98 innings—ratio of 12.5 strikeouts per nine innings. That's some hurling, right there. NL opponents hit only .183 against him for the year—best mark in the league. He threw so hard it seemed his arm might come off—and eventually I guess it almost did. But not in 1990. In 1990, he was a rock. He had a reputation for being wild, and when a guy is hitting 100 m.p.h. on the *slow* radar gun and has a reputation for being wild, and wild-high, you don't get a lot of guys digging in against him. The thing is, even though he had a deserved rep for being wild, that year he was in control in that, yes, he was still wild, but he was *wild in the strike zone.* He didn't always know where the ball was going, so you know the hitters didn't. Our starters—Armstrong, Browning, Jackson, Rijo, Scott Scudder, Rick Mahler—were good, and our relief pitching might have been, for one year, the best in the history of NL ball. We led the league in hitting and defense. We put five men—Dibble, Myers, Armstrong, Larkin, Sabo—on the All Star team, and yet I was the Man on the club, and Rijo had the best stuff on the staff. We had depth, youth, experience, guys who would be postseason veterans for years to come. Most of us were unknown quantities in September, but we were young, our lives and careers ahead of us, which explained why I was the go-to grizzled veteran leader at the ripe old ages of 27 and 28.

Lou Piniella came over to the National League after a career spent in the AL. Lou was an aggressive guy, hot-blooded, didn't manage sitting on his hands, fiery, more of a National League type, seemed to enjoy baseball without the DH. Jackie Moore was a bench coach. He'd managed Oakland for three years in the '80s. Tony Perez was hitting and first-base coach. Sam Perlozzo coached third base, as he did years later when I came to Baltimore. Larry Rothschild, pitching coach for the '97 World Champion Florida Marlins and Tampa Bay Devil Rays manager in '98, was bullpen coach. Always did like hard throwers. Big Stan Williams was pitching coach. Big Stan was—Big Stan. The coaches knew to stay out of the players' way, let 'em do what they did. It was a coming together of talent—more than I'd played with before. Talent alone won't do it. Doesn't happen often, a team clicking. It hadn't happened to me. Now it would. I can't forget that Pete Rose had a lot to do with it—all-time hits leader, leadoff man for the Big Red Machine, the manager who gives us our shots, who was banned from baseball. Every play I made had a little of Pete in it. *Unh!* Line-drive two-run double up the gap in right center . . . Pete, that one's for you.

So, like I said, we won the first nine games of the regular season, busted out of the gate in April, and from there, what we went on to accomplish was unprecedented in National League history at the time. Even the Big Red Machine, the '75 model of the '76 model, didn't lead wire to wire, in first place every day of the 162-game season. Now I'm not seriously comparing the two teams in terms of everyday players. I don't know if *any* team was ever better than the '75–'76 Reds in terms of an everyday lineup. But if you look at our starting lineup with our bench, our pitching staff, our bullpen, we were as good as anybody. I later played on Baltimore teams with some superior personnel, but not all of it in its prime. We were all in our primes—physically, at least.

Where we got the knowledge, I don't know. Like I said, no offense to Lou Piniella, this was Pete Rose's team. I had never known a big-league manager other than Pete. Pete managed the Reds from '84, when I first came up for 57 games, until 1989, when he was fired while I was a regular. So I believe in my heart Pete was more responsible for that World Series Championship than Lou. Pete gave a lot of the young players like me an opportunity, gave the Eric Davises, Barry Larkins, Paul O'Neills, Chris Sabos a shot. Now, not to take away from Lou, or Bob Quinn, because they brought in a Mariano Duncan to play second base for us, a Billy Hatcher to play center when the leg and shoulder injuries kept me from patrolling my position. They brought us in more pitching, brought in Rijo from Oakland for Parker. I missed Pops something terrible, but I was happy for him when the A's won the Series in '89 over the Giants. It was Pete who gave us a chance. It was Pete who had brought us all up when we were young, or younger, and who suffered through the growing pains with us. Pete gave us the time to grow and get it together. And in the summer of '89, when he stepped down, it was hard for, and on, a lot of us. He was the only skipper we'd known.

Peter Edward (I call Hall of Famers—or should-be Hall of Famers—by first and middle names, the way names are listed in the Hall: Henry Louis, Willie Howard, Michael Jack, Reginald

Martinez, Stanley Frank, George Herman—you know who that is, don't you? George Herman Ruth) never allowed things that weighed on him to weigh us down, even when he began to come under fire for gambling. He'd say to me, "E., hit me a couple taters, and it'll be all right." I don't think anybody, and especially Marge Schott, gave Rose the credit for bringing the young players along like he did. Pete developed some great young players and it was sad to see him forced out, because under Pete we finished second four out of five years in the NL West. We hadn't had it in September, when we had those go-to vets you know you can count on. I was still young, still learning how to produce in those types of situations, still finding myself. The '90 season, the playoffs, and the World Series were our team's first real chance to actually say thank you to Pete Rose by our play, although by the time the playoffs rolled around, Pete couldn't even come out to Riverfront. Banned from baseball. Take nothing away from Lou Piniella. He did a fine job. But the '90 team was Pete Rose's team.

Pete predicted almost everything about my career. He was astute about baseball talent. I picked up a lot from him that way. Now I'm astute about it as well. About everyday particulars of lineups, game strategy, matchups, when to go get a guy. I'm an assistant general manager waiting to happen in another life thanks to the likes of Pete, Parker, and Sparky Anderson. As a manager, Pete might slip here and there filling out the scorecard, he wasn't a real pen-and-paper, detail guy. But he wouldn't slip up much evaluating talent. He told people I wouldn't be a guy who played in 162 games a year. He said that not to be denigrating of me but to let people know what to expect because of the wide-open style of baseball I played, how aggressively I played, for how much—or how little—I weighed at the time. Pete said that I would have the wear and tear, the bumps and bruises, would get hurt. It all came true. Pete was just a Yoda-type dude to me. So I knew that I would get hurt inevitably, but I didn't alter my game because of that because I really only knew the one way to be effective, and that was to play hard. Anything less would've been uncivilized.

As a manager, hustle was the only thing he demanded. Charlie Hustle demanded hustle from you. If you had watched Chris Sabo win Rookie of the Year in '88, you had to see he had a lot of Pete Rose in him. He played with reckless abandon, went in headfirst to the bags, emulated Pete. It wasn't a sham, and it got the most out of Spuds. Without Pete's example, Chris was average.

I loved being a Red, and Riverfront Stadium, but some hard things happened to me there—in fact everything in there was hard. The walls of the outfield were unpadded. They were padded later, but only after I kept running into them and other hard fences around the league. It was an unforgiving environment. But maybe the hardest thing about playing in Cincinnati was this: I had become the highest paid player in the whole state of Ohio as far as professional athletes go. I was making a million-three at age 25, and for a young black player with an earring in his ear, wearing leather, diamonds, driving a white Benz, in Cincinnati, it made for angry people. I can honestly say that alone made a lot of people distressed, and I took a lot of heat, which in turn made me all the more stubborn to do things my way. I'm not talking about the heat from the fans in the stands. That's going to be there. I mean heat from the field and front-office management. See, they never really knew me. They didn't know my parents, or my background. They saw a certain style. Only thing they knew about me was what I gave them on the field. My personal style was foreign to them. I was never where they felt I should have been. Never at the Waterfront, where Pete owned a restaurant. When I left the ballpark, they didn't see me. I was at home with Sherrie and Erica or my own set of friends. I didn't mind not making the All Star team in '90 because Sacha was born in July that year, in Ohio. I had a family.

At the same time, some of the other guys would go to Pete's restaurant and occasionally close the bar down. Pete would say, "How stupid can you guys be? You know I own the restaurant and you all are there drinking until it's time to close it down." Only rarely would they see me in there, never closing down the bar, although make no mistake, in the big leagues, alcohol is as big an item as tobacco, smokeless and otherwise, and I'm not trying to come off as a teetotaler. But I didn't want to particularly be seen out clinking glasses and smoking cigarettes. I never missed a team gathering in Cincinnati for any reason—that was in my background and upbringing. Never missed a meeting, a bus, a plane, a workout, a treatment for injury, not so much as a phone call. I came to the post every day. But no matter what I had done up to 1990, it was not enough. It was tough, but with the Larkins coming up behind me, I couldn't let it break me. If I would've broken, I think I would've set back all ballplayers, and black baseball players in Cincinnati by ten years or more. That motivated me. To turn boos into cheers, the question marks into exclamation points, the second-place finishes into something special.

I never ran away from the camera in Cincinnati, either. I shouldered the responsibility. I didn't make excuses about why I didn't succeed on a certain night, or why the team lost. I never shied from the tape recorders the way I saw some guys do. I never spoke and then denied it later. I'd hit game-winning home runs or strike out four times, and as soon as I got out of the shower I talked to all the reporters clustered around my locker. I believed nothing could be written to hurt me. Because I already knew what I'd done if I struck out four times. Well, I did nothing that day, so that's what happened. So all that could be written was I did nothing that night. Or so I thought. Until the *Cincinnati Enquirer* came out with a front-page story in 1988— the front page of the entire paper, not the sports section—and said I was suspected of having a drug problem.

* * *

After the 1987 season, when I put up those great numbers in a short season, all hell broke loose. I had put up such good '87 numbers that people were projecting impossible numbers for me—and then I got off to a slow start in '88. No pitchers were in a hurry to throw me strikes, and I was not yet mature enough to show the greatest patience. Even though I was playing as hard as I could—I always do—the brass didn't really know me, what kind of man I was, my family, and maybe that's what led to off-field politics hurting me as much as I was ever hurt on the field.

The Reds were asking Atlanta—or vice versa—about a trade, Eric Davis for Dale Murphy, straight up. Murphy was a two-time NL MVP, now on toward the end of his career. It could've been interesting. Imagine me being in center field for all the '90s behind the pitching staff of Greg Maddux, John Smoltz, Tommy Glavine . . . *hmm*. But why was Cincinnati interested in trading me? First, Murph was a good player. Second, the Reds had to pay me, I was highest paid, and young, not the likeliest hero for Cincinnati, which was already a small-market team. Meanwhile, the Braves were owned by Ted Turner and he had CNN glue, cable TV glue. Then later on, the Reds were talking about trading me to San Diego for six guys. Then—I don't know whether this happened before the trade discussions, during them, or after—some guys were in Philly talking trades over the phone, and someone said if the Reds are thinking of trading Eric Davis, it must mean he's on drugs. Now whether he was saying it hypothetically, or whether it was a backhanded compliment or not, it was wrong. It was all the way wrong. Maybe he was saying the only way you would trade a guy with this much ability is if something personal was wrong with him. I don't know. The *Cincinnati Enquirer* picked it up and ran with it. All this had to do with money, I believe. I had a great '87, they could build a team around me, which meant, in that marketplace, that I was a million-dollar ballplayer, but I was also young, and what my daddy used to call "colored." Marge Schott was known for complaining on her own conference calls with other baseball officials and management types and owners about her "million-dollar niggers," meaning me and Pops, and allegedly saying she'd rather have a trained monkey working for her than a nigger. I guess she meant in an advisory capacity. So I knew I was fair game. Or should I say unfair game? Anything to tear me down. All for the love of money, or the desire not to pay it to somebody whose people were used to being cheated out of it anyway. That's the way it works. Blacks should work for free. Blacks don't own. Blacks are owned. That's in the back of the minds of some, like Marge, bottom line. You know what I'm saying is true. That's why when rappers like Ice Cube and them came Straight Outta Compton as N.W.A.—Niggers with Attitude— some people got it. Me and my generation, we were the bridge between the Jackson 5, Michael Jackson, Al Green, and hardcore rappers like N.W.A. And if you think it still doesn't happen today, there being a difference drawn between the ballplayers by management, you ask Mo Vaughn of the '98 Boston Red Sox, who was followed by private detectives when it came his time to sign a long-term deal. He was *made* into an N.W.A. Allegations about character flaws are always aired publicly about the black ballplayer at contract time to gain public sympathy over not wanting to pay him. When it was my turn to go through it, it wasn't in the sports section of the *Enquirer.* It was on the front page of the newspaper.

I've never been so confused and devastated by something in the media before or since. At the same time, Jim Bean was doing hard prison time in Chino for slinging dope. Now I had tried to put that and him out of my mind, concentrate on doing what I had to do in baseball, and here it was, haunting me again. Guilt by association. The way I saw it, if the Reds were trying to trade me, *they* must have been on drugs, but nobody was going to rush *my* allegation into print.

I was back in San Diego, trying to follow Parker's advice and let my game do the talking, make my preparations to play the Padres and produce, while the trade rumors are flying. I get a call at 6:30 in the morning, let's just say from an anonymous source. "You see what's in the paper?" the person asked.

"Paper? What paper?"

"Our hometown paper. The *Enquirer*."

"Hard for me to get the *Enquirer* here in San Diego," I said.

"Well, it says you've got a drug problem. Care to comment?"

I snorted and laughed. The voice on the other end of the line didn't laugh.

"Yeah right . . . wait a minute . . . I got a *what*?"

I wasn't commenting on that. I stormed around the hotel looking for Pete, for the traveling secretary, for the director of public relations, for Bob Quinn, Marge, Parker, anybody familiar I could find. I rode the bus to the ballpark fuming. All the Reds' people were like the three monkeys—hear no evil, speak no evil, see no evil. I found the *Enquirer* writers covering the team.

"Why didn't you come to me before you printed it, and at least get my reaction?"

If they were trying to look for players with drug problems, they wouldn't have had to look far, and they knew it. Plenty of good ballplayers obviously had drug problems, and the Reds saw it. Sometimes one guy came to games at 6:45 for a 7:05 game. At the time, some big names in baseball were having a fad trip with cocaine. I don't mean the black players whose names were dragged through the mud in the press. I mean some of the popular white ones, too, who never got named. It's not my job to name them. They know who they are. As for me, I had a deep aversion to going down to that because of my brother. So I've always been careful to stay extra clean. I'm the first one at the ballpark in the morning and the last one to leave at night. I never missed a plane, a meeting, nothing. Knock on wood, I never will. I went off on the reporters, and asked them why they didn't ask me first, and screamed at them not to talk to me the rest of the year. Then I hit two home runs in San Diego that night.

The Reds pulled me off the trading block immediately.

It was like, "No, we're not going to trade him now. He's going to get hot now. He's mad now." So it was like those unfounded allegations against me were all right if they motivated me out of that early slump in '88. I stopped talking to the press immediately, for the first and only time. We get back to Cincinnati. Five days pass. I'm not talking. Hard shell. No pain. Pete calls me in. Murray Cook was there too. They talk to me about giving the reporters what they need, about how I have to talk again. I said, "Pete, I don't talk to them because they didn't talk to me before they wrote that article. My *mother* saw that article. My *father* saw it. My father, Pete."

Pete looked down. He knew how I felt about Ham. I think he had strong feelings for his own father, so he understood. "Well, you know, E., they are the ones who make your career."

"No. W-W-What I do . . ." I remembered what my mother told me about the stuttering, and slowed down. "What I do . . . on the field . . . is going to dictate . . . what my career . . . will be."

Pete smiled. "I don't have to be on the cover of a magazine, Pete," I said. "They don't have to say nothing good about me. As long as they write about what I do on the field, I don't have a problem with any of them." So I did stop talking to the press the rest of the year. I had no other way to fight back. Pete thought he was helping me. "Maybe you'd done a few times recreational, maybe?" I said, "Pete, you've spent time with guys with problems. You saw the symptoms. You're going to sit and tell me, 'maybe you use it recreational?!' I don't need no out. Understand? I don't have to do that. Pete, *you* should know by now, there ain't no such thing as 'recreational.'"

What really bothered me was the embarrassment caused to my parents, who already had my brother on their minds constantly, and then my wife's feelings, and the feelings of all of the people that know me. Dope had already taken my brother down. He'd basically given up his life to be an example to me of what *not* to do. So for them to have to go through this in public about me—this was the kind of stuff that was racial, because they never would have done it to one of their sons, even if he had been *true* and one of their sons was on dope. They never would have dragged him through the mud in public like that. They were all just mean-hearted to me then, the press and the brass. All of 'em. I felt that way when Ham said people were whispering in his ear about me, "You know, after your older son, your younger son must be doing it too, your son is doing that." That's what hurt me most. Ham got a lot of that. Then for my manger and general manager not to back me, it hurt. I know it was rampant in baseball at the time, drug use, cocaine, that wave was just beginning to peak, then bottom out, and I saw the crap, yes, and so did they, the Reds' brass, but because of my personal circumstances, it was not something I could let take me down. They pride themselves on research; they should've known. If they had known me, or my situation with my brother, known how I grew up, they would've known this. All they saw was leather, diamonds, colorful clothes, white luxury car—central casting. They knew symptoms. So these published—what do you call them, rumors, allegations? that just makes them sound true—stories hurt. And down at the root, they were not about drugs. They were about *money.* Let's be clear about that. If something's in the *Cincinnati Enquirer,* people think it's etched in stone. Relationships I forged with local businesses to make it easier for Larkin or the next black star player who came through—all down the drain.

It hurt. But I used that hurt as a motivational tool. Oh, so y'all are trading me, huh? Because I'm on drugs, huh? The *Enquirer* got away with printing that garbage, but it better be happy that the statute of limitations is past. I never got a lawyer, never asked for my legal options, nothing. I just said to myself, "They are going to know they made a big mistake here." I ended up leading the team in home runs and RBI, like I did every year. That goes to show you how inadvertently or not the situation of life was set up to test me—or you—any way it can. It wasn't going to happen on the field. I felt that the first chance they got, they would get rid of me and my $3-million salary that just didn't go down well in the craw in southern Ohio or anywhere in a country where history is that a young man whose family's originally from Natchez, Mississippi, is supposed to be working for nothing. That's bottom line why Marge asked if I was guaranteeing her a World Series as she signed me to a three-year $9-million contract in 1989, why Jerry Reinsdorf told Michael Jordan nobody was worth that kind of money when he signed Michael Jordan to a one-year $31.4-million contract in 1997. The TV networks weren't asking her if she was taking the team to the World Series when they paid her. The customers didn't demand a World Series before they paid to get into Riverfront, or bought beers, hot dogs, and souvenirs. As far as Marge and I were concerned, the well was poisoned. It was like a marriage when things go bad. We stopped communicating. But by 1990, the brass, Quinn, the scouts, had helped put together this good club, with that key piece, Billy Hatcher, coming over from Pittsburgh in April. We were off to the pages of history.

After we beat the Mets at Riverfront on my birthday, May 29, we were 30–11. The baseball season is a long one, six months, and you're going to go through valleys, even when you win a pennant. Not many if any of us ever had, so we had to sort of go with the flow. At the All Star break, we were 50–29, eight games up on the Giants in the National League West. The Giants had won the year before. By game 92, we were 59–33, 26 games over .500 in the toughest division in baseball. But then we hit a little bit of a wall, and lost eight straight. Rijo came back and beat the Dodgers, 5–2, with Myers getting the save, and that was when he became our stopper that year. He had just come over two seasons before, and it took him that long to not only get adjusted to Cincinnati and the National League but also for the Reds to become adjusted to him. The smallest lead we had was on

August 4, when after Mahler lost, the Giants crept to within three and a half. Then at the end of September, the Giants fell away, but the Dodgers got to within three and a half games on September 25, when Atlanta's Tom Glavine shut us out, 10–0. There were eight games left in the regular season; Marge, Quinn, and even Lou fretted about a collapse, a fainting spell, but I'd learned well: it was on me to be the leader because it was a young team. I said, "No El Foldo happenin' here." I could see it in the speed, the defense, the pitching. The rest was a contagion of confidence I was determined to spread. Hitting is iffy—even a hot team can run into a pitcher who's on and get shut down. But speed, pitching, defense will keep you in a lot of games, win many outright. Though I was only 28, I was the Man, it was my team. Even though I had the bad wheel, hip, shoulder, ribs, I sucked it up, we split the last eight, won the division going away, by five games over three good clubs, the Dodgers winding up in second. We had cohesion, spirit, roles. We had young talent. We could run, our pitchers threw very hard, everyone in the lineup could hit the ball out of the ballpark and, probably most important, we played great defense. Now it was on to the postseason October playoffs for us, who were now being called "The Little Red Machine."

The Reds hadn't won the National League West since 1979, which was the end of the line for the Big Red Machine as the world knew it. And now we had the Machine back in full working order. From Fountain Square to Amberly Village, West End to Kennedy Heights to Avondale, the seven hillsides were fired with talk of the Redlegs being on the march again. The fact we were playing the Pittsburgh Pirates, from just up the Ohio River, was even better. It was the Pirates' "Fam-a-lee" with Parker and Stargell that closed the Big Red Machine's era in the playoffs of '79. Parker called me and told me postseason was still baseball, with a nip in the air and a few more frills. He told me to do what I had to do. I asked him if he didn't still harbor some feelings for Pittsburgh. He told me to do my damned job and to flip feelings. Only he didn't say "flip."

Game One against the Pirates was Thursday, October 4, at Riverfront. I was excited. We all were. This was a great challenge. Syd Thrift and the Pirates put together a good squad. They had Jeff King, Jay Bell, steady infielders with pop, Van Slyke in center, good defensively—as good as me, so he thought. And he may have been. When I wasn't in there. I would be in left field in these playoffs, running on that bad right knee, a bad left hip, and with a bum left shoulder. Either they'd have to pad the walls or I'd have to do a better job avoidin' 'em. Eventually they were padded.

Some balls were meant to be hits. Only when I heard the crack of the bat, my body would be off after it automatically. I'd have to think about it *not* to go after it. Now was the time. This was playoff season, the N.L.C.S., and the Pirates could hit, were bound to hit some rockets into the left-center gap, down the left-field line into the corner. I would need to make plays.

The Pirates had Bobby Bonilla, Barry Bonds, Sid Bream, the first baseman hitting for power, a fielding whiz at second in Jose Lind, a good defensive catcher in Spanky LaValliere, although no catcher could keep us from running. The '90 Pirates even had a couple of ex-Reds on their squad, like Gary Redus, one of the Reds' outfielders who took me under his wing when I was younger. We got Hatcher from them, they got Redus from us. It was Redus who hurt us in Game One with a pinch-hit single and a run scored, the winning run in a 4–3 game. O'Neill and I both drove in runs with doubles, but somehow Bob Walk got away from us. We lost, 4–3, not the way to start a seven-game National League Championship Series. Rijo had started. Bream hit a two-run bomb off him. Rijo struck out eight in five innings. Game Two was even tighter but we won it with a go-ahead run in the bottom of the fifth inning. You might ask how can you win in the bottom of the fifth? When your bullpen is as dominant as ours was, you can. O'Neill's RBI double made it 2–1 going into the seventh and the way our pen was stacked, it was like being three runs up. Lind, after tripling in the first game, hit a home run in the top of the fifth to tie it at 1. Browning pitched his guts out for six innings. Dibble and Myers came in and combined for three scalding innings of hitless relief. Dibble, the maniac, struck out two. We were now tied 1–1 in the series.

We won Game Three at Pittsburgh, 6–3, behind Danny Jackson, when Mariano Duncan homered and drove in four runs, more than offsetting his error. Hatcher also went deep, and scored twice. Dibble, Charlton, and Myers combined this time for three and two-thirds innings of one-hit relief.

Myers struck out the side in the ninth, and we won going away, 6–3.

Game Four on October 9 was pivotal. If the Pirates won we'd be tied two games apiece, with Game Five also scheduled for Pittsburgh. More important, they would have beaten Rijo twice in the series. Pittsburgh jumped up 1–0 in the bottom of the first on a home run by Bell, but we came back on homers by O'Neill and Sabo. In the eighth inning, Bonilla led off with a drive over Hatcher's head in center. I don't remember running over there. I did the instinctive thing. It was a 400-foot drive. Hatcher tracked it but he must not have felt the warning track under his feet because he ran full tilt into the wall and was stunned when he bounced off it. The ball seemed to find me. Suddenly I was just there, in center field again. The ball bounced off the fence, took a hop off the turf, and hit my glove. I had no time to think. I turned and threw with all I had to third base. Sabo straddled the bag, the throw came in on a hop—and Bobby Bo was out by five feet.

Barry Bonds was on deck.

The pitchers in our bullpen, the Nasty Boys, went crazy.

Myers's eyes bugged, Dibble's neck bowed, Charlton's head shook. I could see a lot of scarlet and gray dancing around in our dugout. I know confidence is so much of baseball, and of life. Those guys would be even tougher to hit coming out of the pen now, figuring, "Here, go ahead and hit it, dude. Eric Davis is going to run it down anyway." This time Myers, then Dibble, slammed the door—Dibble pitched the ninth, struck out two, and we were in the driver's seat, having won this pivotal fourth game, 5–3, to take a 3–1 lead. You could see the air come out of the Pirates when God made that play through me.

The Pirates came back and took Game Five at Pittsburgh 3–2, Drabek eking out the win over Browning. Tom gave up three hits and three runs in five innings—Barry drove in one and scored one without benefit of a hit—and though Mahler, Charlton, and Scudder pitched three innings of scoreless relief, Drabek made it stand up. Lou rested the Nasties that day, because the Pirates got up on us early, 3–1 and stayed there. Even with Barry Bonds on their club, it was their only way.

That led to Game Six in Cincinnati. I was happy even though I was aching in several places, couldn't run well, was caught stealing once, hit only .174. But we were winning with pitching, particularly relief pitching, and defense. The Pirates made a couple of errors in Game Six, rattled by the 56,079 screaming fans out at Riverfront, and we beat 'em in a tight little 2–1 ballgame, with Charlton and Myers pitching three innings of hitless relief. I had an RBI in the first inning, driving in Larkin, and little-used Rey Quinones drove in little-used Ronnie Oester late, and that was how we won the pennant. You win a pennant with all 25 guys. We were going to the World Series.

Nobody gave us much of a prayer against the mighty, the vaunted, the defending World Champion Oakland A's. But we were forged in the fire. We had a ball club. I hit the ball well in the Pittsburgh series but didn't have a real good batting average. During our first pre-Series workout, Lou comes to me and says, "E., I want to bat you leadoff against Oakland."

I blinked, then said, "Look Lou, what I just did? Don't worry about it. I'll be ready. I hit cleanup. I've hit cleanup all year. We need the power. Don't bat me leadoff."

"Then don't worry about it," Lou said, "if you feel that good."

So Lou left me in the four-hole for the Series.

The outfield at Riverfront Stadium—now its called Cinergy Field, and will be until a new stadium is built—was my place of business. I knew every dip in the turf, I knew the walls. I'd hit many home runs into the yellow seats of the mezzanine. The old Reds came back around for this postseason. They had made history in this same ballpark, which opened in 1970. A lot of people didn't care for the oval-shaped artificial turf parks like Three Rivers in Pittsburgh, the Vet in Philly, and Riverfront, but with the history of the Machine there, it was like some awesome kind of round cathedral. Like church in a way. When Riverfront was full and you had on the white uniform with the Red cap with the white C, you knew you were part of something. A lot of old-timers talked about 1972, when the early version of the Big Red Machine had played the '70s version of the mighty Oakland A's. Those A's didn't take a backseat to the Big Red Machine or the late '80s version of the A's. They won five straight AL West division titles and three straight World Series: in '72, '73, '74, the first coming at the expense of the Reds. Now they were coming in with Rickey Henderson, Jose Canseco, Mark McGwire, Carney Lansford, Dave Henderson, Terry Steinbach, Willie McGee, and they had even brought in the ex-Yankee second baseman Willie Randolph to play second base and steady their infield defense. They were tight, and they could be awesome.

So could we. But what we didn't have an abundance of going against the mighty A's was belief. We weren't finding all that much in the city of Cincinnati, among fans, the local media, the columnists in the local papers; they all picked the A's to not only beat us, but also trample us. Sweep. Even people in our organization believed we didn't have a chance. But I believed we did.

In the first inning of Game One, after the pomp of opening ceremonies, with two outs, my chance came. I'd told the guys after we beat Pittsburgh, "We are not just showing up for this."

Paul O'Neill had looked at me kind of strange. I was the leader. If I folded . . .

Dave Stewart was on the mound here in Game One, on October 16 at Riverfront. At the time, big Stew was the dominant big-game pitcher in baseball, had won more postseason games than anybody since Whitey Ford, former Yankee beneficiary. Stew was MVP of the '89 World Series, conqueror of Roger Clemens in two straight A.L.C.S. meetings between the A's and the Red Sox. The A's had Dennis Eckersley in the pen. Their Game Two starter, Bobby Welch, won something like 25 games. Mike Moore, their Game Three starter, had won 18 games. They were dominant. Rickey Henderson was doing Rolaids commercials, and Rolaids sent a whole box of its product to our catcher, Joe Oliver. We laughed over that. But I told our guys, "We're not going to fear them. We got stars too. What've they done that we can't do?!" I had just been brimming with confidence for some reason. I recall it from the moment we beat the Pirates. Now, as we hit the field, Dave and Rickey Henderson nodded at us, but the rest of the A's, except the manager Tony LaRussa, acted like we didn't belong on the same field, like, "Let's whip 'em and get to our parade."

I'd always admired the big-game home-run heroics. Kirk Gibson launching his game-winning homer in Game One of the 1988 series off Eckersley. Reggie Jackson—Reginald Martinez—hitting three bombs on three consecutive pitches in the final game of the '77 series. Carlton Fisk hitting the game-winner in Game Six of the '75 series against the Reds at Fenway Park. Now Stewart was out on the mound, gazing in with his famous Death Stare, looking like any nonsense on my part, any notion of swinging the bat effectively against him was not part of the game plan. A good pitcher like that, a *great* pitcher like that, you want to get to him before he establishes his rhythm, before he begins to dominate your lineup, finds his arm slot, his location. You get 27 outs to do your business. Rijo would get 21 that day, three hits going to Rickey, including two doubles. Oakland left 11 stranded. Rijo shut down Canseco and McGwire. Held them hitless. It was said you could climb the ladder and get Mark McGwire with high fastballs back then. It wasn't brayed over TV like for me but that was the scouting report. Get the ball up or watch it leave. Both McGwire and Canseco were behind on the right-handed Rijo's pitches all day. I was in left field and didn't record a single putout. Larkin at shortstop recorded one putout. O'Neill, over in right, recorded six putouts, and second baseman Duncan recorded three, though the A's were a right-handed hitting team. They just couldn't get around on Rijo. Couldn't pull him. Well, nobody but Rickey could pull him, and Rijo kept the all-time leading base-stealer and game-leadoff home-run hitter in the ballpark. Rijo got out of the first un-scathed. Then we came up. Lou led off with Larkin, hit Hatcher second, O'Neill third, and me cleanup. Hatcher got a knock, then I was up, with two outs, lining up Stew.

Of all the accumulated battles with big-league pitchers I've had in 14 major-league seasons I don't have that one recorded, not that magic moment, except in my memory. Hard to believe, but CBS, televising the Series, actually missed this. But in my memory, that night, that single at-bat, that moment is crystal clear. Stewart had a hard, heavy fastball, like Scott Erickson later, a slider, a good split, very good control, and he was a mean one; he would buzz you in a minute, high or low, make you duck out of there, make you move your feet, let you know that as far as he was concerned, it was his plate, you were just meat standing next to it. He worked me inside, backed me off the plate, then threw me a fastball down and what was meant to be away. I put a quick swing on it and felt the bomb contact with my hands and my heart leaped as the ball shot away from me on a rising line to center field, went high over the wall, up over the glass-enclosed mezzanine section off the second-deck facing. I didn't watch it after that. Riverfront exploded into my ears and the world tilted as I quickly ran the bases, my feet barely touching the ground. The crew rushed out to greet me at the plate. I slammed high-fives. We led the mighty A's, 2–0.

Riverfront Stadium was rocking with noise and cheers. My teammates pounded on me, and then pounded on me some more. It was more than just a home run. It was more than just a home run to lead off the World Series. It was . . . belief. O'Neill was grinning and looking at me and there was a light in his face and I knew what it was, it was that belief that we had needed, needed from me, we'd needed to see we could hang with and—hey, why not?—beat the mighty Oakland A's.

We ended up winning Game One, 7–0. Wipeout. Dibble and Myers pitched an inning apiece to combine with Rijo on the shutout. Eckersley pitched an inning and our guys took notes. This became important the very next day, October 17. Oakland started Bob Welch, a former Dodger and a good pitcher. We came back with Danny Jackson. Danny didn't have the wicked stuff I used to see sometimes when I would be in the center field laughing at hitters as he was breaking their bats. The A's came to swing in Game Two and led 4–2 after three. Would've been 4–0, but they couldn't get Hatcher out. After two games, he was 7-for-7, with five runs scored. It was still 4–3 Oakland in the bottom of the eighth, when LaRussa brought in Rick Honey-cutt. We scratched out a couple of hits, tied it, sent it into extra innings, where we got to Eckersley in the bottom of the tenth, when Bates singled for Dibble. I drove in a run, but they pitched me good and careful.

We strung together three hits off Eck in the tenth, and won, 5–4.

When we went up three games to none, after Tom Browning pitched six innings and Dibble and Myers again combined for

three scoreless innings of relief in Oakland, the handwriting was
on the wall. It was a six-inning game. If you weren't in front of
us at the end of six innings—forget it. The A's were accustomed
to the heavy weight of their batting order breaking a team down
over nine innings, but nobody except Rickey in their lineup was
accustomed to forcing the action. The A's scored three off Tom
but that was all they'd get; meanwhile, we pecked six different
Oakland pitchers to death, starting with Moore, the starter. He
didn't make it past the third inning, when we put a big seven-
spot on the board and cruised in with an 8–3 win in Game Three
of the Series out at the Oakland-Alameda County Coliseum.
Even after shocking the baseball world and being up three games
to none, some A's were still talking. Saying we had small chance
to beat them four straight. There was dissension over there.
Canseco's then girlfriend had said, "Maybe I should've worn a
red dress." They were thinking, "We're gonna win the next two
in Oakland, then go back to Riverfront down three games to
two, and we'll see." But once we took Game Two, I knew it was
over because we had already beaten the very best they had. We
had beaten Dave Stewart, and then we had beaten Bob Welch
and Eckersley in Game Two, when Joe Oliver got a knock in the
tenth inning to drive in Bates. We knew were faster than them,
much faster, as a team. They had Rickey at the top, and we still
haven't gotten him out, but the rest of their team speed couldn't
be compared to ours, and we took advantage. Even though they
had Eckersley, and he had the hype, our bullpen was superior to
theirs. It wasn't even close. Now in career saves and victories,
that might not be so, but that's how statistics can be deceiving in
baseball. That year, there was no comparing the Nasty Boys
of the Reds bullpen to Eck and the A's. We were just flat better. We had two relievers that year who were better than Eck.
Defensively we were better. Speed-wise. Every ball hit to the
outfield—we got on our horses and went to take the extra base.
Every ball they hit toward the gap, Hatcher, Paul O'Neill, or I
would race to cut it off. We knew every game could be won on

the base paths and in the gaps. That was the way we approached it. Every chance we got, we went from first to third. That year we had at least six guys that had stolen 40 or more bases. I did it, Sabo did it, Larkin, Mariano, Billy Hatcher, O'Neill could run. They just couldn't stop us. Earlier, I'd gone to Lou and asked him to turn us loose. During the year Lou had wanted to shut things down and control the action and tempo. I went into Lou's office at Riverfront in September and said, "Lou, great job you're doing. We didn't get this lead by hanging back. If you don't want us to run, give us the hold sign in a certain situation where you think they have something on, but for the most part, let us go. This is the edge we have." He did. That's when we ended up kicking the lead back up in September and won the division easily. Speed was the difference in the postseason against the Pirates and A's.

Game Four now. The impossible was happening. We were in position to sweep. All along, leading up to the World Series, when people said, "Gee, I hope the A's don't sweep," I would think, and sometimes say, "The A's have to be careful they don't *get* swept."

Hatcher had gone 9-for-12 in the first three games; he was just on fire, they couldn't get the brother out. In fact, Billy Hatcher in that World Series amassed the highest batting average in World Series history for players with 10 or more ABs. He hit .750. George Herman had hit .625 back in '27. Hal Morris, Paul O'Neill, our lefty bats, gave the A's right-handed starters fits. Larkin was getting on at the top of the lineup and picking up everything at shortstop. Sabo had nine hits in the series. Role players from Todd Benzinger to Bill Bates to Herm Winningham to Glenn Braggs did their jobs. The bullpen was untouchable. To start Game Four, Stew sent us a message and he brushed Hatcher back. Don't think he was trying to hit him on purpose, but he was getting him to back off the plate, and he hit him in the hand. Then I was up at the plate, thinking, Wouldn't it be nice to hit a home run in Game Four, to sort of cap it off. After the two-run blast in Game One set the tone for this reincarnation of the Big Red Machine, the A's had been very careful with me. I was hitting .286 for the series, three runs scored, five RBI. Stewart was looking at me like I could hit him and hit him hard again. I had 16 people up in Oakland, including my parents, Sherrie, and our babies. My relatives and friends were there; this was to be a celebration that would take us from Oakland to the airport on to Cincinnati to the parade at Fountain Square, trailing confetti and champagne all the way. This was to be the peak of my life in baseball, the realization of a prophecy my father made 20 years earlier, when he came home from work one day and I had hit a ball over his head and he had called me a natural. I was ready to take Dave Stewart deep again. Everything, every muscle and bone and nerve ending in my body was primed.

And then . . . Hatch got thrown out stealing. I could have wrung his neck, but then being aggressive was our style. Live by the sword . . . quietly, I reracked my bat until the next inning.

Well, as we used to say in the neighborhood, it bees that way sometimes. I was scheduled to lead off the next inning when we went out in the field for the bottom of the first. Then, in the field it would be. A complete ballplayer, a natural, can affect the game from many places, not just from the batter's box. Hatch was in center, I was in left, we were up three games to none in the 1990 World Series over the Oakland A's, Jose Rijo was on the mound and on top of his game, fastball riding high, slider snapping like a bear trap. I was standing out in left field with my knees bent, my hands on them, a little smile playing on my face, relaxed until Jose went into his motion, and at that point you prepare, tense like a coiled spring, ready to pursue the well-hit ball, hoping Willie McGee would hit it to me. You just never know what God has in the storehouse for you.

McGee hit a line drive, low, in the left-center-field gap, and dying fast. I'm the only one who can get it. Nobody can get to it but me. Hatcher has no chance. I could play it on one hop for a single, but I can get it on the fly for an out. I broke on it true all the way, broke on contact, and it was dying, and I didn't waste a step, really it was a base hit all the way unless I could make an impossible play, a sure double or triple if it gets by me, but I liked trying for the impossible. That was my whole game. No way a 165-pound converted shortstop could hit 475-foot home runs to right center until his manager, greatest hitter by volume in history, Pete Rose, said, "He's got more power to the opposite field than anybody I ever saw!" No way can you jump over walls in Shea, Three Rivers, Riverfront, the Vet, routinely bringing home runs back into the park, turning them into outs. I'd brought a Darryl Strawberry homer back into the park in '87 in Shea, making Straw kick up dirt halfway between first and second and shake his fist at me. I had brought *two* Jack Clark home runs back into the park that same season. So nobody could catch this base hit? Without thinking, doing what came naturally, I got a good break on the ball off the bat, attacked the ball at the right angle and I dove, stretched out, full extension, parallel to the ground, opened the glove and snapped it, catching the ball. I already had the bad left shoulder from hitting the wall in September going after a foul ball in Riverfront. As I catch McGee's ball I'm compensating and trying to avoid landing on that bum left shoulder, the shoulder at the base of the extended arm, on the end of which is a glove with a newly caught ball. All this happens in a split second. I could hear Hatcher yelling, "Yeah boy! Yeah!" I'm landing now. Can't land on that bum shoulder. I'm trying to protect myself so I'm going to catch it and roll toward the right. I dove, extended, and hit the ground with great force, hit directly on the elbow of my lower arm, inner elbow particularly. The force of hitting the ground hammered the bone into my side so hard that I immediately saw stars.

I rolled over and my mind immediately went first white then black with pain and I saw the ball come out of my glove in slow motion as I lay there. Somehow I picked it up and flipped it to the cutoff man, Larkin. I had to see this later on videotape to know that I did it. Don't remember it. I just remember these waves of pain in my side. But I didn't just stay down even though when I hit I knew something was wrong immediately, but my instinct was to retrieve the ball and flip it back in to Barry Larkin. Willie McGee got a double out of it, and I recall thinking of the pain, but mostly being mad because Willie McGee got a double out a ball that I felt I had caught.

I didn't know what was going on from there. I couldn't separate my consciousness from my pain. The field seemed to tilt to one side again; I realized I was back down, first on a knee, then on my back. The pain knocked me down. I didn't know what was going on inside me but I knew I was in tremendous pain. I knew the normal pains of baseball. This was something else. More. It didn't subside. It wouldn't subside. It intensified. "You all right?" somebody asked. Maybe it was Hatcher. I couldn't even answer. Hatcher frantically motioned to the club-house, but the team trainers Larry Starr and Dan Wright and Lou were already on their way out. People today tell me how courageous I was for staying in the game at the time, but that was hindsight. At the time, even though I couldn't see straight because of the pain, I also knew this was Game Four of the World Series, the World Series I had promised to Marge Schott when I signed a three-year $9-million deal the year before, the World Series Pete Rose had predicted we would win one day when he brought up six rookies back in 1986. We were in the process of sweeping the Oakland A's of Henderson, Canseco, McGwire, Eckersley, and Dave Stewart. It had taken 10 long years in pro ball, five years being bridesmaids and best men, and now our time was here. You think I wanted to come out of that game? Never was there a game I wanted to come out of less.

I finished that half inning out in left field, even though it felt like my side was on fire—so much I had finally even tried to signal the umpire for time to get me out of the game. It seemed like my stomach swelled up tremendously. I didn't know the swelling was from my own blood. I was yelling at the umpire, but when I opened my mouth, nothing came out. God was with me. No one hit a ball to me. If they had, I couldn't have done a thing about it. I was paralyzed. Somehow I made it to the dugout at the end of the inning. I sat down on a bench running along the back of the dugout, took a deep breath, and said, "Okay, E., you're up," and I tried to get up—and couldn't. I was supposed to lead off, and I couldn't even get up off the bench. The pain was mind numbing.

"Hey man," I said. My voice surprised me. Just a rasp. "Hey man, I can't even move!"

My teammates carried me up the narrow incline to the visitors' clubhouse beneath Oakland-Alameda County Coliseum. They took my spikes off. Suddenly I had to go to the bathroom. I couldn't move so they brought me a plastic cup—in case of internal bleeding, they wanted to know. It was like a big beer cup. I passed straight blood into it. No urine. Straight blood. When I saw that, I began to cry, and it seemed like I cried then for all the times I hadn't cried.

My mother, father, and Sherrie were led into the clubhouse, anxiously awaiting transportation for me to the hospital. I heard a lot of panicked voices, talking of helicopters, ambulances, and the last game of the World Series. I'd reconciled with my mom after being estranged from her for a while after she and Ham broke up. They were all in there when I urinated straight blood. Sherrie saw it. The whole big beer cup full. They couldn't wait for an ambulance. So I went to Merritt Hospital in a plain, unmarked van. No IV, no nothing. Only thing that got me through was my wife and my mother trying to keep me calm. If they hadn't been trying hard to keep me calm and conscious they may have flown more off the handle themselves. But they are clutch people, you know. We did get a police escort—only the escort, a lone motorcycle, stopped at every red light! Now my mother was really going off, completely and totally going off in the van. I could've died in the back of that van. God did not want me then.

Finally we turned off onto the hospital grounds. That was when the motorcycle cop's siren came on. My mother was hysterical by this point. If she could've gotten to that motorcycle cop, he would've needed a van to take him to another hospital. My mother, I hadn't really heard her curse like that. She was cursing up a storm in that van. My heavens, was she.

Everybody was in that van. My life was in that van. Sherrie was there. Shirley was there. Ham was there. This was going to be my validation for the life I had chosen, or the life that had been given to me by God. I didn't know why I'd been chosen. I just wanted the people I cared about to be there. Now it was like I had invited everybody to my own funeral. They wheeled me in and stopped at the registration desk. A lady tried to register me, asking me all these questions, but once again somebody is underestimating Shirley, who goes off on this lady.

"If you all don't take my son . . . into this hospital . . . and see what is wrong with him . . . This is my *son*! This is my son and he's bleeding internally and you're talking about filling out forms!"

By that time a doctor on call came out and they rushed me in for treatment. And that's when they found out that I had lacerated my kidney. One of the doctors at Merritt Hospital said it looked as if my kidney was a "tomato that had been thrown to a sidewalk." Soon they had me hooked up to tubes, catheters, IVs, monitors, machines; I looked like the Frankenstein monster and felt a little like him, too. I'm in intensive care, and it's going to be my home for the next 200 hours or so. The only thing that saved me was that a blood clot formed around my kidney.

I was in great pain, in and out of consciousness, and they medicated me for the pain because it became unbearable, unceasing, wouldn't stop. Have you ever been hurting to the point where you'd do anything to make it stop? My family, prayer,

God, baseball—there they all were again, at once. I don't know if we've won the World Series, but I'm asking about it in my lucid moments. In fact, this was on Saturday, and I didn't find out that we won the World Series until Monday or Tuesday the following week. I had a vague sense only of coming in and out of consciousness and of great pain for the next few days. Every time I opened my eyes, somebody that I loved was right there, and I could see them pulling for me, could see it on their faces. And then I went back out. Fading, in and out, in and out. My mother said she couldn't be sure if I was going to live or die.

I was vaguely there for the next few days. I think my Reds' trainer Larry Starr came in, and a couple of other people from the ball club, maybe. I think I remember Ronnie Oester coming in. Ronnie was a utility infielder on our club. For some reason I remember seeing his face, seeing him pulling for me. It might have been Ronnie who first told me that we had won the World Series, 2–1. I was in and out, so this isn't clear. Later I found out what had happened. Glenn Braggs hit for me in the second inning and flew out and it was 1–0 Oakland until the eighth. Larkin and Herm Winningham scored the runs. Braggs drove in one run, Morris drove in the game-winner with a sacrifice fly. Rijo went eight and a half, struck out nine, gave up only two hits, one on the ball that McGee hit to me, one on a bomb by Rickey. Rijo, who we had gotten from these same Oakland A's for Dave Parker two seasons earlier, was dominant. Randy Myers got the final two outs, and the 1990 Cincinnati Reds were World Series champions, and had started celebrating right on the spot, right on the grass at the Oakland-Alameda County Coliseum. By that time, I was in surgery.

The team left for Cincinnati the next day. I don't know if any of the other players came to the hospital to see me. I just can't recall. My family says a few of my teammates did come by, but I was in no shape to recognize or even acknowledge them. Later I asked my wife and my mother when Marge came. They didn't say anything and by that I knew that Marge hadn't come. "Did she call?" I asked. They said nothing. "Did Lou call?" Nothing. I ended up staying at Merritt Hospital in Oakland about nine days. There was a victory parade I'd always wanted to be a part of, ending at Fountain Square in downtown Cincinnati. Tony Perez took one of my jerseys to the parade, and held it up as he rode in the motorcade, and again at the fountain. The crowd had roared its approvals. Later a team contingent went to Washington, D.C., invited to the White House by the president, George Bush. It was Marge's second trip to the White House. Marge is a Cincinnati native and being able to own the Cincinnati Reds was probably the highlight of her life and had helped her gain access to some of the most powerful men in the world. Marge knows how to treat powerful men, and had learned a lot from them. Everything but compassion. She was honored by President Reagan at a White House reception in '86. She had gotten all this in 1968 when Charles Schott, her husband, died, leaving her in charge of his business holdings. I don't really blame Marge for forgetting me. It's probably what any good businessman would do.

I couldn't leave Merritt Hospital until I could show the doctors I could eliminate properly. That would let them know my insides were functioning okay. But even then I'd be on medication, a catheter, in a wheelchair, hooked up to tubes and wires. I couldn't travel on a domestic airline. So now I'm coming out of the ICU after nine days. Mind you, I have my people in Oakland all this time, in a state of anxiety. The Reds had left Sunday morning. Nobody had come to check on my family, on my wife and little girls. Sacha was only about three months old at the time. The next week after I started coming around, feeling not good, but not dead either, the doctors came and asked if I thought the Reds would fly me to Cincinnati. They thought I might heal up faster in familiar surroundings. The doctors felt like I was getting antsy and worried, which was true.

"Yeah Doc, that would be great. The team will fly me back," I said.

So the doctor instigated what would be my greatest pain. I was so confident when I told the doctor that of course the Reds would fly me back to Cincinnati. I'd be the Man. We had won the World Series over the Mighty Oakland A's. Oh, they'd fly me back. I've helped them go from losing a hundred games in 1983 to the World Championship in 1990. I'd told Marge Schott when I signed in 1989 that we would try to win the World Series. We had delivered. But it was almost like, what do you mean we? The doctors asked me if the Reds would pay for me to go back on a chartered plane, so the medical hookups could be brought for me. I'm saying, "Yes, they'll do it." See, as far as I'm concerned, I'm the mayor of Cincinnati, even though they had the big parade, a civic celebration, without me. I'd been waiting all my career for that. I was a World Champion ballplayer. One of the doctors said, "Maybe *you* can call the Reds. See what they want to do."

"What they want to do? Why ... they want me there," I said. No answer.

So I called. I called everybody. Got nobody. So I called my agent. He called Bob Quinn.

Mr. Quinn told him, "He's making over $3 million. Let him get his own plane." My agent, Eric Goldschmidt, relayed the comment. I sank down and brooded. Later I called the Reds.

"Get me Marge."

"Who should I say is calling, sir?"

"I want to talk to Marge. Tell her it's her million-dollar ... outfielder."

I tell Marge the situation. She tells me, "Well, I don't know anybody with a private plane here in Cincinnati." I couldn't ride a commercial flight because I couldn't sit up. I had to remain prone, and have two nurses with me, and the machinery. "Marge, you don't know anybody with a plane? You know Proctor and Gamble people in Cincinnati; Carl Lender is one of the percentage owners. I've given them all a good ride, Marge. I gave *you* a good ride. You know I did."

"I know you did, honey. I know you did, sweetie. I'll get back to you."

Marge never called back. The Reds never called back.

So I chartered my own plane and sent her the bill. When I got back the media found out about it and all hell broke loose. I went straight from the airport to Christ Hospital downtown. Bob Quinn comes to the hospital. It's not inconvenient to come by, now that I'm back in Cincinnati and all. My family is in my hospital room with me. Quinn comes in, brings a World Championship baseball cap or two and a couple of T-shirts, doesn't say 10 words to me. Talks to everybody else in the room. Later, he went to the television stations and told them he and Eric Davis had a good lengthy conversation and had resolved all our differences. It was all so much baloney. I saw him on TV saying it. My mouth was a straight line. All feeling I had for the Reds was temporarily buried. I asked Sherrie to get me the number to the television station, Channel 5, that had just had Quinn on air. I called up a sportscaster named Greg Horn and I said, "Look, Bob Quinn has not said two words to me." The television station sent a crew down and I blasted the Reds' brass. No, it wasn't very Christian of me to blast them, but I wasn't feeling very Christian at the time. I let 'em have it. I said that Bob Quinn was lying. He hadn't talked to me. He brought me two hats and a couple of T-shirts and left. So it blows up again. I'm in the hospital about another 40 days. Mind you, the doctor in Oakland told me it was going to take anywhere from 12 to 18 months to heal up properly, and that was with complete rest. He suggested I not do anything at all off-season, take the next season, 1991, off, and then that off-season, and then come back.

Marge eventually comes by to see me at home, with a Wheaties box with a team picture on it, and another hat. She comes by, there's a media parade behind her. I know it was all orchestrated. Everybody was there. CNN, ESPN, the local stations. Marge does all the talking. I said only a few words. I didn't appreciate it. It was obviously face saving for her. It dawned on me then that I was in a sense really nothing more than a million-dollar nigger. When Marge called me and Pops those names, it was more than just name calling. It was the way it worked. Marge tried to drop a guilt trip on me, saying she didn't know. She says that "the people" wouldn't allow her up into the hospital in Oakland or Cincinnati. Maybe they wouldn't. But I've never seen a place where Marge wasn't allowed—especially if somebody tried to keep her out. She thought I believed that. She said, "We've reconciled, haven't we?" I just looked at her. Didn't know whether to laugh or cry.

I never answered her question.

Don King, the fight promoter, called. He wanted to get into the sports agency thing. At that time I had to make decisions—career decisions. Whether I wanted to pursue that aspect, force it, maybe lose my career. Or swallow my pride and pursue baseball. I prayed. I asked God, "What should I do?" I talked to my parents. I talked to Sherrie. But it was a decision I had to ultimately make alone. Then the Reverend Jesse Jackson called. The Reverend Jackson wanted to bring down all the legal means on Marge. Don King's was basically a general conversation about representation, what he could do. But baseball is not boxing. Baseball, hot dogs, apple pie, Chevrolet. It's America's game in good ways, and bad ways. Whether we want to accept it or not, there are certain things that are not allowed in baseball yet, and I'm not talking about crying. I've seen plenty of crying in baseball, but I don't know of any black team owners, or agents, and I didn't think that having Don King represent me was going to be good for my image. My only answer was to play on. That was all I could do. That's not to say King is not good at what he does, or that the Reverend Jackson is not good at what he does. But baseball is set up in a totally different way; really, it's been exclusive off the field, sadly, and I didn't feel like I wanted to jeopardize whatever might be left of my playing career, even though when I talked to them both I was still so weak physically I didn't know if I'd have much of a playing career left. I'm not saying having Don King as my representative would have jeopardized it. But honestly I felt deep down that it probably would, not reflecting on Don so much as on the way the structure of the game is maintained. I have an agent as an extension of me. Straw and I had the same baseball agent for a long time. Straw and I tried to do some things together. We started Custom Interiors, a decorating business, around 1989. But things didn't turn out well. And I had to get my agent straight a few times on what was happening to my money. So it's not like it's all one way, like one way is good, and the other way isn't. At the time, I just felt my agent was an emissary to baseball. Goldschmidt was my emissary. And I had to watch him. In my experience, trust God, and watch everybody else. All this came in the wake of the '90 World Series, getting left behind. It stayed with me. Had it not been for my family and God, I would've been completely devastated. And there was nothing the Reverend Jackson or Don King could do to help.

Time goes by and spring training rolls around, February 21, 1991, when everyday players report. And even though all the doctors have their doubts (the ones in Oakland said I should sit out the whole season), my last official doctor's appointment in Cincinnati was on February 19. The team doctors gave me the green light. That was the first trip in when all the blood had disappeared from my urine. Took until two days before spring training for it to become okay. In the meantime, I haven't worked out, done anything. Didn't rehab at all, and I had always worked out, always rehabbed, I never was idle during the off-season. I come to the post every day. But my insides would not let me this time. My abdominal wall structure softened. I go down to spring training anyway. I didn't see a doctor once I got there. I went down there and started playing—or trying to play. Later, as the '91 season went on, I just got weaker and weaker and weaker until I couldn't even pick up my baby girl, much less be myself on the baseball field. I couldn't even hit a ball out of the park in batting practice. That's like Michael Jordan being held scoreless in a pickup game. In Florida I know something's wrong. I go see the team trainer, ask to see a doctor, say I have no strength. I tell Lou. He says, "Well, maybe . . . you're drinking too much. Kidneys you know, you can't drink. Maybe that's it." I told Lou, "Come on, Lou. I've been in the big leagues ten years. What do you mean, drinking too much, partying too much? That has nothing to do with how I'm feeling."

Marge arranged to send me to her doctor at a Jewish hospital. I go in and talk to him. He's supposed to be examining me. Never touches me. Never takes a test. Never pulls out so much as a thermometer. He talked for about 15 or 20 minutes and he sends me on my way. He calls me and tells her, according to her people, "There's nothing wrong with Mr. Davis."

I get a second opinion from one of the doctors who said that when he saw me dive after the ball and land the way I did on my arm, he figured what was wrong; he said that they shouldn't have moved me, they should have brought out the stretcher because I could have died right there. "You shouldn't play at all this season," he says. "Now if you had a regular desk job, something of that nature, I might let you go back. But because you are in a high velocity, high intensity, very physical occupation . . . no way. You shouldn't be playing at all. What's it been, seven months?"

I let the Reds know this and we have a powwow. Lou came in, and Bob Quinn came in, and a team doctor came in, and Doctor Melman, who told everyone what he had told me. He said, "Gentlemen, I don't work for the Cincinnati Reds. I'm a physician first and foremost. And as a physician, straightforward, Eric Davis should not be playing *any* baseball this season. He had no rehab, his abdominal muscles have atrophied because of damage to his kidney, the kidney and the entire elimination system haven't recovered yet. He should not be playing."

They listened, then asked me not to talk to the press.

And it was at that time, I believe, they decided they were going to trade me.

"Okay," I said, continually naive, "I won't talk to the press."

Almost before I come out of the meeting, there's a press release saying I'm going on the disabled list because I am "chronically tired." That's when I fell out of grace with Lou Piniella. Actually I should have sat out the whole year, but because we had won the World Series, and I'm the team veteran, the Man, the Spokesman, the Stand-Up Guy, I wanted to be part of defending that title. But if somebody smart in the organization had seen me as a human being instead of as a machine and had told me, "No, you're not playing, you're too valuable down the road, we've got too much time, money, experience, and manpower invested in you to risk it foolishly," I would've heard that as common sense and listened. I wouldn't have played. You know, I'd never torn a kidney. Not many people have. I didn't know what it took to come back from it. I didn't know just how critical the abdominal muscles were to the swing. Mine were in no shape for the rigors of the season. I knew pulled muscles, strained ligaments, sprained wrists and ankles. I didn't know about rehabbing torn vital internal organs. I didn't know how to rehab this. And I also didn't know what was going on with the brass, but I do know that's when I fell out of grace with Cincinnati.

I played in 89 games in '91. Gave Sweet Lou Piniella all I had. I only hit .235 in 289 ABs. It took me two season to shake off the effects of lacerating my kidney. I hit .228 in '92, and .234 in '93. In '91, I hit 11 home runs. All arms. No turn. No leverage. Sheer force of will got it done a few times. I couldn't sustain. So weak. The Cincinnati fans were booing me hard, even though we won the World Series the year before. I didn't blame the fans. They didn't know that I shouldn't have been out there.

If you're out there in a big-league uniform, the paying cus-
tomers have every right to demand some production out of you.
I blamed myself. I thought less of the organization for putting
me in that position. I'd been injured, but my body had never
failed me before. It was inconceivable. Ever since I'd been left in
Oakland, the end in Cincinnati was in sight. I grieved without
knowing it over the loss of that part of my life that was con-
nected to the Reds. Inevitably, in mid-summer of 1991, I was
traded from the Reds to the Los Angeles Dodgers, our rivals,
my hometown team, traded for two good young arms, Tim
Belcher and John Wetteland. I told myself I didn't care. That's
what you have to tell yourself. If you are going to be traded you
are going to be traded. It's up to you to adjust, move, live on.
You have no choice. I decided to look at it as a challenge, a
chance to start all over again. But a sadness I couldn't shake
went with me to L.A.

PART IV
Winter

ELEVEN / WINTER 1993

ADVERSITY/BLESSING
Has-Been

LIFE LESSON/STRATEGY
Don't Buy into All Outside—and Inside—Assessments

Lou Piniella orchestrated the trade, me to the Dodgers for Tim Belcher and John Wetteland, two young big-league arms. Live arms. I don't care if you're traded for Willie Mays and Mickey Mantle, it doesn't feel good unless you want it and, being honest, I didn't want to be traded from the Reds. But it does kind of matter, if you've got to be traded, whom you're traded *for.* So Belcher and Wetteland were outstanding pitchers. I'd gotten to the point where being traded was the only thing that could happen. Lou has told me many times since that he regrets it; he didn't realize my level of commitment to the team, the history, the town, the Reds organization, because you can't be committed to all that and not be committed to the Reds. I sold out my body any number of times while Lou was managing. He saw that. It's a what-have-you-done-for-me-lately business.

At the time, Reggie Sanders was the number one prospect in the Cincinnati system. They were grooming him to play center because he's a talented individual, reminded me of myself when I came up. When Reggie was brought up I had a tough season and the focus was on him replacing me. I went to Reggie and talked to him. "I might not be here next year, Reggie, and you might be the center fielder. Don't feel like it's wrong for you to replace me, because really you're not—you're just stepping out on your own. Just play ball. Just play hard and do your best. Get ready to drive in some runs," I said. Then I told him how to prepare for that, just as it had been done for me.

A few members of the Reds' hierarchy seemed upset that Reggie and I were getting along. They seemed not to like the fact that I was educating him as I had been educated. They wanted me to be mad at Reggie, to get into it with Reggie, even fight with Reggie, where they could egg that on. Being who I was raised to be, and knowing the things I had learned from men like Ken Griffey Sr. and Dave Parker, I would never have done that to a youngster with potential. Some old-school stuff is ridiculous, too. I knew I could still play once I finally healed. In my mind I was saying, "I'm going to play somewhere eventually and play well, Reggie, so you aren't taking anything away from me. Don't worry about me. Worry about Reggie. Do your thing. I'll help as long as I'm here. Whatever it is, if you need to talk, wanna know something, I'm gonna help you because the players I came in under didn't shy away from me." I didn't bash Lou, or the general managers, or Marge, or anybody else. I felt like I came in a whole man, and I'd go out a whole man.

Of course Reggie was compared to me. I suppose it was as tough on him as it had been on me to be compared to Mays, and the accomplishments of the Big Red Machine. They wanted to give him my Reds' number, double fours, 44. Reggie was wising up. He said, "I want my own number."

I wasn't surprised when I was traded; I was surprised to go to the Los Angeles Dodgers. I was a little surprised they traded me within the division, and trading me to the Dodgers wasn't like trading me to Siberia or the Texas Rangers, but sending me home in a way. And Straw was with the Dodgers now, too. But because I'd been spending off-seasons in Cincinnati, it was like my home now. I tried to make it as though I didn't care, but I'm a caring person, how could I not? I *acted* like it didn't matter. I never tried to defend myself because I didn't feel like I had to do that. They were waiting for me to say, "I don't want to leave." I did say I liked playing in Cincinnati because I did. In spite of it all, in spite of what happened in 1990, I did like it. To me, Riverfront Stadium was a great ballpark in baseball history. I enjoyed playing there. But I wasn't going to beg. I wanted to stay but I wouldn't beg. I'm going to play hard no matter what uniform I wear.

When I was traded, not everybody in Cincinnati was happy about it, either. It was hot there for a minute on the radio and in the newspapers. You know how it is, you can beat up your brother, but you don't want anybody else beating him up. Some of the same people who were all over me about my earring, anything they could latch on to about me, and my lack of production as they saw it in the 1991 season—many of them still didn't want to see me go because they knew deep down what kind of ballplayer I am. So even some of the same ones who were often beating me up on the radio call-in shows were now saying, "Wait now, whoa, wait a minute, don't let *him* go."

The reporters on the beat said, "Too bad. Eric Davis is a good quote." The Reds would become a young team, and an unproven team, and what fun is it for the press to beat up on unproven players? None. Some of the guys, they don't like talking to the press, and sometimes they don't have to, they cut them off. But no matter what I did on the field I always had time for them and told them like it was or how I felt it was. So for a lot of different reasons—and I believe familial affection was one of the reasons—a lot of people in Cincinnati didn't want to see me go. From fans to baseball writers to the general population, they knew they had a guy who caught the eye, brought heat and light to the town, brought a high level of play, who played hard, played to win, could do the slap-your-forehead spectacular sometimes, the essential Five-Tool Ballplayer. I was somebody they came out to see, no matter whether I hit a home run or struck out. Parker once said he would pay to see me play. So I played as if Parker had paid to get in, and was sitting there with his son, and wanted his son to know what a helluva ballplayer looked like in motion.

In some ways, I was my own worst enemy in a sense in Cincinnati because of my own athletic ability. I remember early on in my career, once we were playing the Atlanta Braves when Chuck Tanner was the manager. Glenn Hubbard was playing second base. Chuck had Hubbard hold me on. I mean hold me on the bag the way a first baseman is on the bag when a runner is on first. I had never seen it before. It was like I was on first base. It was like, forget the whole right side. Hubbard wasn't going back and forth. He was at second base, holding me on! I looked over in the dugout at Chuck Tanner, and he smiled slyly at me, then tipped his cap. Chuck Tanner had been Dick Allen's manager on the Chicago White Sox in '72, and manager of the 1979 World Champion Pittsburgh Pirates. I didn't steal third and I didn't score. Score one for Chuck.

I'd always gotten injured playing defense, not offense. In L.A. I broke my collarbone diving after a ball in the outfield. I had people tell me later this was one of the greatest catches they ever saw in Dodger Stadium—only not that many people saw it. I was playing in right. Straw had hurt his back, and I was the only outfielder we had who could play all three outfield positions. I think Andy Van Slyke was at the plate, we were playing the Pirates, bases were juiced, and he hit one into the right-center gap. I laid out for it, about twelve inches off the ground, parallel to the turf; I caught it, tried to tuck but was too close to the ground, hit and bounced and ended up breaking my collarbone.

If I don't make that play it's three runs. If you're the pitcher, you go to arbitration; you're gonna win because your ERA is now under four where if that ball gets by me it's over four. That's why pitchers liked me. I was always helping somebody's ERA. Could've played that on a hop, nobody says anything. But my philosophy in Cincinnati, L.A., Detroit, Baltimore, wherever it may be, was always this: *My teammate is out here trying to feed his children, I'm out here trying to feed mine. We're in the same battle, I've got to help him. That's my job.* So I did it.

It's always been automatic, going to get the ball. I don't think I can help it. Sometimes I have to consciously say, "Ease down, E. Ease down." I can still hear Pops Parker: "Boy, I saw you wide open, so I pulled up sweet 'cause I knew my son had that one in his hip pocket, hellfire, boy! I started to fade toward the infield, just be your cutoff man. You a bad man, boy. Bad man." I've seen outfielders in my time that were good outfielders but I've also seen some manipulating the play, like slowing up so they could dive after a ball so it could look good on the highlights, and some announcer who didn't really know ball would say, "What a great play!" Yeah right.

Peter O'Malley was a good owner in that you never really saw Peter all that much. The only time you'd see Peter was maybe at one or two games down in Vero Beach during spring training. He would come down with his family, but never went around saying, "This is my team. You are my property." The Dodgers had a great family environment. If you didn't know who Peter O'Malley was, you never would've known. He was unassuming. He'd stand back. He had Christmas for the kids in spring training. His family has sold the Dodgers now. I don't know how it is anymore.

I bought season tickets for my mom, my dad, my wife, my brother, and Rochea to come anytime. There were promotional pictures of me and Straw on RTD city transit buses. My brother and my sister took hits for that. Their friends would be, "So? It don't mean nothin'." Everybody else that came to Dodger Stadium had to pay. I could not allow myself to get into a pattern of giving everybody tickets, so I took care of my family and the people close to me, because I knew too many people: "Hey, if you wanna see me, spend the five dollars. If you can't spend five dollars, you don't need to come to see me play. Why do I have to give you something for you to come see me play?"

My only problem playing in L.A. was breaking my collarbone. And Tommy Lasorda.

I think Tommy had too much control, and I loved Tommy. Tommy was a fine human being, I believe he'd do anything in the world for you, but he had too much power, and his focus by this time was on his A-list of celebrities in the clubhouse, glad-handing, eating, and asking for pictures, autographs, and handshakes. Now it was all about Tommy's office being lined with A-listers, how things were so much better in the good ol' days, so much so that one veteran cracked, "Yeah, things were so much better then they left Brooklyn quicker than you could say Jackie Robinson."

Baseball got mostly lip service by the time I arrived. One guy told Tommy I couldn't hit where my hands were, that he should change where I held my hands when I hit. I'd hit like this for 10 years. But Tommy tried to change my approach. Tommy, in his day, had been a pitcher.

"Tommy, I don't believe my approach to hitting is wrong. If it was, why would you trade good pitchers like Belcher and Wetteland for me?" I asked. If I get beat by a high fastball, then it's my fault for swinging at it, but that's my own aggressiveness that I had to learn to control. And in time, I will. As a hitter you feel like you can hit anything. But the reality of it is you can't. Tommy appeared to be listening to me, but unfortunately he probably wasn't, because as I recall some nice guy was standing there waiting for a hug. I was hitting .320 in '92 when I broke my collarbone. That killed the rest of '92. I came back but wasn't the same. I had restrictions on my swing, my turn, the kidney was still not right, but my drive to play was there, so I came back and played. That year I had surgery on my shoulder, I tore a ligament in my hand, got hit by a pitch in the wrist, fracturing it. I didn't have these surgeries until September. I tried to play on. My average plummeted. Didn't have the surgery until after I just got to the point where three cortisone shots weren't doing me any good. One of my many doctors told me, "You know what? I admire you."

"Why?"

"Because if the public knew what you had to go through just to suit up—you have *got* to be the toughest guy I know because of the things you play with."

That's why I feel like I was born to play. If not, I'd have quit a long time ago.

Sparky Anderson always did want me, ever since way back when I was in the Cincinnati chain. Sparky had managed the Big Red Machine, had managed the Tigers for 10 years. He was trying to get me. Sparky was like a Casey Stengel. He knew. Tommy was an icon—if you go back and look, everybody in baseball gets bashed except maybe Joe DiMaggio. Not Tommy. Because of the power he had. In '93, early on, I tried to change, just to cut down on the static. That might have been the biggest mistake of my career, trying to oblige Tommy about my hitting. Tommy was having problems with Straw, and I don't know if this is true, but I'm not sure Tommy could always make the distinction between me and Straw as far as our approaches to the game. Tommy wasn't there on those nights when Straw and I would be driving and would split up, with me coming home to Woodland Hills, Straw going off into the night. Straw had not been as lucky in his home life as I had been in mine. His personal life was unstable at that time, while mine was anything but; Sherrie's always been there for me, and the girls. The thing about being in L.A. I regretted was that I felt the fans and our teammates didn't get a chance to see Straw and me play our best, at the level we were supposed to display. In my case, physical injury and the handicap of trying to hit the way Tommy wanted me to hit held me back. I can't speak for Straw. I know he had back problems, but I also know Straw hadn't been as lucky as I'd been at first when I hooked up with Sherrie. And a relationship going bad can really screw up a ballplayer. I think of the season and a half I was in L.A., Straw and I may have played in 20 games total together. We might have won 16 of the 20 when in the lineup together. Hitting a healthy Eric Davis third and a healthy Darryl Strawberry cleanup and vice versa never really happened. I wish it had. But Straw hurt his back, and I was messed up, trying to recover from a broken collarbone, damaged wrist, really just now getting back right from the lacerated kidney of 1990, so I was never really able to deliver the kind of play I was capable of, and for that I'm sorry, sorry that the city of Los Angeles, my hometown, and the Dodger franchise never were to see my best. That's the only thing in my career I'd ever apologize for, not being able to give the L.A. fans the showcase they deserved, because if Darryl and I were healthy, we would've produced. Simple as that. That's my only regret.

I did try to oblige Tommy Lasorda. I tried to move my hands way up by my neck. It just wasn't working for me. I was hitting about .180 in '93. Missing fastballs right down the chute.

Tommy said, "Keep trying it."

But what really hurt and confused me was his lack of public support at the same time. He'd tell me behind closed doors: "Keep trying it." We'd lose, I'm 0-for-4, Tommy would say to the press, "Eric ain't playing up to his capabilities." I'm trying to make this adjustment because he asked me to. I'm a team player, trying to do what the manager says I gotta do. He didn't support that. I was close to walking away from the game in '93 because it got to the point where I was getting no support and struggling, trying to do something that Tommy had asked me to do.

I called up the then Dodgers' general manager, Fred Claire,

and asked why Tommy was hanging me out to dry like that. I wouldn't have a problem walking away with honor but I'm not going to be humiliated in this game by Tommy or anybody else. I've done too much and given too much of myself to go through that. Just let me heal, then let me play, the numbers will come. Fred said, "No, we're not releasing you. I know you can still play. Who do you want to work with?"

I thought for a minute, then said, "Reggie Smith," the hitting coach, a former outfielder. I knew Reggie. We were seeing eye to eye in spring training. At that time I might have had one home run. I was struggling big time. I didn't want to be struggling at home. You have your pride. You want your family and your people and your friends to be proud. So we had a meeting. Fred told Tommy, "We're gonna give Eric a week without playing, let Reggie work with him so he can get his stroke back. If you want to pinch-run with him, okay, but he's not gonna get any ABs." This was at 4 P.M. on a Monday afternoon. We were playing Cincinnati. Smiley was pitching. I come to the park. I'm in there. I said to Reggie, shaking my head, "Reggie, I'm playing." He was hot, he went to talk to Tommy. Tommy said, "I need him in there." I said, "You put my name in the lineup, I'm gonna play. But I'm going back to the way I know how." I dropped my hands, held them in front of me—and ended up crushing a grand slam off Smiley, driving in six runs.

Tommy and I could not agree on my swing, so finally he agreed I could work exclusively with Reggie, the batting coach. Reggie Smith was the only hitting instructor I ever worked with in the big leagues that asked me, "What do you want to accomplish?" as opposed to "I want you to do this, or that." Reggie said, "What kind of hitter do you think you are, and what kind do you want to be?" I said, "I'm a power hitter, and a run producer. I hit the ball out of the ballpark."

Reggie took me to the cage, stood 10 feet away from me, and

fired balls at me. "Get in your stance," he said. "Put your hands where Tommy wants 'em." I did, and he fired ball after ball past me. "Now, put 'em where you want 'em." I did, and he's throwing and nothing is getting past me. I'm peppering him. "Whoa, E.D.," Reggie said. "Ain't nothing wrong with your swing." He said the only thing wrong mechanically was that I was setting up too late, causing me to rush, making the swing too long. Cleared that up in no time. I come back around with 14 home runs and 50-some RBI by August.

And that's when the Dodgers up and traded me to Detroit.

In Pittsburgh, Tommy called me into the manager's office in the visiting clubhouse. He put the general manager, Fred Claire, on the telephone to tell me I'd been traded. Tommy couldn't even tell me himself. All he said was, "Telephone." So I talked to Fred Claire at Three Rivers Stadium in Pittsburgh. Tommy couldn't even look me in the eye. I don't know why not, though. I looked down at the Dodger blue script on the gray road uni. I was always proud to put on that uniform. Jackie Robinson's uniform. When Fred told me I'd been traded, he said he was sorry. I told him not to be, the Dodgers had been fair enough to me. Then I asked, "Where?" Fred said, "Detroit."

That meant Sparky Anderson. Sparky had been phased out of managing the Reds before I got there. He had been the manager of the Big Red Machine. He was originally from L.A., had gone to Dorsey High. He'd always spoken to me in spring training: "Son, they should just let you be . . . why, if I had you . . . why don't they just put you out there in the pasture and let you play?"

If I was getting traded anywhere, Detroit and Sparky looked pretty good.

TWELVE / WINTER 1996

ADVERSITY/BLESSING
Sabbatical

LIFE LESSON/STRATEGY
Rejuvenation

So I got traded from the Dodgers for nothing really, for a box of Cracker Jack—for a pitcher named John DeSilva. Don't know if he ever even made the Show. The Dodgers were just looking to unload me. At the time, August 31, 1993, the Tigers were five games out in the AL East, and Sparky had been trying to get me over the years, and finally had an opportunity, so he traded for me, figuring I could work out my problems at the plate that stemmed from my injuries in the '90 World Series and the '92 collarbone injury. I went over there and played extremely well from the jump. My first game was September 3, against the White Sox. I homered and doubled. On September 10, I had a double pump—two home runs—off Chicago's Alex Fernandez. Sparky was licking his chops thinking about the next season. I had a wonderful time playing with Cecil Fielder, Tony Phillips, Alan Trammell, Lou Whitaker, Kirk Gibson, and Dan Gladden. That was talent. Sparky said what was holding them back was enough pitching and having the kind of center fielder you need in Tiger Stadium, telling the press, "I always said if I could just get a healthy Eric Davis in center field here, before we get too old as a team." The Detroit nucleus had won a World Series 10 years earlier, in 1984. Chet Lemon, a fellow alum from Fremont High, was the center fielder when they won it all in '84. Closing in on 10 years later, it was still an outstanding club.

Then I had a tremendous spring training in '94. I'd signed on with the Tigers and felt great. I was 32, had a wealth of experience, finally felt physically and emotionally healed from that terrible and freak 1990 injury in the World Series. The only difficulty was that I was unfamiliar with the ballparks and the pitchers in the American League. And that would be my undoing. Right off the bat, first series of the year, we played in Boston. Fenway Park. I'd never played there. I was in center. Andre Dawson hit a bullet straightaway and deep. I took off instinctively and ran the ball down, but being unfamiliar with the dimensions of the park I couldn't tell how close I was to that particular segment of center-field wall. I caught the ball but then ran flush into the center-field wall and dropped it—more important, I slammed into that wall so hard I really messed up my neck and shoulder. I was all jacked up after that. But I kept on playing, and it just kept getting worse until by May I was taking six and seven cortisone shots in my neck just to go out there and play, until it got to a point in June where I couldn't play at all because I couldn't even turn my head. Not at all. It happened in the very first series of the year. Sparky had had such high hopes—this was going to be his last Tigers team—and yet Sparky never bailed on me, never blamed me. He saw what had happened. He knew I was injured. Never heard him say anything but "Eric Davis is a great kid."

I never wanted more to play all-out for a manager. But I ran into the wall at Fenway, and as badly as I wanted to produce for Sparky and all of Detroit, I couldn't. I would've given anything to have played center injury-free for Sparky. I wanted to open his eyes some more. I came off a year having battles with Tommy Lasorda, and before that the debacle in Cincinnati at the end of the triumph of the World Series. There'd been a lot of stress on me and I didn't feel like putting up with it, then to come to Detroit physically unable to perform—it had gotten depressing, these yo-yoing injuries. I lost my zest for the game. I had a collapsed vertebrae and a bulging disc in my neck, along the spinal column, which holds the nerves, and mine was so bruised that there were times I had no feeling in my left arm. I'd have to have surgery. That was the strike year—1994. I ended up getting the surgery done in Los Angeles when we went out on strike. That was the last straw for me physically—eight surgeries in seven years. Six years straight I'd had surgery every off-season, whether it was a knee, a shoulder, my neck, something. When I suffered the kidney injury, I'd had to go back in for orthoscopic knee surgery soon after, the next month. I got to feeling like the poster child for surgery. Now an attending physician said, "If you go out there and dive again, there's a possibility of paralysis." At that point I had to make a choice of what was more important to me: my career or my family. Being able to play with my girls, pick them up, hug them, have our enjoyment of each other. I told myself, "That's more important to me now." So at 32 I retired.

My body told me no. That's why I left. My mind was saying maybe because mentally I was still in tune with the game—more in tune than I'd ever been. I knew more and had wanted so badly to play center field in Tiger Stadium for Sparky. But I ran into the wall at Fenway Park chasing a line drive the first week of the season and had the bulging disc in my neck, and I tried to play but just couldn't in '94. Physically, I wasn't able to do it. It bothered me, because Sparky saw this and didn't bail on me, and I respected what he'd done in baseball, yet I couldn't perform. The lack of being able to do it physically affected my mental makeup and that's what caused me to walk away from the game after neck surgery—the nagging feeling I was letting people down.

My family supported me:

"Well, you played long enough."

"You don't need to play no more."

"If you don't want to play, you don't have to play."

"You really have done everything a man can do in baseball, haven't you?"

That last one got to me, because I didn't know if I had or not. I'd been Player of the Week, the Month, never Most Valuable Player, but in '87, if I hadn't gotten hurt, I might've been, and in 1990, whether elected or not, we won the World Series in the biggest upset in 30 years. It wasn't a matter of my career seeming incomplete. I had done enough things to feel accomplished. And my friends and family were really supportive. To play as long as I had was a blessing in itself, my mother and father said that. Being able to accomplish what I had accomplished in the game was another blessing. From others, I didn't get a lot of slack. Some people were upset with me. *How could you quit a good job like that? Wish I had me a good job like that.* I could play once I was surgically repaired, but I'd never taken time to heal from everything, I was always right back out there and now I was mentally burned out from dealing with injuries, rehabs, the brass, who in the end see you as a commodity. After going through what I went through in L.A., then going to Detroit, being disappointed by getting hurt again, I said, "I have to walk away from the game I love. Even though I love it—it's not as important to me as my life." I'd made a good living and supported my family so it was a decision I made for myself. I didn't want my family, my wife, or my girls to make the decision—then it wouldn't be right. I wanted to make the decision myself. But I would keep running into people after I decided to hang 'em up. *"Davis, man, you too young to be retired, look at you, man; you look good, you know the game—this is you. I appreciate the way you play, you always play 100 percent,"* Hearing this worked on me, too.

I did a lot of things in this game that my peers understand, and to me that was the most important thing. They're the people not only that you locker with and spend eight months out of the year with, but also the people you play against and respect.

That's really more important to me even than what the fans think. Numbers don't define me. My dynamic was different. I play gung ho. If I'd been in the military, I would have been a Marine. A Green Beret. A Navy Seal. No guts, no glory—and maybe no kidney. I did what I had to do to get the job done. When I came into the big leagues, I was 160 pounds. Like a stick of dynamite. I'm 200 pounds now, but that comes with age. I played. I'm the one that caused them to put padding on the walls all around National League ballparks. The outfield walls were once just hard boards. But I ran into so many of them, hurt myself so bad, that now the walls are all padded. That's not a stat, but it's impact.

It's very difficult to give up what you feel is your calling, no matter what the circumstances are, especially when you've been doing it for a long time. The hardest thing is to find something to do that's as absorbing, as time consuming, and as gratifying. People look at you differently when you're a retired ballplayer. Remember, I had been playing professionally since I was 18 years old, and now here I was, 33; I'd been a major leaguer for ten years. Basically, you get everyday stuff handed to you on a silver platter once you make the big leagues. Now repairmen left bills. I had to wait for tables at restaurants. That took some getting used to. Mostly it's the bulk of free time to fill. Baseball is a vocation, avocation, and hobby—it fills up so much of your time. So if you don't have major hobbies or business operations you can step right into, it's a tough transition. You don't know exactly what to do. You can clean out the garage just so many times.

My family was happy, Sherrie and the girls. Well, they were happy for a while. Then they were ready for me to go somewhere. Sherrie would ask, "Eric, don't you have anywhere to go?" Aren't you going somewhere, honey?" It was a transitional period for them, too. They were just not accustomed to having me around in the summer. You really have to work on your marriage when you're at home every day. When you're a big leaguer, or just a professional with a traveling job, you're guaranteed some time away, and we'd gotten used to having space. But when you're there every day, it can get to be like, "Don't you have anywhere to go?" "No. Don't *you*?" "You need to go do something because you're getting on my nerves." "Well, you *already* got on mine."

Now I had to fit into Sherrie's schedule and the girls' schedules, and Erica, my oldest, really was starting to have an active one. She is a lot like me. She can play anything and loves to participate in sports. She's a feminine girl, but she has athletic ability like her daddy and she likes to use it. She was just about eight years old at this time. I was picking her up from school and taking her to activities. I'm not a big get-up-and-go guy. I'm content to be at home, do what I'm doing right now. Sacha is more like me in that way, a little family homebody, too. She's the little model with the fingernail and toenail polish and all the frilly things, and she can be fussy. She might well be athletic one day, but right now she wants nothing to do with that, she likes her dolls, her nails, her earrings, and she isn't trying to get dirty at all. If her sneakers are dirty, she doesn't even want to put them on. She already wants the six-inch heels. Modeling, that's her bag. As for the rest of my family, they'd never lived their lives through me—when we were together we didn't talk about baseball that much. They've never really been that caught up in what I did for a living. They enjoyed coming to ball games, but the job of baseball was never even discussed unless I was hurt or something. It was always "How are you feeling, Keith?" not "You're playing?" During off-seasons, we had never sat around and discussed any exploits of mine, positively or negatively. That's how my family was, and it started with my father and mother. I'd grown distant from my parents between the time I left for the minors and the time I retired. They were both remarried, and they both lived close to us, my dad and his wife in

Woodland Hills, my mom and her husband in West Hills. When I told my mother and father I was going to retire they said, "Oh. Okay. If that's what you want to do, it's up to you."

And that was the extent of it. Sherrie's reaction was similar. You have some guys' wives saying, "No, we can't quit, we gotta keep playing." But Sherrie and I have been together so long, she has a good feel and read on me. We're not insecure in our relationship. And she knew it wasn't a family decision because the family wasn't out there taking that day-to-day pounding. I was. I don't think any player ever plays pain-free. You're never going to play this game pain-free. That doesn't happen at the major-league level. You're going to have nicks, scrapes, bruises, sprains, and breaks and tears. The only time I played pain-free was back in Little League. It's just impossible to do for me, or really for anybody outside of Cal Ripken Jr. You play a hundred games, something's going to happen. Something's going to hurt. But soon I began to heal up. I started beating up on my barbecue grill. I beat it up. For the first time, I got a chance to enjoy my own house. Because I had never been home in the spring and summer, and that's when a house really opens up. I got to enjoy the swimming pool, the outdoor grill, the basketball court, the game room. I got a chance to enjoy life in '95, being home for the Memorial Day, Fourth of July, the girls' birthdays, having a pool party for my oldest daughter's birthday, a lot of things I had missed. To be able to do that at age 33, when my girls where small, that was great, to see the satisfied looks on their faces, that I was there with them. I got a chance to go to some of Erica's activities, some of the games in all of the sports she participates in. I could tell she was proud I was there, and I was proud of her, too.

When I was out of the game, people sometimes asked me to pick my ideal team. Not an all-time team, necessarily, but a team of guys I'd played with or against or watched, a team I'd want to be on if we were playing for the world championship. I'd build it for defense first.

At first base it probably would be Keith Hernandez, who played with the St. Louis Cardinals and the New York Mets. In addition to winning 10 or 11 Gold Gloves, he was a clutch hitter. As an opponent, you didn't want to see him up there with the game on the line. Lefty, righty—didn't matter to Keith. More than that, he went to a new level for first basemen in terms of aggression on defense—charging sacrifice bunts, throwing out lead runners. I still have vivid images in my mind of him charging fearlessly and as a left-hander making that throw to second or third base to get a lead runner when a lot of left-handers wouldn't want to make that throw. Again, I'm thinking of a player I could've complemented. Once I was in Candlestick Park, Reds against the Giants, must've been 1987 or so. Score tied, bottom of the ninth, Giants have runners on first and third, one out. Will Clark at the plate. I'm in center, playing shallow. *Way* in. Will hits a bullet base hit up the middle, a game-winning hit—only I'm charging hard, pick up Will's hit on one hop and in two bounds I beat the runner from first into second base and then I jump into the air, set to fire over to first and try to double up Will. Only our first basement was Todd Benzinger, more a hitter than a fielder; he gave up on the play, wasn't playing attention, about to walk off. And so I had to eat the ball and the winning run scored easily. Hernandez would've been stretching for my throw (as it is, Clark gets on me every time I see him, even 10 years later, for turning his RBI single into an RBI force-out). Hernandez was the best at coming off the bag and starting a double play. As for hitting, he didn't hit with a lot of power, but if you needed a knock, a knock was coming. If you asked anybody on that 1986 Mets' World Championship team what or who exactly fueled them, I think mostly they would tell you it was Keith. I know Straw would. That's what he told me. Straw and Doc Gooden were young then, and Keith had a veteran's will to be successful and he spread it around. The premier defensive player at his position. If you get the premier defensive players at their positions, that usually means they can play, period, and will hit, and you'll win.

That's why at second base I have to take Robby Alomar hands down no question, and I say that even though I watched and then played with Lou Whitaker at Detroit, and watched the great Joe Morgan, who was the second baseman with the Big Red Machine in the '70s and played all over the National League in the early '80s—just slightly ahead of my time. Between Joe and Sweet Lou, well, that's two of the best second basemen ever to play. But still I have to take Robby. It's not that I think it's that big a gap between them, but I think Bay-Bay is that far head and shoulders above everybody defensively. If you look at the total package of what he possesses I don't think there's ever been anybody close. Talent-wise, yes, but in terms of understanding of the game and imagination, he is the best. I don't think there's been anybody that positioned himself like Robby does, that can anticipate like he does, that plays with the fearlessness that he does. He knows where he is and what kind of play he has to make at every second of a ballgame. Some guys, as the play starts to develop, they're thinking about what they're going to do as the ball's coming to them. He already knows. He knows if he's going to use a flip, a shovel, a toss, that if it's here, he has to go behind his back—he knows all of that. He's got a great arm. I had no way of knowing it all then, but with me in right field and him as my cut-off man, we'd throw out more than one guy at third base on a hit or a fly ball out to right. The Blue Jays had won two World Series back to back in '92 and '93 with him, so I'd seen him operate even by the time I was retired in '94. Later, when I played with him, I'd watch him and think "What's he going to do before the ball even gets there?" I watched him on some of those relay throws where he can calculate speed of runner and distance and time and I've seen him throw behind the rear runner, get him lots of times, right as a guy is rounding first base. Because of his anticipation. He knows, "Okay, you're coming around first, I can catch this relay throw as if I'm going to throw to third, only I can't get the guy at third, but I can spin and gun you out before you can get back to first base." I've seen him do it. And his knowledge of the game is great. Always talking baseball. Always trying to figure out how he can get an advantage over a pitcher, how he can do this and that. You can't really fully appreciate it until you watch him work day in and day out. I wasn't with the Orioles in 1996 when he had the unfortunate name-calling, spitting incident with umpire John Hirschbeck. It's sad that people won't allow him to move on now. Granted, he was wrong, and he'd be the first one to tell you that. But even as it went on, he got the playoff-clinching home run, and then he helped the Orioles beat the Indians in the playoffs with another late game-winning homer, all the while the press and the fans in lockstep came down on him. Robby played right through that, and he's still playing through it, and he'll play through it until he decides to retire. At second base on my team, write him in. Or Morgan, really. I'm going to sell tickets, too, because purists will come just to watch them play.

Shortstop? The Wizard. Ozzala. Ozzie Smith. I can't even describe the plays I've seen from dugouts or have been on bases and watched Ozzie make. I've seen ones on the Game of the Week and *This Week in Baseball* that everybody saw, but I'm talking about the ones I saw him make live, when he was with the Cardinals playing the Reds.

Ozzie was all glove when he first came up, but as he got older he became a better hitter. He taught himself how to hit. Defensively—there's not another word besides "great" to describe him.

Third base might be the hardest choice. I saw Mike Schmidt, on toward the end, but he was still clubbing with the Phillies when I came up. I went on to play with Cal Jr. for a couple of years. But when I retired, I would've said Buddy Bell. I had a chance to play with Buddy for three years in Cincinnati, and watching his overall gracefulness in fielding the position, I could imagine what he must've been like at 25 and 26 years old. Buddy could pick it real clean. Bell probably had the softest hands of any man I've ever seen, in a sense of receiving the baseball, even after he'd gotten older. Seldom did I ever see Buddy Bell get angry. When he came to play with us in Cincinnati, he didn't have the arm like I heard he'd had earlier in his career, but I've never seen a third baseman who could dive and get up as quickly as he could and throw as accurately. I never saw Brooks Robinson play, but to watch Buddy dive behind the bag and throw to first in one motion—it was just tremendous. He made the tough plays look routine. His hands were never behind the play.

Behind the plate, I'd have to take Mike Scoscia of the Dodgers for his defensive abilities, for his ability to handle the pitchers, and for things I saw him do before I saw any other catcher do them. I've seen him block the plate before he gets the ball, block the plate and lock a guy up. You had to literally run him over to get to home plate. That plate was his and you weren't getting in there. If you watch a lot of catchers now, they'll invite you to slide and then try to knock you off your line to the plate. They're going to get the ball and then try to come back and tag you. But Scoscia was just planted in front of the plate. My goodness, you couldn't even see the plate. I know. I've come in on a play at the plate against him, and I know *I* couldn't see it.

Right field. That's a tough call, too. That's a really tough call. Dave Parker played right field. By the time I played with Pops his knees were shot to hell, his arm wasn't what it was, but I grew up watching his teams in the '70s in Pittsburgh. I never saw Roberto Clemente play. Wish I had. I'm talking only about guys I played with or against or saw. I'd have to say for right field, Andre Dawson. He had one of the strongest arms in the game. And when his knees were right, he was fast. He knew how to position himself. Offensively, his numbers speak for themselves. In 1987, when I had my career year, Hawk was NL MVP with the Cubs, and hit 49 home runs.

Center field, I would have to leave that one open for you.

In left field, I would have to say Barry Bonds, because of his throwing ability, his ability to be aggressive and attack the ball defensively. You don't see a lot of outfielders attacking the ball defensively. I always did it, and Barry Bonds always did it, too, anticipated and positioned himself very well, and his eight Gold Gloves and his offensive numbers speak for themselves. He didn't win three National League MVP awards because of a public relations campaign. Barry can *play.*

My father's never really told me how proud he is of the things I've done. He'd tell me what the guys at his job had said. He always did it that way. When I retired, he'd report to me on what they guys on his job were saying: "Man, your son's too young to be retired. These guys, they don't play the game the way your son did. They *can't* play the game the way your son did." I think my father knew what he was doing, because those things stayed with me whenever I watched a game. He knew my body needed rest. But he also knew I had always played like he had always worked.

I started to think about playing again partly because I was intrigued by the challenge of being able to see if I could do it. Once I felt good physically again, that improved my mental makeup. It wasn't dwindling ability that forced me to hang up my spikes, it was just physical and then mental attrition. And if you never do it again, you always ask yourself, "What if?" I wasn't prepared to go the rest of my life asking, "What if?" and "Could I have done it?" So I said I'd give it a shot again. If I'd continued to have any kind of discomfort in my neck, I wouldn't have come back. But my neck felt better by the time of the 1995 play-offs, and internally I felt better than I had since 1990.

I hadn't gone to a single game that season. I had told myself,

"You're not going over there," meaning to Dodger Stadium at Chavez Ravine. It was almost funny, because every time the Reds came to town, Lenny Harris would call me up, always with the same thing, trying to get me out to the ballpark. I told him and Barry Larkin, "If you go to the play-offs and meet the Dodgers, then I'll come see if you and Barry learned anything, Lenny." I never thought those two teams would make it to the play-offs, but that's what happened in 1995. Barry and Lenny had kept after me, and lo and behold—the Dodgers and Reds played in the first round of the '95 play-offs.

I didn't consciously take that as a sign, but I did make plans to go over to Dodger Stadium for the first time since my retirement. It was a joyous occasion, a play-off atmosphere down on the field. I knew almost everybody on both teams: "Ah man, you look good. When you coming back, man? These outfielders can't play compared to you, E.D." If I hadn't gone to that game, maybe I would not have come back to baseball. But I did go back to Dodger Stadium, where even Tommy Lasorda was smiling and seemed happy to see me. I walked on the field and felt that pregame atmosphere, and just the smell of the pine tar and the wood, the sound of the wood on the ball, and the excitement of late-season, championship, top-end, big-league baseball took me back to where I belonged. For me, being back out there, and all that talking to myself I did to get away from the game, all that pain and frustration I felt, within one half hour at the ball park, just melted away in my memory, back into a place where I could easily recall them but not feel them so much.

That day Jim Bowden, now the Cincinnati general manager, saw me, and I ended up sitting next to Marge Schott, of all people, for a little while, and Jim asked me then if I had contemplated coming back to baseball. I said no. Then he asked again. I said I might, nothing was etched in stone either way. He asked me to give the Reds the first shot at signing me. I told Bowden to give me a month to work on it because at that point I hadn't even picked up a bat in a year and a half. Bowden was insistent. I told him to give me a month to work out, and if my neck responded and I didn't have any problems physically, especially with my neck, I'd come to spring training and then we'd all see.

The Reds beat the Dodgers three straight. Then the Reds lost four straight to the Braves. "With you, we could've gotten 'em," Lenny told me. So I started working out in October and November of 1995, gingerly swinging the bat. Reggie Smith had a baseball camp over near my home; I worked out every day. I ran, stretched, did calisthenics, normal things, waiting with dread for that feeling of my neck seeming like it was broken, turning it slowly, like mechanized armor, a turret on a tank. But it gave me no pain. The doctors' handiwork on my neck held up.

My hitting felt great. My hands went back to where they were normally but up a little, above my waist now. My mind was clearer than it had been in years. I concentrated on executing the five skills without intense pain blocking me and hindering my movements. When I stepped into the batter's box it felt like this is the man who stepped into the batter's box before he hurt his kidney, before he hurt his neck. It was the first time in five years I'd swung without pain. The swing was there. The stride was there. I called up Jim Bowden and said, "Everything is back."

I signed a deal with the Reds in December 1995. I knew it was probably going to be a courtesy look, more than anything, for an old heir to the Big Red Machine. Davey Johnson was manager of the Reds' play-off team, and I had spoken to him on the field just before the play-off game at Dodger Stadium, and he really wanted me to play for him, and I really wanted to play for him. But even then people were saying Ray Knight was going to take over for him, and he did. I knew Ray Knight hadn't liked me much when he was playing and had started swinging his fists at me for no reason back in '86. I figured, what the hell. I'm not a grudge holder. I just figured that was a competitive thing. Eight years had passed. I was too old for that now. I wasn't going to say, "I don't want to sign with the Reds because of Ray Knight." That would've been ridiculous. I was going back to play baseball. I wasn't going back to forge relationships with managers. I could've signed with some other teams, but I wanted to go back to Cincinnati because of Barry Larkin and Lenny Harris, my protégés, and because of the fans, knowing the lay of the land. Besides, Sparky was gone from Detroit now. I guess you can tell, part of my heart will always be with the Reds no matter where I play. It's like a first love. You can go through things, be hurt, be devastated, move on, marry somebody else, whatever—but part of you will always love that person like you can love no one else. This was so with me and the Reds, regardless of GMs, regardless of Marge, because I gave that organization 12 years, and the first and best years of my professional baseball life. Anytime you spend that much time you don't blow it off and say, "Fine then, it's over." Deep down, if you helped that individual or institution, or they helped you, it's always going to be a strong part of your heart. It was that way between E. Davis and the Cincinnati Reds. On both parts, I think.

I love the Reds' tradition, but unfortunately they don't understand the value of it. The Reds finally retired the numbers of Frank Robinson, Joe Morgan, and Ted Kluzsewski recently. They should have retired Davey Concepcion's number. How can you have a shortstop play 20 years and not have a day for that man? Joe Morgan never had much interaction with the Reds organization while I was there because they didn't recognize him. Riverfront is one of the only ballparks I've walked into where you had no sense of who played there. You're talking about a tradition that, outside of the Yankees, is unparalleled. Unparalleled. Second to none. You take a 25-man roster of Cincinnati Reds all-time players, you're second to none, except maybe the Yankees, and that's a maybe. Look at the outfielders you can choose from: Frank Robinson, Curt Flood, Vada Pinson, Ken Griffey, Cesar Geronimo, Bobby Tolan, Klu, Parker, and, if I can say so, Eric Davis. Look at the infielders—Concepcion, Morgan, Rose,

Perez. Look at Johnny Bench behind the plate. That's what you're looking at. You walk into Riverfront Stadium—Cinergy Field—you don't even know what team played there, let alone what great individual talent wore that uniform. If you didn't know, if you were a guest, or a foreigner, if you came in from out of town doing business and you weren't a baseball fan and you saw that stadium or you went to the game, you wouldn't even know who played there. You're talking about a team that once put eight men on a National League All Star team. Seven started. If you walk into Yankee Stadium, you're gonna know. You walk into Dodger Stadium, Baltimore's Camden Yards, you're gonna know. Somewhere, you're gonna see some pictures hanging. I can tell you there's no picture of Joe Morgan in Cincinnati at the ballpark. Between all these guys, somebody had to do something on every single day of the summer there. Somebody had to do something on every day of the baseball season, down through history, something that could be commemorated. Very rarely did you see any recognition of this.

Tom Browning became a friend. He threw a perfect game once, and I was in center behind him. Made some plays. Helped him. He helped me. We were teammates. Marge gave him a gift. Gave his wife a mink coat when he threw the perfect game. I did something that hadn't been done in Cincinnati for 40 years, since Frank Robinson. I hit for the cycle, back in '89. What do you think Marge gave Sherrie? To me she gave a pat on the back. To Sherrie, not even that. Just, "Good job." I think Tom Browning understood this. He took time to say, "Great way to go, E."

By the way, I would've hit for the cycle for Cincinnati again in '96—I needed a double in the last at-bat, and hit a bullet down the right-field line and Eric Anthony laid out and caught it. Eric Anthony never made a better play. The score was 15–2 at the time. I admit I cussed him out all the way around the stadium. Boy, that would've been sweet—hit for the cycle twice, for the same team, after being traded by that team. That would've been worth remembering, wouldn't it?

* * *

When I got to spring training in 1996, I felt good about the situation with the Reds because I knew the players and I didn't think there was anything there that would keep me from making the team. Reggie Sanders was the only outfielder there who had done anything, the only one you could say had a job. There were a couple of others, Mike Kelly, now with the Tampa Bay Devil Rays, and Vince Coleman, the old ex-Cardinal. That wasn't going to be a problem for me; all Vince ever had was wheels and since he was getting older those were going. That's about all.

Ray would be managing the Reds now, for Marge, saying that there were two outfield jobs open, and I would be there. The center-field job and the left-field job. I was still 33, young enough to play either, and with my body healthy, talented enough to play either. The chance to compete excited me, because I hadn't had this competition for a couple of years. For 10 years, whenever I went to camp, I'd known I was getting 450 ABs, bat third or fourth, be in the field, so now it was one of those things where I was welcoming that challenge of having to compete. We had an intrasquad game right away and Mike Kelly hit a home run, and immediately Ray was saying Kelly was going to be the everyday center fielder, that he was going to get 500 ABs, how he reminded Ray of George Foster, raving on and on about a guy who, God bless him, was unproven on the big-league level. One intrasquad game dinger and now Kelly's getting 500 ABs in the big leagues? Playing center field every day? On a play-off team? It's all I can do to keep from laughing.

I had re-signed with the Reds for $500,000 for the 1996 season. No option. Sink or swim. Fair enough. I'd gone down to Plant City for spring training. Plant City is like Mayberry, only with fewer stores. It's not the kind of place where you say, "Hey, think I'll go to Plant City to hang out." No. It's not one of those places and to me that was good because there weren't many distractions. You had to focus on baseball. When I first got down there I felt like I wasn't in their plans. They had me hitting in the last group of guys that wore the big numbers, number 73. You know that poor guy won't make the team. There were about seven or eight outfielders, but I didn't see anything that would keep me from playing, Even though my career numbers have been curtailed because of injuries, still, as deceivingly low as they were, they were still more than all their career big-league numbers combined. I knew in my heart if I got a chance, none of those outfielders would prevent me from playing. But I couldn't write my name on the lineup card. That was Ray Knight's job.

But Ray seemed to be doing everything in his power to prevent me from making that team. Had me batting ninth, taking B-squad road trips that veterans rarely take, caddying for Vince, Reggie, and Mike Kelly. Normally you could trade all three of those baseball cards for one Eric Davis, but retirement humbled me, I had to check my ego at the door, which was good, because I was able to recognize what obstacles I had in front of me in this comeback attempt. In no way did this discourage me. It let me know I was alive. This was what I was accustomed to. Obstacles.

I started working out on my own. Staying late on my own. Hitting off the tee on my own. Going back to my oldest habits of success. And with this preparation, even batting ninth, I started hitting tape-measure home runs that spring, I started making plays in the outfield. Started stealing bases. Ray said, "Well, maybe he has got a possibility of making the team as a fifth outfielder." But there was something nobody else knew that I knew. I was confident now because I knew more. I had become that veteran that Dave Parker and Pete Rose and all those old guys from the Big Red Machine had built me up to be. If only my body wouldn't betray me again . . .

So Kelly hit a home run in an intrasquad game and Ray got so geeked he guaranteed him 500 ABs. I'm sitting there saying to myself, "A manager promises a guy 500 ABs for a dinger in an intrasquad game? That won't hold past April. Mike hasn't proven he can handle big-league pitching on an everyday basis—two games into camp and he's given him a job? Ohhhhh-kay."

I never sat down with Knight to say, "Why can't bygones be bygones here, Ray?" or to discuss whether I'd get a fair shot in '96. That spring, I could see Ray didn't want me to make the squad. I can't say if Jim Bowden, the general manager, or Marge didn't want me to make it. But I'm pretty clear Ray didn't. Here you have a player of my proven caliber that hadn't played for a year and a half. Seems to me a smart baseball man, logically, would do everything that he could to get me as many ABs as possible, get me to playing as much as I could, so I could make the team or not make the team based on performance. So he could see whether I still had it or not. That didn't happen. I knew something was wrong when I got in my first hitting group. You can tell by the group you're in. You can tell where on the totem pole you fall. Like I said, I'm in with some guys that I know the first cut is coming from. That's the hitting group I'm in. The print's pretty big between the lines here, and I'm thinking to myself, "Dog, it's going to be like this?" I started off swinging slowly, bringing myself around slowly; I know this is not going to last, these unproven guys. It will come back around to me because I'm a hitter. I'm wondering whether Ray Knight knows this or not, but I'm figuring that he *should* know it, if he's the manager. But Ray would take me on trips and I wouldn't even play. And if I would play, I would bat eighth.

I used it as a motivating factor, a challenge. To come back and have the manager totally disrespecting me, it made me say: "Okay, we'll see. We'll see who comes to the post."

When we played the Kansas City Royals in a split-squad game, I hit a home run over the scoreboard. I was told Ray told the reporters, "That was on a 3-and-0 pitch. Anybody can hit a home run on a 3-and-0 pitch." I can tell right away this is going to be hard to swallow for Ray. Because I could feel myself coming around. I knew I still had it. Now if Ray denied I still had it, it would be to the detriment of his ball club. There was no way these unproven guys or an aging slap hitter like Vince, or Reggie Sanders, who I raised, were going to outperform me. So I told the reporters like Hal McCoy of Dayton, still on the beat, and a newer guy named Rob Parker, from the *Enquirer*, "Well, I'd say, by Memorial Day, I'll either be the everyday center fielder, or the everyday left fielder. Bank on it." Then Reggie hurt his back and I got a chance to play right field. Then I played center and left field. One game we were playing the Tigers. Biggest yard in Florida, Ray put me in center. I thought, "Well, well, are we trying to show that I can't run anymore? Can't cover ground?" I ran down about six balls in the gaps and turned four doubles into outs. Really, I thought it was funny, except that when the grind started, I knew no one would want to win more than Ray Knight. So I'm starting to swing the bat well. Hit a couple more homers. I can feel the vibe changing around the clubhouse—coaches talking to me, including me in this and that, where before I was being excluded from everything. I can see it. I've got a good sense of awareness of what's going on around me; everything is starting to pick up now that I'm clubbing. Everything is starting to revolve around me now, and so I went from not having much of a chance to make the team—Ray's exact quote was, "If Eric Davis makes the team, it'll be as a fifth outfielder"—to being the tonic, the fulcrum, the Man the team needed if it was going to continue to at least contend.

I ended up hitting around .400 that spring.

Ray called me into his office at the end of spring and said, "I know you had a better spring than Vince, but I made a commitment to Vince that he would start." I said, "Ray, there's no way. The job should be open to the best man. But I understand." Ray said, "I promised." I wasn't in a position to bargain. I accepted what Ray told me. But I knew eventually I would be in there.

At first, not playing was hard, but I had to focus on preparation for when I would be in there, because sooner or later I would be. Ray Knight doesn't like to lose ball games any more than any manager does. When the bombs start going off, you get less particular about who is in the foxhole with you, especially if they're helping you win firefights. I had to study the pitchers because I had been out of the game for a year and a half, and out of the National League for over two years. Sure enough, Ray started sneaking me in there against lefties. I started hammering them. By May I was really revving, and in center every day. Kelly struggled, Vince struggled; it got to a point where the pitchers started complaining to Ray about me not being in there because I'm in the outfield making plays to help them, throwing people out like I did when I was a young stud, patrolling the gaps, not to mention beating the breaks off the ball, protecting Larkin, getting him better pitches to hit just by being in the on-deck circle, while Kelly is losing balls in the lights and Vince can't get it out of the infield. Later on, in the middle of May, McCoy came up to me one day at Riverfront and said, "Remember what you told me in spring training? That by the middle of this month you'd be the everyday center fielder?" I was on my seventh straight center-field start. Ray had tried his best to get by with Vince and Kelly. But they didn't hit. And there was no one in the lineup who could protect Larkin hitting third, so we went straight to the bottom of the NL West. Ray had to put me in there. The muscles in his jaw worked, but he had to do it. I wind up having the club on my back. Ray loosens up after a few wins, talks about how he needs me. It's funny how things can evolve in one season. Not only was I again quickly a big fan favorite in my old baseball home of Cincinnati, Ohio, I was also a pitcher's favorite, too.

Ray didn't have much choice in playing me because I started beating on that baseball so much there was no comparison between me and the other outfielders we had. None at all. That's just the way it was. If I was on a team with Clemente, Frank Robinson, Hank Aaron, then yeah, I'm the fourth outfielder and there's no comparison between me and them. But between me and Mike Kelly, Vince Coleman, and Reggie Sanders, it's the same thing, only a little more in my favor. Ray reluctantly put me in the lineup. The season goes on and either Larkin or me is performing as the best player on the team. It got to the point where Ray needed me to help secure his job. All of a sudden I'm a team leader. All of a sudden I'm a main focal point of the offense. He was reluctant, but he saw the numbers every day unfolding, how the pitchers and managers on the other teams wanted to avoid pitching to me, and how I added to our confidence, how I balanced the whole batting order, how I forced them to pitch to our number three hitter, Barry Larkin. Then I got dinged and was out a few games. Quickly Ray's position was, we need Eric in there because he's doing this and that. He needed me. You can get into that situation in your work environment. It can happen, in baseball and everywhere else. Sometimes your boss needs you but for some reason he doesn't like you. I'd gone from having Ray not speak to me to asking me who I thought we should sign.

As the season goes along, I'm doing my thing, and being especially helpful to Barry Larkin, who ends up with 33 home runs, a career high. See, I'm hitting cleanup, right behind him, and I ended up with 26 home runs, 83 RBI, 81 runs scored, 20 doubles, and 23 steals in only 129 games and 415 ABs. But in spite of my play, Barry's play, we really didn't have much else, particularly pitching, and so we were struggling to reach .500 for the year, and it was starting to settle in on Ray. Then he told me and Larkin something I don't think I've ever heard any manager say. I know I had never heard any manager say it to me. The last three games of the season were in St. Louis, and it was already etched in stone that neither Larkin nor I was going to play. We had September call-ups and the young guys were going to play. No big deal. Last series of the year. We're going nowhere. We were at .500 going into this last series with the Cardinals, and then we lost the first game. So Ray called me and Larkin into his office and tells us that he needs us to play the last two games so that it would look better on our record, being 81–81 instead of 80–82, or 79–83. I never had a manager tell me that. Especially not a manager who tried to punch me out when he was a player because he didn't like me or the fact that I'd played the game hard, or the fact God had given me talent. Funny how things come around, how everything comes out in the wash. Ray didn't say he thought it would be better if the team finished at .500 or above. He said he felt it would look better on the team's record. So I looked at Larkin and Larkin looked at me, and I started laughing. I couldn't help it. And, well, we ended up playing, and getting the two wins, and Ray ended up looking like he wanted to look.

Ray had called me into the office just before that to tell me how the Reds were going to re-sign me for '97, and how they want me back because I'm an intrinsic part of the offense, and how I'm a leader, and he never knew that about me before. Ray is also telling me who he wants to break in, and asking my opinion of them and who he doesn't want to re-sign, and what do I think of that.

So I'm saying, okay, I'll do whatever you need me to do. All of a sudden I'm a Man again in Cincinnati, Larkin and me. I did want to stay in Cincinnati. I felt that was where I should be. I felt vindicated, comfortable, having gone from a guy they think is washed up, who they're giving just a courtesy look to, to a guy they're consulting with about the lineup, to an integral part of the offense. And I'm sitting there going along, saying, "Okay, all right, I can do this. I can do that."

I tried to school the younger players, although in some cases, advice does no good and you have to learn for yourself. Willie Greene, a good young player, an infielder, third baseman, came up. He ordered a limo one day, had it brought to the ball-park, and had it parked right outside the clubhouse door. We happened to lose a game that day. I asked him if was he crazy. I told him to tell the limo driver to meet him over at his house. "You haven't even been in every bathroom in the league yet and you've got a big white stretch outside the clubhouse picking you up, just after we just got beat on?" "It's my birthday, E.D."

Will protested. "Willie, I don't care." He was setting himself up for unnecessary criticism he didn't deserve. You're going to get criticized enough.

During the month of September, everybody is talking about contract extensions and some players had already gotten them, though by now we know that Marge is a thrifty sort, putting it mildly. Once she banned Rob Parker from the press room where the media eats because he had written critically. I called for a pizza and had it delivered to Parker in the press box. Marge didn't like that too much, but, like Hal McCoy, Parker had been fair with me. Why starve the man?

Cincinnati is a small-market town and it'll be a long time, if ever, before there's another year like 1990. Bowden said that to some degree his hands were tied. They gave light-hitting infielder Jeff Brantly an extension. They gave reliever Jeff Shaw an extension. They gave starting pitcher Mike Morgan an extension. Lenny Harris, Thomas Howard, and I were also free agents. But we were also African American free agents. None of us got extensions. I'm not judging it, I'm just telling you the way it is and what it is you have to deal with. Everyone has obstacles. While we're being asked to win a couple for Ray Knight, I'm asking, "Are you going to give Thomas Howard and Lenny Harris [a hell of a utility ballplayer, can hit, can play everywhere, ended up helping the Mets in the run for the NL wild card in '98] and Eric Davis extensions?"

I ended up talking to Reds' team president John Allen. Jim Bowden and his assistants were talking to me and saying we were going to work it out, it would all work out, just as soon as they got a couple of the other guys done, just as soon as the smoke clears, just as soon as they can get with Ray and formulate a strategy, just as soon as they can run the numbers by Marge. Meantime, Davey Johnson had designs. Davey managed the Reds while I was in Detroit and was retired. It was Davey, not Ray, who took the Reds to the play-offs in '95 when I went to Chavez Ravine and the fellows were telling me to come back. Davey left and Ray came in. Davey was in Baltimore now. There's history of players moving from Cincinnati to Baltimore and Baltimore to Cincinnati, from Frank Robinson to Chris Sabo, with mixed results. Some teams get comfortable trading players, and the trades somehow seem to fit, to help both clubs. Baltimore and Cincinnati are two such clubs. Lee May played for both back in the day. F. Robinson was an All Star outfielder that the Reds traded to Baltimore in the early '60s and Frank went on to be a Triple Crown winner for the Orioles. There was no real need to trade for me. Cincinnati wasn't going to re-sign me. I'd been in the game long enough to trust my instincts, not just about what goes on out on the field, but also behind the scenes. I knew enough about talent and how a team is put together to be an assistant general manager myself. The baseball education of Eric Davis was hard but complete.

I flew to Cincinnati around December 15. I met with Marge, even though at the time Marge was suspended. She can't do anything, her hands are tied, in a baseball sense. I think Marge has always admired me as a baseball player. All those things she said—I think Marge was just trying to fit in, be one of the boys, be tough, show how hard she could be. But I always thought deep down she admired me, was a closet Eric Davis fan. That's what I like to think.

"Eric," she says, "I want you to come back and play for me. It's all in the papers here how the Indians are trying to sign you. Is that true? You know I can't let Cleveland get you."

"Cleveland, Marge?" I said. I wasn't really being coy. I'd heard Cleveland was interested, to some degree, but then I'd also heard that Bake, Dusty Baker, the manager of the San Francisco Giants, was interested, too. I'd heard the Boston Red Sox were interested. And I'd also heard Davey Johnson and Baltimore were interested.

"Don't act like you don't know, Eric. You hurt me."

"Aw, Marge. You know I would never do that."

"I couldn't bear it, Eric," she said. "I couldn't bear you going to play in another city in Ohio." I knew if I went to Cleveland and did well, the sports columnists and editorial page writers wouldn't let her bear it for very long. Marge has always been a favorite pincushion of theirs and I have to say, the old girl usually brought it on herself. But at the end of the day, Marge was always cool with me—except for that one time, that one time in 1990, in the aftermath of the World Series.

"You know you'll be a Red all your life, Eric. You know that."

"I know what you're saying, Marge." I told Marge what I thought was fair, which was much less than what I was making when I left the game. Two million for the numbers I put up in 1996 is a bargain. I told Marge that was what I needed. I wasn't trying to break the bank. I knew how she was. Marge told me that since she was officially suspended for some of her off-color remarks, she couldn't really get into the contract negotiations. I told Marge I had always thought she could do whatever she wanted to do. That's what she had always done—what she wanted to do. She smiled.

I ended up going back down to Jim Bowden's office and talking to him; he's a nice enough fellow, and he offers me a million two per, for two. I happened to be second on the club in just about all important numbers, homers, batting average, runs scored, RBI, stolen bases. So I said, "Jim, that can't be right. Come on now. Check your figures. You've got all of these role players you've signed for guaranteed money, but for me, you got to check the budget. Two mil a year for three years, for the numbers I'm bringing, the attitude I'm bringing, the help I'm going to give your young players, for the mound meetings I'm going to cause the other team to have. Come on Jim, I didn't just fall off the onion truck. I've been here a while." Jim says he has to check the budget.

So it came down to that Friday, December 13, 1996. I

wanted to stay in Cincinnati. A part of me will always be a Cincinnati Red. So I suggested deferring some money. Bowden ended it up by telling me he'd talk to Marge on Monday. But Monday's too late. He knows it, and I know it.

A week later I'm at home in Woodland Hills helping Erica with some of her homework while Sacha is trying to get me to pay attention to her latest nail polish. My agent calls talking Baltimore. I know Davey Johnson can manage a ball club. He came to Baltimore and they were a pitch or two away from the World Series in '96. I'm intrigued by Camden Yards, by the fact they have Roberto Alomar, Rafael Palmeiro, Cal Ripken Jr. I wasn't keen about coming back to the American League, but if I had to come back to the AL, it would be in Baltimore. The Orioles had players I admired and respected, and they had Davey. Even if you have talent, you have to mold and shape it, deploy it properly. I don't get caught up in managers but I know you're at their mercy. You can have the biggest jewel in the world, but if you don't chisel that jewel right you're going to crack that jewel and it's going to be worthless. It's the same way with a talented team. The Orioles had a talented team. Exciting players. Even in a different league, you admire them. You're like, "Ah . . . he's at it again," watching them play on those highlights.

When I signed with Baltimore, Jim Bowden told some of the Cincinnati reporters he would've signed me for the same thing. And if that's what he had to say, to save face with the baseball fans of Cincinnati—that's okay by me. Baltimore offered me two mil and change plus an option year at the same speed.

I'll always cherish being a Cincinnati Red. I won't cherish everything that happened to me there, because some bad things did happen. But Cincinnati was like—a first car. I still got that '66 Mustang in my heart, even though I was going to play in a Porsche in Baltimore. I've still got that Mustang deep in my heart. Though I wouldn't trade the Porsche. Cincinnati was my town, didn't matter the scenario, the radio bashing, the revolving-door GMs, all the water under the bridge between '80 and '96. Cincinnati was my town—I knew it, Marge knew it, and it was just hard to leave when something is yours and you've grasped it, and then it's gone. It's hard to walk away from something like that twice—it was for me. But I guess that's just the kind of brother I am.

But now all that was over, and I was on my way to Baltimore. New life. There was a reason God was taking me there. I didn't know what it was then. I thought it had to do with me playing baseball. I had never heard of or had heard very little about Johns Hopkins University Hospital.

I talked to Davey before I got to spring training. He called me at home. He told me that I was going to play right field for the Baltimore Orioles. "I know you're gonna be ready, E.D. Been waiting a long time to be able to write your name on my lineup card," Davey said. Reminded me of Sparky Anderson, him saying it that way. Made me feel good. "Thanks, Davey," I said.

"No, thank *you*, Eric. Come in ready. We're gonna have fun. Let's play baseball."

So I signed with Baltimore. Why? Cal Jr., Roberto Alomar, Davey, Raffy Palmeiro. I could've gone to a rebuilding team. But having the opportunity to go to postseason, with a chance to go to the World Series, being managed by one of the better managers to run a club in recent times—I thought it might be a perfect fit for me. I wanted to see what a perfect fit felt like.

THIRTEEN / WINTER 1998

Coming from Behind

Give It Your Best and All

In July of 1998, at the All Star break, the Orioles were 38–50, 30 games behind the Yankees, 17 behind the Red Sox in the loss column. We'd lost 1–0 on Sunday, July 5, to New York in the last game before the break. That Yankee rookie outfielder Ricky Ledee threw me out at third from the left-field wall. It took a perfect throw. The ump called me out. We lost. Coming off being in the American League Championship Series and a pitch or two away from the World Series in '97 with the Orioles, it was disappointing to play so badly in the first half of the '98 season, particularly with the Yankees playing .750 ball. But after the break, the Orioles turned around. The AL had won the All Star Game at Coors Field in Denver, 13–8. Robby was elected MVP for going 3-for-4 with a homer, two runs scored, a stolen bag, and creative defense. Basic Bay-Bay. Cal drove in two, Raffy had two knocks. It's not like we haven't got guns. Ray Miller had a meeting, told us he wanted us to be more aggressive, to take the extra base, not just go station to station and wait. Ray praised the American League for being aggressive on the bags, stealing, playing hit-and-run—National League-style ball instead of station-to-station baseball. "I think the three guys in the All Star Game showed what kind of ability we have," Ray said. "I think you'll see results. I think you'll see these guys come together."

One problem was not our coming together; it was that it took us 82 games to figure out a batting order that could score runs and strike fear in our opponents with contact and speed up top—Robby leading off; then Brady, hard to double up, seeing fastballs when Robby's on; Robby a threat to steal. Hitting second allows Brady's batting average to creep up, then me in the three-hole, then Raffy Palmeiro at clean up, or vice versa. Then Harold Baines, Cal Jr., B. J. Surhoff, Chris Hoiles or Lenny Webster, Joe Carter hitting five through eight. Nobody hurt except the opposition. I'd been hitting second, when I had played at all, and when your leadoff hitter is slumping and your eight-nine hitters don't run well, hitting an RBI man second doesn't generate you much at all.

"Who's your leader?" someone asked me over the All Star break.

Without thinking, I said what I'm accustomed to saying: "I am."

Later on, I prayed about it. "God, let me be me again."

I came into the clubhouse for the first Boston game at home after the All Star break and saw the batting order. I was hitting third. The Orioles began the second half by sweeping Boston four straight games at Camden Yards. Then we won 9 straight, 14 out of 15, 17 out of the 20. In those 20 games I hit .435 (tops in the big leagues), scored 23 runs (second), had 28 RBI (first), nine homers (fourth), 37 hits (first), and a slugging percentage of .729 (second). In 21 days, I doubled an RBI total it had taken three months to amass. At the end of the first 20 games after the All Star break, I was on a 17-game hitting streak, my longest since I was 24. I wasn't named Player of the Month for July, Albert Belle was. He broke the July record for home runs with 16 and drove in 32. Numbers don't accrue all at once. Each hit, each run scored, each RBI, is the result of a single challenge. When you go to the park every day, one city to the next, you don't know what's going to happen, whether the opposing pitcher is throwing well, how the manager is using you, injury status, what kind of defense you're facing, how tough the pitcher is on you, how tough he is that day, what he tries to do to you generally, what he tried to do to you in each specific situation. You try to prepare professionally, apply what you've learned over the years, hope the manager gives the ball club every chance to win. Each situation occupies its own time and space, and you have to conquer it. A game lasts two and a half hours, three and a half in the American League. Each at-bat is a little epic, and a lot of little epics make up a season.

I'll try and show you what I mean.

Against the Red Sox on July 9 in the first game after the break, Robby went deep leading off, yanked a change-up over the right-field scoreboard. Later on, Mike Bordick pulls a ball into the left-field seats at Camden Yards. Mussina was still not himself after getting hit in the face by that liner, but he was throwing strikes, not walking anybody. That's half the battle. They get solo shots from John Valentin and Darren Bragg. I'm at designated hitter, DHing, wearing a protective sleeve over my sore right elbow. Hard to do, DHing, when you're an everyday player accustomed to affecting a game on defense. Had to watch Bainesy to see how he handles it. I didn't get three Gold Gloves for DHing. Maybe it's a blessing in disguise. Most things are. Find a way. So I come up in the eighth, already had a knock, been stranded twice. Tie game. Fight off a 2–2 pitch, hit it fair down the right-field line. It drops. Bragg fumbles it. Not an error, a bobble as he picks it up. I see this as I round first. I jet. This is my style. If Ray's come to appreciate it, good. I beat the ball into second. Raffy hits a fly ball to medium center, to Darren Lewis, who doesn't have a great arm. I'm off for third. In standing. One good thing about the injuries is that there's miles left on my legs. My body has been injured, but not worn down. Thirteen years in the Show, and I feel fresh.

One out later, Cal fought off a Jim Corsi pitch, dumped it into short center. I scored the winning run as the Orioles won 3–2. The ball club can win if it pitches. If I have to carry us for a month and can do it, so be it. And then, if we are a good team, somebody will pick me up.

Sherrie and the girls had come in, and Sacha's birthday was a couple of days away. I got to take both my girls to lunch with the outstanding students of the Baltimore Educational Scholarship Trust (BEST), a program that provides promising kids with tuition to private schools. Of all the awards I've received and programs I'm involved with, from Reviving Baseball in Inner Cities to the Roberto Clemente Award for the most inspirational player in the big leagues after the '97 season, to the Fred Hutchinson Award, to being a national spokesperson for the American Cancer Society—this takes a backseat to none. It's for the education of children. That's my home training coming out. I ate with 20 minority students, my girls, and Sherrie. They were smart. I made them laugh.

"Hey! He's . . . he's joking around with us! He's . . . cool!"

"I think your leg kick is too high, Eric! That's why you get jammed like you did last night," said one high-pitched yodel from a bespectacled beanpole adolescent.

"Fought it off though. Now what did you say your name was? Earl Weaver?"

He giggled. "No. Joel Chambers."

We played some trivia, had some fun, and gave out prizes. We organized the lunch where the children would have a fine dining experience, something they were unaccustomed to since they were from underprivileged homes. The children had a three-course meal, got instruction on silverware from the restaurant staff at the Sheraton Inner Harbor Hotel. How could I look around me and not feel blessed? How could I not feel like I was in the palm of the hand of God?

The next night the Red Sox threw their ace, Pedro Martinez, who they signed for six years, $74 million, in the off-season.

I played with Pedro on the Dodgers in the early '90s. Great stuff. Command. Three pitches, works fast, comes right after you. Can beat you with the fastball alone, can spot it up, down, in, out, in the strike zone, or take a little off, slide you, curve you, change you up. L.A. didn't think he had the physical stature to hold up as a starter. The kids from BEST were in attendance. I'd given them game tickets. Sherrie and the girls were there. Ray didn't start me. Mo Vaughn came up in the seventh and touched one off against Sid Ponson, a line shot to left. Bainsey strained his hamstring running the bases, so in the sixth, Ray tapped me and I was in there again, DHing, grounding out to short. In the bottom of the eighth, I came up again, with none on, two out in a 2–2 game. The pressure was on; Pedro was 11–2 at the time, and 7–0 on the road. If we lost this game, the season would be all but over.

All I can say about what happened next is God was with me again. Pedro made a three-inch mistake with his curve; got it a little bit up, about kneecap high, and I was able to lift it 420 feet over the center-field wall into the home bullpen. Camden Yards went crazy. As I got back to the dugout there was something extra in the way Cal put his palm on top of my head. We had been embarrassed the first half of the season. Let's play some ball. Nobody understands the psyche of everyday ballplayers better than Cal. Robby gave me a pound. Raffy said, "That's what I'm talking about, kid!" echoing what I say after he comes through. We won 3–2. I got a good night's sleep.

We won again the next day, behind Scotty Erickson, 2–1, against Timmy Wakefield. Joe Carter, playing right, hit a solo shot. I was happy for Joe. That knuckler messes up my timing. I can hit the breaking ball, but knuckleballers mess me up. I'm not running up there to face change-up artists like Doug Jones either. I almost got to Tim once, but flew to the track in center. I did not get a hit. And that was the last game for over a month where I didn't get a hit.

Fans at Camden Yards had booed Joe the night before. He

was scuffling, hitting .246. One of us is going. The Giants were sniffing around for a right fielder. Brian Sabean, general manager, and Dusty Baker wanted me in '97 before I signed in Baltimore. I wouldn't mind playing with Barry Bonds. Junior Griffey is coming fast, but for now Bonds is still the best. Pitchers respect and are in awe of Junior—Sparky had made no bones in walking him whenever he came to Tiger Stadium—but pitchers and managers *fear* Bonds. In an earlier game, Buck Showalter, manager of the Arizona Diamondbacks, walked Bonds with the bases loaded in a two-run game with two out in the bottom of the ninth at Candlestick Park. Walked in a run just to keep Bonds from having a chance to beat him! It worked, too. Arizona got the next guy to fly to right. If it came down to a choice between me or Joe being here, Joe might get chosen if it was a personality contest. Joe's happy-go-lucky. I love life, I make people laugh, but it's all about production in the big leagues. On production, Joe was more likely to be traded. But it figured the Giants were asking for me.

On Sunday, July 12, third inning against Boston, with Korean right-hander Jin Ho Cho on the mound, I hit my tenth career grand slam, a towering fly ball that landed 412 feet away, dropping over the center-field wall, beyond the reach of Darren Lewis. After I got back to the dugout and my teammates had given me hands, fist-to-fists, pats on the back, Ray called me over, "E.D."

He was holding the white clubhouse phone. "For you."

It was reliever Jesse Orosco in the bullpen. Mike Mussina wanted me. "I woulda caught it," Moose said. If you knew Mussina, you'd understand. He's a different kind of guy. So am I, so in my own way, I kind of understand him. Let's put it this way: I try. So I snorted and laughed with him. I got the feeling Moose was liking watching me swing the bat. Moose is easy to play behind. I guess some would say he sure is, throwing a good heater and that Frisbee like he does. He's not the kind to come in and slam his glove on the bench if somebody makes an error behind him. I think maybe he stays to himself too much, but that's him, his preparation, and his unusual sense of humor.

The tension that comes with losing is leaving us. We're starting to relax.

I drove in five runs—batting third, the RBI would come—and we won, 8–6.

We sweep the Red Sox four games.

The Blue Jays come in for two. We sweep them. Web and Raffy carried us. We went to Texas and sweep two. Arrived at LAX at 2:30 A.M., July 17. I didn't get home until about 4 A.M., with a game scheduled the next evening, but it's an afternoon game by my body clock. I spent a night at home before heading to Anaheim. The first game of the set I singled, doubled, scored twice, once on Raffy's bomb to win it. Umpire Ken Kaiser asked me how I was doing, if I was staying at home in Woodland Hills. He was umpiring at first. Ken is a big guy, big basketball fan.

We're rolling now. Nine straight. My mother, my wife and girls, and a dozen or so friends and relatives waited for me after the game, along with the southern California fans, some regulars who are always there when I visit, some with photos of me as a Dodger. I came in the next day feeling good, strong. Locked in. Mom was cooking for the multitudes, and that night we'd have one of our traditional neighborhood cookouts, only over at the team hotel, the Doubletree, not in the backyard. But that's what it would remind me of. I couldn't wait to see friends and relatives I hadn't seen for a while. Ma insisted on setting up shop in a suite at the hotel so I wouldn't have to travel up to West Hills, or even to Rochea's—she lives with her husband not far from Anaheim.

I came into the clubhouse; checked the work of the clubhouse boys on my gear—good enough work, have to give each of 'em an extra $20—got taped up, black tape over ankles, wrists; then checked out the posted batting order. I was back in the two-hole? Times like that are frustrating. More than being disappointed, I was confused. The order of Alomar, Anderson,

Davis/Palmeiro, Palmeiro/Davis, Baines, Surhoff, Rip, Webster/Hoiles had been working. Baines was out on the DL, but this enabled me to be the everyday designated hitter, and I'd come to the conclusion that pride was not as important as rest. Four ABs is four ABs. I was adjusting to a DH role.

"Ray is tripping," I thought. But then I just let it go. God is good. We just find a way. The batting order sequence was off again, so we finally lost a game, after nine straight wins to start the second half. I went 1-for-5. Changed my whole approach trying to advance runners by hitting to right instead of trying to score runners with an extra-base hit or a home run. But I didn't brood like I might have when I was a younger player, full of misunderstanding. There was too much in life to enjoy. That night we enjoyed our "cookout." Almost everybody was there: my wife; Sacha; my mother; her husband; my sister, Rochea, and her husband, Richard Miles; Cubby Brown and his wife Juanita and their daughters; Renard Young, my cousin; and my old buddy from the neighborhood Derrell Spann and his son; plenty of other folks. Shirley cooked up a storm—smothered chicken, barbecued ribs (meat falling off the bone) collard greens, turnip greens, macaroni and cheese, potato salad, rice and gravy, creamed corn, candied yams. I played the music. Had a *good* time. I walked around with Sacha at my side. She put my face in her little hands and examined it. "What are you looking for?" I asked. "Daddy took it on the chin today," she said, echoing one of my sayings. "I just wanted to see if you were okay." Lenny Webster and Jeff Hammonds stopped in. Hammer had his fiancée and their daughter with him. When I talk to Hammer, I think about me being young, and Parker talking to me, and showing me the way. I tell Hammer to hang in there, his day will come soon.

Next day I'm back in there, hitting third. We fell behind the Angels 1–0. I led off the sixth against Omar Olivares with a homer to center. He got me the first time with a breaking ball, but then he made the mistake of coming back with it the next

time up, on the pitch I knew he wanted to get me on. We fell behind again, 4–2. I homered again, this time in the seventh, a two-
run bomb, a shot—the crowd oohed at the sound of contact and
the sight of the ball going out on a line, bouncing off the red
rocks behind the center-field wall to tie it at 4–4. We were patient in the ninth, drew four walks; Cal got to Troy Percival for a
two-run single. We won again, 7–4.

We came home for three games against the Oakland A's.
First night Raffy cranked a three-run bomb and I had a two-run
job, and we won 7–1. The hitting was contagious now, we were
hitting .316 as a team since the break. We lost Robby for two
weeks; he jammed his little finger on second base while stealing
on getaway day in Anaheim. He's on the 15-day DL. Reboulet is
a good fill-in, but he ain't Bay-Bay. Lenny Web's been hitting
.600 for a week. He drove in six runs and I drove in one and we
won again, 9–7, after Raffy hit a walk-off piece the next night.
Then Web hit another walk-off home run the next night, off the
same guy, the Oakland closer, Mike Fetters. So we swept Oakland, too. We won 14 out of 15 ball games—.930 ball—after the
All Star break. We went from 15½ games behind the Red Sox for
the last play-off spot to seven games back, in 15 games. The
Lord works in mysterious ways, his wonders to perform. Junior
Griffey and Alex "A-Rod" Rodriguez came in and did their
thing and won the last two of a three-game battle, then we hit
the road again. The days were now hot and long but the mission
was clear.

There's always something happening to keep me grounded. I
found out Donald Royal, a forward with the Orlando Magic,
had been diagnosed with colon cancer. I called him and told him
things to expect, and to let God help him.

We lined up to play Detroit, then managed by my old teammate
Buddy Bell. I sat in the tiny little Tiger Stadium dugout, closed
my eyes, saw the smiling mug of Sparky Anderson peering in at

me, smiling, saying, "You're a great kid. By God, can you go get 'em." Good ol' Spark. Wish I could've gotten hot for him—hot like I was right now. We won the first night after falling behind 5–0 in the first inning. In the third, I pulled a three-run shot on a line inside the left-field foul pole to bring us to 5–4, and we scratched it out from there, 6–5. Ray put a squeeze on with the game tied 5–5, runners at first and third, no outs, a 3–1 count on Mike Bordick. Pac-Man popped the bunt up for an out, no run scoring, but he came back and got the game-winning single later on. After the game, when Ray went to shake his hand and say something to him, Pac-Man didn't waste much time getting off the field. The next game was more of a party, 14–2. Hoiles hit two bombs, Cal Jr. drove in two, Raffy had three knocks, two doubles. I was happy to table set with three singles. The Tiger first baseman, Tony Clark, gives me regards after the first, told me I was swinging the wood unbelievable for . . . then he sort of stumbled over what he wanted to say, but I knew he meant well, so I just thanked him, then I shot off around the bases on Cal's triple. When you're going through the dog days like this, the rhythm of the ball games takes over. Baseball becomes life, becomes living, and all the in-between becomes the brief rest and recreation.

Buddy had his ace Justin Thompson going in the last game against Jimmy Key, coming off the 60-day DL. As for me, I'm seeing it all so much better. I know what I'm doing so much better than I did 10 years ago. Ray says it looks like I'm about to go to sleep up at the plate, I'm so relaxed. I take Justin out, upper tank in right, in the first inning, fastball away, solo job. We build a 4–0 lead. Hammer's in there. He triples. The Tigers tie it 4–4. Bobby Higginson—he sure can hit. In the seventh, they bring in a flamethrower, the number one pick in the 1997 amateur draft, kid named Matt Anderson. Raffy and I had faced him the night before, in the blowout. He'd pitched an inning and sailed right through us like we weren't even there. Grounded me out. Punched out Raffy.

"That boy throws *hard*," I thought.

But being an old National Leaguer, hard throwers don't bother me. It's a league of hard throwers. I'd have to ratchet up my bat speed, if I could. B.J. walked. Tiger Stadium stirred a little. On a 1–1 pitch, Matt Anderson brought me 100-m.p.h cheese, belt-high. I swung on it with an A swing. I should be tired. I *am* tired, but this is the big leagues and I'm an RBI man and we need this game. Somebody said it sounded like an M-80 explosive going off. I felt a wave run through my entire body. Perfect contact. The bat snapped back across my body after the follow-through and pointed at our dugout, and I looked over in there to see my teammates rising up off the bench as they followed the flight of the ball, shouting, making Os with their mouths. I knew it was in the upper tank in left center when I hit it. I looked up. *My God.* It was 15 rows deep, upper deck, in left-center field, toward center. A 500-foot shot, easy, if the upper tank didn't stop it. Don't know if I've ever hit a ball harder than that. We win, 6–4.

Ray told the press he didn't watch it after I hit it, just said, "That's gone." Said a ball always made a loud sound on ground level when I hit it. Said I was one of his favorites; if it was his decision, it'd be easy—he'd bring me back in '99 because I was electric, a draw, said sometimes you judged players by thinking about them on the other bench, whether or not it would bother you. Ray said if I was sitting over there he'd be scared to death. I wondered why all this talking was going on for a game-winning homer. In the other clubhouse, Buddy Bell just said, "Looks like E.'s got his bat speed back."

Seventeen out of 20 since the break. Back in the hunt. Blessed.

We lost the first two in Kansas City. Pat Rapp hit me in the right elbow with a pitch in the first game. Oh, he intended to do it. The other players read box scores and get scouting reports. They know who's hot on the other teams. Nothing happened. No Royal got buzzed in return. I'm not saying they had to get

hit but that's three times I've been hit and we can't buzz somebody? Am I going to have to go out to the mound? We lost the
first two games out of three. Rapp pitched against the Yanks at
Yankee Stadium on August 8. Straw was all over one of his fastballs, so much so that Rapp fell down on the mound, afraid the
ball was coming back through the box. It landed in the third
deck at Yankee Stadium instead. Saw it on *SportsCenter*. I
laughed. I'd have to thank Straw later. He had six straight hits
during this time—all dingos. He and I have always competed.
And I had started to hit. So he started to hit. Don't know who
started first, me or him, but he hit a couple of pinch-hit grand
slams, had 20-something home runs, just like me. I knew he
wouldn't take me doing well lying down without doing something himself. It's been that way between us.

Now, both slowly and suddenly, because that's the way
baseball happens, I was in the midst of a 30-game hitting streak.
At the same time, the Orioles were going 30–8 at the beginning
of the second half. A 30-game hitting streak today must be
equivalent of a 40- or 45-game hitting streak in the old days.
Back then, players could see the same pitcher four times a game.
That won't happen to me, to see the same tired arm. There are
games when I'll see four different pitchers, when it seems the
manager makes a change every time I come up. It's a compliment, really. No manager is going to let me see any of these lefties three times, and there ain't no more Steve Carltons, except
for the Unit, Randy Johnson. But it was a thrill, going on this
streak, and I wanted it to keep going even under what were impossible conditions. Jim Palmer said he once saw Luis Aparicio
have
a 20-game hitting streak and his batting average went *down*.
Mine didn't go down. Went from .287 at the break to .332 on
August 23, a Sunday. Over the 30-game streak, I hit .400. What
does it feel like to hit .400 against big-league pitching for a solid
month? Feels like you're in the groove, in the Zone.

By then, the team had traded Joe Carter to the Giants and

Hammer to Cincinnati, where he could play every day, every young player's dream. In there every day, show what you can do over a full season. I told Hammer it was the best thing, maybe not for the Orioles, but for him, and we spoke daily for quite some time as he got adjusted. It was funny—Jeffrey started in Baltimore, now for the shank of his career he'd play center field in Cincinnati—where I had started. In return for Jeffrey Hammonds, the Orioles got Willie Greene, my teammate in Cincinnati in '96, once the jewel of the Cincinnati farm system, as Hammer was for Baltimore. Willie has a good left-handed bat; he's not an outfielder, he plays third. Specific to our situation of trying to catch the Boston Red Sox for a postseason berth, the trades took a good outfielder and two righty bats with pop from us, and gave us a lefty bat with pop. Now our whole team batted lefty, except me, Cal, Tractor Man Hoiles, and Web. And I was the only right-handed hitting outfielder we had left.

We took the first three games of a four-game set in Cleveland, August 13 to 16. Scott Kameniecki started the fourth game for us. Kammy won 10 games the season before and had pitched well in Game Five of the playoffs against this same Cleveland team. He was pitching hurt now, problems with his neck. I'd gone 4-for-4 the day before. Ray had pulled me in the sixth inning. I had to be in there every day because I was hot and driving in runs. Sixteen of the 30 games in the hitting streak were multihit games. But because of the hitting streak and the makeup of the roster, we were in a bad situation. I couldn't be rested at all. The 4-for-4 game had to be won first, before I could come out. On the fourth hit, Ray took me out to rest my legs. Even DHing a lot, my hamstrings were barking now. I can't run wide open now or I'll pop one of them if not both of them. Even though we were up 5–0 when Ray took me out, we almost lost the game. But B.A. homered off the change-up artist Doug Jones in the tenth inning and we won, 9–8.

The next game the streak ended, at 30 games. Jaret Wright was on the hill for the Indians. We had taken the first three of four. This is where average teams relax, saying we already got three. But you might as well get that fourth one if you can. Joe Morgan and Jon Miller came into Cleveland to broadcast the game on ESPN. Any of the old stars from the Big Red Machine always make me sit up straight. That's the way I was trained. Joe caught me around the cage. We talked. He congratulated me. I felt proud, like I was part of the history of the game. I wanted to get a knock that night in the worst way. Wright got me the first time with a fastball up on a 3–2 count. Should've laid off, but I didn't. In the later innings, in my third at-bat, Cleveland manager Mike Hargrove brought in a right-handed sidewheeler named Steve Reed to face me. Reed ran a fastball inside, then a slider away. I was all over that slider away, that was my pitch to hit. Reed had an ERA of less than 2.00 at the time, holding right-handed hitters to a .130 average. But I still had my pitch to hit. And I hit it hard, to right, on a line, but just foul, and that was the end of the streak. Instead of trying to hit it that way, I should've just hit it, and it would've gone that way, because that's where it was pitched. But I tried to steer it and it went foul. Two strikes now. I wouldn't get cheated. Reed came with a fastball under my hands and I swung over the top of it, I mean I swung *hard;* if I *had* hit it, it would've landed in Lake Erie. Strike three swinging.

The game ended with me in the on-deck circle as Raffy flew out to the wall in left.

I'm proud of that 30-game streak, the team record for the Baltimore Orioles' franchise and longest in the big leagues in '98, but I would have liked to have kept it going a little while longer. Well, that's how the streak ended, in Cleveland, the same place DiMaggio's streak ended, and I was sorry to see it end. Under different circumstances, I think I could have kept it going up to 40 games. Or more. As it was, the 30-game streak was the longest in the '90s, along with Nomar Garciaparra of the Red Sox, who had a 30-gamer in '97. If I could have gotten past that game, I think I could have gotten to 40. Several guys in history had a 30-game streak, and only 25 guys in all baseball history had more than a 30-game streak, the last one I think being Paul Molitor in 1987—he had a 39-gamer and looked wrung out when it was over. One guy whose longest streak was 30 games was Stan Musial. Stanley Frank. Once of the St. Louis Cardinals. Now I may not know everything, but I know enough to be impressed by that kind of company.

To me the amazing thing was not that I hit in 30 straight games, but that I *played* in 30 straight. I couldn't forget I was coming back from cancer surgery and chemo. I hoped my streak had shown people what can happen. You can survive cancer and resume your life—live even *better* because now you can appreciate life much more. There are no limitations on human beings. For a month, I had carried the team. A month is about as long as you can carry a team, as long as is humanly possible. When you're in your twenties you might have the physical strength to do it for two months—that would be superhuman—but you don't know enough about the game to do it. When you're in your thirties and experienced enough to do it, to know what it is, you can physically do it for a month, if that. For one month, for the 30-game hitting streak, I hit .400, 52 for 170, with 13 homers, 36 RBI, 33 runs scored. Extrapolate those numbers— times five would be a 150-game season, the numbers would be .400 batting average, 65 home runs, 190 RBI, 165 runs scored. Those are not Hall of Fame numbers. Those are wrath of God numbers. For 30 days I had played as the wrath of God. I had asked and it was given unto me. I had sought and I found. I had knocked and the door was opened unto me. I had started to hear the name Joe DiMaggio mentioned toward the end of the hitting streak. The *Baltimore Sun* even called me "Joltin' Eric" in one of its headlines—which doesn't have the same ring as "Joltin' Joe," I know. I don't see how DiMaggio did it, not even back then. I don't see how he hit in 56 straight big-league baseball games, even with no night games, no air travel, facing just the one pitcher for four at-bats every game instead of these relievers throwing ungodly breaking BBs that they throw today. Still, I can tell you—what a grind it must have been for him. What a feat Joe DiMaggio pulled off. I can only tip my cap to him. Two months of at least a hit every day. Amazing.

As for records themselves, this was a great season for breaking them. One of the best records (and most accessible in an expansion year) was Roger Maris's 61 home runs in one season. As we know, Mark McGwire of the Cardinals and Sammy Sosa of the Cubs ended up breaking that record—shattering it—and revitalizing baseball. Barry Bonds and John Olerud of the Mets came within one successful AB of reaching base in 16 straight trips to the plate. Ted Williams's all-time record is 16. Each ended up with the National League record of 15. And I had managed to get over halfway to Joe D.

I took the next day off. Came back the following day with two home runs in a 7–1 victory over the Minnesota Twins at Camden Yards that moved us nine games over .500 on Tuesday, August 18. Brad Radke was the Minnesota ace. I took him out the opposite way on a line over the 373-foot sign in right center in the first inning, then pulled him deep into the seats, to the walkway in the left-field stands for a three-run bomb in the seventh. He threw me high fastballs that at-bat, but I was fresher, my reflexes were sharp. I laid off and he had to bring it down and *bang*—outta here.

"He's a fan favorite, a team favorite, and a personal favorite," Ray Miller said in the papers. "Managers aren't supposed to have those, but it's fun to watch him play . . . Something good is going to happen when he's around." I appreciated the compliment, but I knew I was a favorite because I'd hit two taters and was producing. Being somebody's favorite isn't always a help to them. A favorite can be asked to get one hitter too many. A favorite can be asked to play when he's injured and shouldn't be in there because he's hurting the team more than helping it.

The Devil Rays came in. We won the first game but lost the second and the season series—inexcusable, since this was a first-year expansion team. Kammy lost the second game. Shouldn't even be out there. Kammy's hurt, got a bulging disc, and shouldn't be starting if we're trying to catch anybody. He's nibbling around the plate so much I started calling him "Three-and-Two." We came back Saturday, August 22, and beat Cleveland and Bartolo Colon, 6–3. I got 2-for-5, hit a fastball off the left-field wall to drive in Robby. Saw no more fastballs that day. Cal hit a two-run homer. Scotty pitched a complete game.

Doc Gooden beat us on Sunday. Not overpowering, but in command of the strike zone.

We go to Chicago. The plane ride is happy; Ray is swaggering because we've got Moose, Juan Guzman, and Scotty lined up to pitch. But Chicago has just lost four straight on the road to Seattle, and their professional pride is stung. And Albert Belle is swinging a hot bat—Albert was named July AL Player of the Month over me and he deserved it because he set a league monthly record for home runs with 16 and drove in four more runs than I did with 38. Frank Thomas, even in a down year, always swings the bat well against Mussina. Must be hitting a million off Moose. Sends a limo for Moose whenever we hit town—not really, but he would if they let him, probably.

The season ended for us in that series. Not because we got swept, but because of how it was handled. You are going to get swept occasionally. Can't let it throw you. First game, Moose gives up four early, we lose 6–4. Don't know if Moose is fully over getting hit in the face by the liner off Sandy Alomar's bat. He seems to have become more of a breaking-ball pitcher. I'm out there thinking, "Hope he don't throw no breaking ball to this guy." Breaking ball. Knock. And sure enough, Frank Thomas, Big Hurt, takes him deep. So does Albert. Moose is death on some teams, but Chicago gives him trouble at this stage in his career. But even if we lose three, we're playing well enough. There was still time. What happened in and after the next game really decided the season—apart from it being decided last February. Earl Weaver, the old Orioles' manager, says you decide your team's success the preceding winter, when you put your team together. After that, you're just playing it out. We traded Hammer. We've got one utility infielder, Reboulet. No back-up first baseman. No back-up third baseman. Even if Cal starts every game, there's a lot of games you can get him out of early as long as you're not hurting yourself defensively. With Rich Becker and Willie Greene—good men, and major leaguers, but it should've been Brady in left, Hammer in center, me in right, with Becker, B.J., or another outfielder helping out, B.J. rotating in and out with Cal at third, giving Raffy a blow at first. We could have done it in such a way where our guys would all be getting strong at that right time. Unfortunately, we didn't.

So Guzman gives up six runs in the second inning, we lose 12–5. But it was *how* it happened. Caruso pushed a bunt toward Robby, which he went to field, only Guzman got to it and threw it past Raffy, but I had the play backed up, so Caruso didn't get to second base. Later in that inning, in an attempted rundown between first and second, Ray Durham broke for home from third. Raffy threw to the plate. His throw to Web was slightly up the line, but mostly it was Durham's speed that beat the play. It happens. Tip your cap. We gave up six in the inning, came off the field, and Ray is yelling at Raffy, "Let's get our head out of our asses!" Durham had scored from second base on an overthrow to second base into center earlier in the year. Nobody got hollered at then.

Ray decides to hold this meeting before the next day's game. He held the meeting on August 27. If it had been me, I would've said, "Fellas, you've played great ball the second half. I know you're tired. Hang in there. I'm resting everybody I can rest tomorrow. I don't care if we play seventeen innings, Raffy, you don't pick up a bat. Robby, take a day off. Sit on the bench, talk to me about what you see is going on. No hitting for the next two days. Late bus, 5:30 P.M. And fellas. Don't worry. We'll get 'em." Instead, Ray says he was proud of the way we've played, and how he stood up for us when they wanted to break up the team, and now we're letting him down. He says he doesn't want to start pointing fingers—which means he's about to start—and he starts in on, of all people, Robby, all over Robby about the bunt play, about why didn't he back up first base, and where's his head. Now, Robby, like any great artist, can be overly sensitive to criticism. It was obvious Robby was trying to make a play on the ball, and even he can't be two places at once. We are veterans and we *like* each other, and we know what each can do, and we're not going to pass blame around to each other. "Wait a minute, I'm not taking the blame for that loss, later for that," Robby said. He can have brain lock on the field and make a mistake like everybody else, he knows that, but he had also been playing a great second base for us throughout most of the streak and his feeling was this is a whole team. Don't pick me out. Ray says if Robby doesn't like being singled out he can get out. Robby says no, *you* get out. Bridge burned. So Ray finished it by saying he was pulling himself and the other coaches out of the meeting, and that if we needed to fight each other, then go ahead and fight. Then he left. Like we're supposed to fight. We're looking at each other in confusion. Even Cal Jr. is scratching his head. We were a couple of pitches away from the World Series last year. We've won together. The same guys. To-gether. So we know. We're not going to fight over a bad game after going 30–8. Somebody said, "We ought to kick *Ray's* ass for not realizing his inexperience is part of the problem." Ray is learning how to manage. We realize that. None of us is getting any younger. Ray will grow into the job, but Cal doesn't have that time, I don't have that time, Raffy doesn't have that time, Robby doesn't have that time. Ray would be better off with a team full of rookies. Then they could all learn at once. We were brought here to win. So whenever I got a big hit, and Ray told the press I was one of his "favorites," it made me feel uneasy. In my experience, a vote of confidence is the kiss of death.

That meeting killed the will of a team struggling to get back in it. Everybody, the manager included, had to pull together for us to have a shot, because we were short. We went on to lose 10 straight. The wheels came off the pitching, the everyday players were tired because we only had 13 spots for position players. Even though we've got 12 arms, and four lefties, none of the lefty pitchers are starters. This is what happens when you try to do too much for too long. Yes, we had gone 30–8, but it took a toll. The whole outfield was dropping like flies. B.J.'s batting average has been in free fall for about a month. I love him, but his parachute won't open. Playing left field every single day wore him down. Brady injured a knee going after a fly ball the last game of the Cleveland series. We could use Hammer. I thought of Parker being in right when I was young and in center for Cincinnati, how Pops would say, "Go get it, son!" I thought of Hammer not being out there so I could yell, "Go get it, son!" Hammer was in Cincinnati, playing center every day, wearing number 4. He told the Cincinnati press he was wearing number 4—half my Reds' number 44—because if he could be half the player Eric Davis was, he'd be doing all right.

Once we got back to Baltimore, we had three against the Kansas City Royals. The first game was Sidney Ponson's. I sat out. Sidney was in a 3–3 tie with Rapp in the seventh. Two outs, runner on first, Johnny Damon, a lefty hitter who hurt us in Kansas City by jerking one out, is up. Arthur Lee is heated in the pen. Now Sparky would take Sidney out right there. Lou Piniella would take Sidney out. Joe Torre and Felipe Alou would take Sidney out. Davey Johnson would take Sidney out. But Ray leaves Sidney in. Damon jerks one off the right-field scoreboard. Greene plays the carom not as well as a more experienced outfielder might. Damon rolls all the way around to score; 5–3, Royals. That night we hit into five double plays. Five DPs, all to end innings. Becker homered twice in Chicago and is probably the only healthy outfielder we have left other than me. He hits into a double play and we lose, 6–5. Ray says it was obvious he was one batter late in removing Sidney. Says it was the kind of game where a manager wants to go home and shoot himself. This year is about gone now. After that ill-fated meeting in Chicago, we fall 11.5 games back of the Red Sox by the first week of September. This is when the September call-ups come, and rosters expand from 25 to 40.

We go to Seattle for three over the Labor Day weekend. Junior Griffey hit his fiftieth home run, I hit my twenty-seventh, we split four games, go on to Oakland. While we're in the Oakland clubhouse, we watch McGwire club his sixty-second home run on September 8, at 5:18 P.M, Pacific time. After Mark launched his sixty-second at home against the Cubs, we watched the celebration while he rounded the bases, hugged Roger Maris's family, Sammy coming in from right field, and then them doing their thing, with us watching in the visiting clubhouse on the West Coast and applauding, and saying, "Good job." Sammy hits his sixty-first and sixty-second a few days later, September 13, in Wrigley Field, and wound up with 66 for the season. McGwire ended up with that unreal total of 70. Now, baseball is a six-month season. In five of six months, Mark hit double figures in homers, and the one month he didn't, June, he hit eight. I've seen many Player of the Month awards handed out to guys with eight home runs. Sammy hit *20* in June, so he is the one-month Home Run King. Twenty in a month is the pace of a 120-home run season. Wow. Sammy ended up 158 ribbies, .302 average, and the National League MVP. Home Run King Hank Aaron wrote in *Newsweek*: "Look at the number of players on track to hit 40 or more homers this year. Can it be this easy to hit in the major leagues? It never was when I played. Not taking anything away from McGwire or Sosa, this year's expansion to more teams has a lot to do with that. The year Maris hit his 61 was an expansion year, too ... pitching is nothing compared with 30 years ago. We had Sandy Koufax, Don Drysdale,

Bob Gibson, Juan Marichal in the National League alone! The thin pitching today has to affect the number of home runs."

Now I respect Hank Aaron—Henry Louis—but I'm out here trying to hit pitching today, and let me tell you, there's no big difference. In Hank's day, all the pitchers weren't Koufax, Gibson, Marichal. Top-end players might hit .250 against number one starters. If all Hank faced were number ones, he wouldn't be in the Hall of Fame. If all the pitchers had been like Koufax, Gibsons, and Marichal, wouldn't be *any* hitters from that era in the Hall of Fame. Today, when you go to New York City, you gotta face David Cone, Boomer Wells, Andy Pettitte. Go to Arizona, you gotta face the Big Unit, Randy Johnson; you go to Boston, you've got to face Pedro Martinez; you go to Toronto, you've got Roger Clemens; go to Baltimore, you've got Moose Mike Mussina. There's more speciality arms, relievers designed to get you, righty or lefty. I'm not saying expansion wasn't a factor, but it's been a great year, and Mark McGwire and Sammy Sosa made interest greater by taking the long ball to the next level.

Everybody is not going to win every year. There are other rewards and responsibilities to being major leaguers. First thing I have to do is chin-check some of these young brothers coming up from the minors—the first baseman Calvin Pickering, outfielder Danny Clyburn, Ryan Minor, the six-seven heir apparent to Cal at third base. I chin-check 'em, just as Parker once chinchecked me. Except maybe Jerry Hairston. His father played infield for the White Sox; his grandfather played in the Negro Leagues, got four or five ABs with the White Sox. Hairston knows to be seen and not heard. The others, I have to tell 'em, "You're not the Man. You have to learn how." Some don't even want to get up for the national anthem. You better get out of that clubhouse and get out here on that bench and learn something about big-league baseball and how to produce. When I came up you wouldn't dare talk about what you did in the minor leagues. Nobody cares what you did in Bowie or Rochester. I'm trying to figure out not what you did there, but what you can do here.

And if you're going to talk, talk to somebody about what you should be doing up here.

The first night of that final homestand, we're down 3–0, seems like the season is over right there. The next game we lose, it's over. I hit a three-run bomb off Angels' ace, Chuck Finley, over the scoreboard the opposite way in right, then hit a two-run single to center. Raffy goes 4-for-4 and we beat the Angels, 8–3. The next day we're down 2–0 in the bottom of the ninth, but Bordick hit his twelfth homer, a career high, a two-run job. I follow with an RBI single up the middle off Troy Percival, scoring B. A. Brady, and we win 3–2. On Sunday I draw a walk leading off the ninth after we let a 7–1 lead evaporate into a 7–7 tie with the Angels, who are fighting for the postseason with the Rangers in the AL West. I draw a walk to lead off the eighth, Ray pinch-runs me, Harold gets a hit while going 4-for-4, the floodgates open, we win 12–7. The Rangers come in. We are six and a half games behind the Red Sox with 12 games to play, including six with them. We beat the Rangers the first night, 1–0, behind Juan Guzman. I pinch-hit for Rich Becker in the bottom of the eighth, knock in B.J. with a sacrifice fly to right. The next day the bubble bursts. Too much to overcome, the Red Sox, the law of averages, Ray's inexperience, the hole we dug. We lead 5–0, but blow it. Ivan Rodriguez takes Armando deep—hitting a hung slider—for a 6–5 lead in the top of the ninth after we were up 5–4. Once again, I don't start. Ray was trying to save me for the Red Sox, who come in for two the next day, September 16. I pinch-hit leading off the ninth. I'm a tough out.

I single up the middle off Rangers' reliever John Wetteland—once traded from the Dodgers to the Reds, along with Tim Belcher, for yours truly, back in '91. Ray pinch-runs for me. But we've let it slip away. We can't get the runner home. Lose, 6–5. Game over.

The Yankees came in and they put us to sleep in the first game, 15–5, on Friday, September 18. One game from elimination. Now, the next game, Saturday, September 19, seemed relatively unimportant, yet it turned out to be historic. In baseball, you just never know. It was just a game, a 5–3 victory over the Yankees. David Cone started for the Yankees, didn't pitch too bad, but we beat him. I was 3-for 4 with a double, and two RBI, and also a run scored, putting me at .325.

What was significant about this game beyond batting titles and home runs was that this was the last of Cal Ripken Jr.'s immortal record of 2,632 consecutive games played. Amazing. I didn't know it until the next day, on Sunday, September 20. Neither one of us, me or Cal, was in there that Sunday. I saw Cal sitting in the dugout as the Orioles took the field. I looked out on the field and saw one of the rookies, Ryan Minor, warming up at third base. It dawned on me.

A change had come. I smiled and said to Cal, "Say man. Wait a minute. What do you call yourself doing? What are you doing sitting over here with mere human-being ballplayers?"

Cal smiled, but didn't budge. I didn't know he had decided to end to streak. Then, after the first out, the Yankees stood on the top step of their dugout and applauded Cal, and he took a short curtain call. Sixteen years of playing every day, never missing a start.

Ray tacked up the scorecard. There it was—Rip's name blacked out, MINOR in with the starters. On the list of substitutes RIPKEN was squeezed in on the bottom right. On top of his name was DAVIS. So there it was, September 20, 1998—The Unbreakable Man and The Man Who Wouldn't Stay Broken; the Iron Man of baseball and me, E.D., who'd never been able to get in as many as 500 at-bats in a season. There we are on that immortal scorecard, as historic as the scorecard of the day before, Cal's last game of the incredible streak. Both scorecards one day may even be as historic as the seventieth home-run ball of Mark McGwire.

In that September 20 game, the first one Cal missed in 16 seasons, I pinch-hit, got a knock, drove in a run, thought of the times I'd seen Cal with his son, Ryan, around the batting cage and in the clubhouse. You could see his son picking it up, as I'm sure Cal did with his father, who was once an Orioles' coach and manager. Then I thought of Cal bantering—he can be a merciless critic. I remembered the frustration on his face after a loss. But he never got too far up or down. I remembered Matt Anderson, the 100-m.p.h. kid pitcher of the Tigers, coming to Baltimore. Cal got a line-shot base hit to left off him. Bullet. After the game I said, "Say, that was a hundred-mile-per-hour fastball you turned around today, Cal," and Cal had visibly brightened up and said, "Yeah, E.D. Maybe I'm not washed up after all." He was my teammate, and a good one. Cal would be perfect for managing, only I know he still wants to play. I'd heard under some managers, Cal would be out at shortstop calling pitches, and that under another manager, he once said to an umpire, "Why don't you throw this guy out of here, so we'll have a chance to win this game?" You wouldn't be surprised if I told you *which* manager, either. Cal's only 130 or so knocks away from 3,000 hits, and I know he wants that, just like I'm 30-odd bombs away from 300 home runs. And in the context of trying to win ball games, I'm sure we'll reach our goals, as teammates in a larger cause.

I finished the season with a .327 average, and although I wouldn't catch Bernie Williams at .339 for the American League batting title, I did finish fourth, behind Bernie, Mo Vaughn (.337), and Albert Belle (.328). I had 89 RBIs, 81 runs scored, 28 homers, was eighth in the league in on-base percentage (.388), ninth in slugging percentage (.582) in 452 ABs, a season after colon cancer. I'd rather play in the World Series, though. Nothing in baseball compares to that. There's always next year. After this, who knows? I just know I still want to win. God, I still want to win. Still blessed.

FOURTEEN / WINTER 1999

Reborn Again to Play

Make Proper Adjustments

The Orioles played an exhibition game against the Toronto Blue Jays in July 1998, up at Cooperstown, New York, at the Baseball Hall of Fame. We had a pregame Home Run Derby. I hit three out. Brady Anderson hit five. Later on, I went to the Hall of Fame, alone. I looked at the plaques and exhibits. For me, it was like going in the Reds' clubhouse down at Al Lopez Field in Tampa for the first time, back in the spring of 1983. In Cooperstown, I slowly walked through the section they have dedicated to George Herman "Babe" Ruth. Did you know that back in 1921, George Herman had the monster year of life with the bat? He did. He hit .378, with 59 homers, 44 doubles, 16 triples, 17 steals, 144 walks, 171 RBI, 177 runs scored, and 457 total bases, the all-time record for total bases. I'm feeling you, George Herman! Now that's what I call a *Year.*

There at the Hall of Fame is a special room for Henry Louis Aaron, along with the other guys who hit 500 home runs. Men, all of'em. But only the original Hammer hit the 755.

"You just don't know what's waiting for you inside there."

Now I know good and well that I'm not going to be inducted into the Hall of Fame. I think about that sometimes. I've always been about finding my level of competition. While we were there, Don Sutton and Larry Doby, among others, were inducted into the Hall. I was surprised when I looked at Doby's numbers. Doby hit 253 home runs. I hit my 253rd during that July '98 hot streak. Got 266 now. I'll get 300. Doby had just under 1,000 RBI in his career. So do I. I'll get 1,000. He hit a homer to help win the World Series for Cleveland in 1948. I hit a homer to help win a World Series for Cincinnati in 1990. He was an infielder turned outfielder. So was I. He had trials I could not imagine as the second black player after Jackie Robinson to play in the big leagues, first in the American League, having only team owner Bill Veeck, a few teammates, and his family to count on. It was different later on, for ballplayers like me. It was easier in some ways—not in others. Seeing his numbers and thinking of Doby made me smile. His numbers were like mine. My numbers were not like Willie Howard Mays's. But it was Mays who said, "All they'll do is compare numbers on paper, and that's not always the game." It was Willie Mays who said that *he* was honored, to be compared to *me*. It was a veteran move. Taking some pressure off of a young player. They say one reason Larry Doby made the Hall was because he beat the odds.

No, I won't get to the Hall of Fame. But I have a Hall in my own mind, where greats reside—greats like Ham; Shirley; my grandparents; Rochea; Ms. Marshall; Sherrie; Erica; Sacha; Aunt Tee; Renard; Earl Brown; Coach Dickson; my brother, Jim; his daughter and granddaughter, Laquisha; Straw, Larkin, O'Neill, Pops Parker, Bay-Bay, Hammer, Raffy, Cal . . . Standing alone in the Hall of Fame in Cooperstown, New York, I thought, "It *is* a game of blessings . . . for everybody."

When the Yankees came into Camden Yards at the end of September and Cal finally sat out a game, I didn't see much of

Straw. He was back in the visiting clubhouse. He didn't play. I didn't know he was hurting. As a player, you don't let on when you are hurt, you don't complain about pain, not as a top-ender. He didn't say anything to me about feeling stomach distress, but later he told me he remembered what I'd told him after I'd been diagnosed. He said what I'd gone through helped save his life because without that experience he would've gutted it out. I'd been in New York at Yankee Stadium when I'd been in pain to the point where I had to leave the ballpark in May of '97. Now it was September of '98, and Straw was leading the Yankees in homers, and they were about to go to the World Series. But they would go without Straw. He had been chugging over-the-counter antacids, and thinking about what I'd gone through. He was having abdominal pain and serious cramping and because of what happened to me he didn't put off going to see a doctor about it. Good thing he didn't wait. He was diagnosed with colon cancer on October 1.

On that same day, young Joel Stephens, the 23-year-old minor leaguer in the Orioles chain who threw out the first pitch with me and Boog Powell back in April, died of colon cancer.

I first heard about Straw checking into the hospital for tests and a colonoscopy just after the regular season was over. Straw's wife, Charisse, called me up. She was distressed. It was the day before their series with Cleveland, the ALCS. Then she ended up telling me the diagnosis. She is a good wife to Straw, mother of their young children, Jordan and Jade. Straw has two others from his first marriage. Straw and I have been through some things. We came up together. We have helped each other. Then we grew apart. We're not alike. But we came up together. I wanted to tell Straw he'd be fighting now for his children and all those people like Joel Stephens. We got on the phone and we talked for a good half hour or more. It had been years since we'd talked that long. When I got sick, he was sympathetic, but like many who are healthy, he avoided the idea of illness, as well as the people who are ill. I understood. He thanked me, and he said it was much less scary to him now, the idea of cancer, and recovery, because I had gone through it. I make a play, then he makes a play. It's always been that way between us. So my going through cancer recovery had turned out to be a blessing. Straw's mother died of cancer two years before; I know he was feeling mortal. A couple of times when we talked he got quiet, and I knew he was crying, but I also knew he had hope from me being there, talking to him, proof that life goes on.

"You're gonna be all right, Straw," I said. "This is something you will beat. Not *can*. *Will*."

Straw had surgery on October 3, at Columbia Presbyterian Hospital in New York City. They found a walnut-sized tumor and removed it, along with 16 inches of his colon. He was put on chemotherapy—Leucovorin, 5FU. I told him there'd be days when he'd want to say, "I ain't going." I told him to focus on his children. The Yankees, wearing his number 39 stitched into their caps, beat the Texas Rangers and the Cleveland Indians, then swept the San Diego Padres in four games in the World Series. Straw spent 10 days in the hospital, but he and Charisse were in a candy-apple red Cadillac convertible when they had the parade in lower Manhattan on Friday, October 23.

On that same day, Marge Schott agreed to sell her interest in the Reds or face indefinite continuance of a two-year suspension for statements unbecoming to baseball. She had until December 31, 1998, to sell her interest. I took no pleasure in hearing this.

Brady Anderson had a tough 1998. Hit in the .230s. He was making $7 million a year. B.J. turned down a three-year, $12 million contract to test the market, turned down $4 million a year, and stood to get around $4.5 million a year for three years from the Orioles, Mets, or Pirates. The Orioles offered 31-year-old outfielder Brian Jordan a five-year contract at $8 million a year.

Brian played with the St. Louis Cardinals in 1998, hit .316 with 25 homers and 92 RBI. As you know, I hit .327 with 28 home runs and 89 RBI. Eighth in the AL in on-base percentage (.388), ninth in slugging (.582). Asking price—two years, averaging $4 million a year. The Orioles hired a general manager, Frank Wren. I couldn't blame Frank that my negotiations didn't work out. He'd just been hired by Peter Angelos. He wasn't there in '98, in the dugout, on the field; he hadn't seen what Ray Miller saw. In 173 games, 610 ABs with the Orioles over two seasons, I hit .321, 36 homers, 114 RBI, 118 runs scored, a franchise record 30-game hitting streak, and one case of cancer, beaten.

Off Ray's suggestion that he didn't think I could do it again, the Orioles' offer was an average of $2.81 million for two years. Ellis Burks had comparable numbers in 1998, and got a two-year $10 million deal from the Giants. Jordan's numbers were not better than mine. The O's offered me a two-year contract for $5.62 million—forcing me to sign for less than market or leave Baltimore.

I'll always respect Orioles majority owner Peter Angelos, and I will never, ever forget what he did for me in '97 and '98, especially in '98, when he brought me back for the season after cancer at $2.5 million, which was my "well" option price. He could have cut me, then brought me back for $1 mil. But he didn't. I'd like to think the year I had in '98 might have been worth $2.5 million. But, like I said, all year long, once Ray Miller started saying I was one of his "favorites" when I was winning games for him during the dog days of summer, deep down I figured that was the kiss of death for me in Baltimore. Ray said he needed somebody who could play every day. I'll let you in on a little secret: What you need to win in the big leagues are people who produce. Simple as that. It's not who plays every day. It's who produces *any* day. Ray said they wanted to "get more athletic." You're not going to find many people more athletic than me. I wish I could've had one last conversation with Peter Angelos like we had at Johns Hopkins hospital that time, where I could get around to telling him that while I might not be the be-all-and-end-all, I could help. Once Jordan signed with Atlanta, Robby Alomar signed with Cleveland, Alan Mills signed with the Dodgers, and Rafael Palmeiro signed with Texas, the Orioles would need help. They got some when they signed Albert Belle for five years at $13 million a year. But that meant Brady still had to play center. Albert would be in left. Unless the Orioles got more, the American League would pitch around Albert. Maybe Ray could find himself some outfielders and a second baseman, but whether or not they would produce was another matter. Either way, I wished the Orioles well.

On November 19, 1998, I signed a two-year, $8 million contract with the St. Louis Cardinals of the National League. The Cardinals' famed manager, Tony LaRussa, had called me. In fact, he called *twice.* He'd said the Cards *wanted* me; he knew what I could do, he'd paid attention during the '98 season. I'd helped beat LaRussa's A's in the 1990 World Series, but Tony held no grudge. He respected me. I heard it in his voice. There were other offers from other teams, offers for a bit more money, but I signed with the Cardinals for all the right reasons. Tony said they needed a leader; they had a lot of young players with talent, but they were inexperienced. Tony said they wanted me to lead. Half the battle is being somewhere you're wanted. Tony might hit me behind Mark McGwire to protect Big Mac. The only guys I knew in St. Louis were Mac, Ray Lankford, and Willie McGee. I'm told the young outfielder J. D. Drew has a nice stroke; with good tutelage he'll be productive. Not as productive as Stanley Frank Musial, but nobody was comparing J.D. to Musial—not like they'd compared me to Mays. Good. He doesn't need that. The game of baseball is hard enough. I don't know how tight our pitching and defense will be, but with Drew in right, Lankford in center, me in left, Big Mac at first, I'm speculating we'll score our share of runs.

On November 20, the *Baltimore Sun* reported:

Eric Davis, who in only two seasons graduated from Orioles right fielder to cancer survivor to civic treasure, officially parted ways with the franchise yesterday when he signed a two-year, $8 million contract with the St. Louis Cardinals. Davis, as inspirational a figure as he was productive with the Orioles, became a central piece in a sweeping Cardinals makeover that included a five-player trade immediately before his signing. Though the Cardinals met his asking price, Davis maintained he was "disappointed" that the Orioles had deleted him from their plans for 1999.

"I enjoyed the city, the fans and the media in Baltimore. I can be disappointed in the [negotiating] process . . . but it doesn't mean I didn't have a good time there," I told the *Sun*. "I was made to feel like part of that team and part of the city. I'll always cherish that."

Just before the New Year, I returned to Baltimore. I had an appointment. A youngster wrote me, asking me to give one of his baseball teammates a call. His teammate was 15, named Frankie March. Frankie had contracted a most vicious sarcoma of the lungs. He'd had a lung, three ribs, and a portion of his spleen removed. He was an Oriole fan and an Eric Davis fan. He had terminal cancer. Sometimes a call won't do. I went to his house to see him. His mother and grandmother greeted me with open arms. They knew I was there for Frankie. He was shy, almost unbelieving that I was with him. He was undergoing extensive chemo, and had lost 42 pounds. We talked for hours, with his mother and grandmother and all the relatives crying with joy when they weren't smiling to beat the band. After his sister left for work, a bunch of her co-workers called or jumped into their cars to come by. "Oh, nice, you came to see Frankie," I said, hoping they took my point. And Frankie . . . Frankie was great. I told him he had strength he didn't know he had, asked him to keep up with the St. Louis Cardinals as well as the Orioles next season. As I left, his mother, her eyes shining, grabbed my arm and told me, "You are the best medicine in the world for him." I told her she was the best medicine in the world for him, along with all the people that loved him.

While I was in Baltimore that day, I called up Orioles' owner Peter Angelos. He seemed pleasantly surprised to hear from me. "Eric," he said, "I've never had a ballplayer call me before."

"Well, Mr. Angelos, I just wanted to thank you again for what you did for me and my family in the last two years. I just wanted to thank you for that kind of faith and support."

"My pleasure . . . Eric . . . they told me they were going to sign you . . ."

It's all water under the bridge now. Soon after I hung up with Mr. Angelos, as I was preparing to leave the Sheraton Inner Harbor Hotel Baltimore, the phone rang. It was Cal.

"What happened, E.D.?" he asked, talking about my aborted negotiations with the Orioles and me signing on in St. Louis. It didn't seem to be his favorite roster move in Orioles' history.

"Aw, Cal, you know how it is. They told me signing me wasn't a priority. Then after I signed in St. Louis, Mr. Wren wanted to know why I didn't give them a chance to match what St. Louis offered. It's all aftermath now, brother. But let me tell you, man, I had a great time here. I'll never forget it. I'll never forget you. You helped me in ways you didn't even know, Cal."

"So did you, E.D., so did you. I want you to come to Hawaii to coach at my camp . . ."

After I got off the phone with Cal, that very same day the St. Louis Cardinals traded for Edgar Renteria, the gifted young shortstop who had helped the Florida Marlins win the World Series in 1997. I smiled when I heard this. So the Cardinals were serious about 1999. Good enough. In the limo on the way to BWI, the Baltimore-Washington Airport, I broke out my New

Era size 7⅛ red St. Louis Cardinals baseball cap and placed it snugly on my head. New day.

The sun is warm, the colors are vivid, and I'm grateful again, happy to be in Jupiter, Florida, in the spring of 1999, for another go-round. Now I'm playing with this edition of the storied St. Louis Cardinals baseball franchise. This is what I know, do, have done for a while. This is me.

I don't know all my teammates' nicknames yet, other than Big Mac. But Tony LaRussa is here. I started smiling as soon as I saw him. I'm coming in humble, yet knowing what I can do. I feel lucky to be back among top-end big leaguers, by the grace of God.

When you join a club, you get to see how another big leaguer gets his numbers. You can read box scores, watch highlights, but that doesn't tell you how a guy gets his numbers, where his mass is, in what situations he thrives, where his holes are, how umpiring affects him, what he believes in, how he came up in the game, what he can joke about, what he can't. I'll learn my new teammates, how to complement their play, help them be successful as the time goes by. The first thing I'll learn is their batting stances. Had 'em down by the end of spring training in '99. I had Big Mac and Willie McGee dying of laughter as I mimicked Big Mac's stance on the dugout steps. When you play with a guy every day, you find out who he is. You know him then.

Just like those of you who read this book now know me.

I don't often go back to Denver Avenue, west of Figueroa, east of Hoover and Vermont, South Central. My family isn't there any longer. I don't look at it as though we "got out," however. I can remember when getting there was all my parents wanted to do. It's not just the bad place some people make it out to be. Among the storefronts are bright lights like Redeeming Love Temple of Faith; big complexes like the Crenshaw Christian Center and Ever-Increasing Faith Ministries. All that is there, too. The spiritual is there in abundance. It never was all bad, and shouldn't be played that way. There's a spirituality in that place—just as there's spirituality to hitting a ball out of a big-league ballpark. I hope someone will remember me that way, as a big leaguer; remember that I played hard and sometimes maybe well enough to bear watching. Of all the things I learned, the most important is to live your life understanding that God is in charge, and be humble under it.

Whatever the year 2000 and beyond brings me, I hope to continue to give and receive half as much as I have given and been given in the decades of the '80s and '90s, when I was blessed in many ways by the touch of the hand of God, and was also in my prime as a big-league ballplayer.

And this book? This is in case my memory fails me one day, and my girls want to know.

AFTERWORD

"Eric is the one guy who can lead the [National] League in home runs and stolen bases. Name me another cleanup hitter in either league who can steal one hundred bases. Name one. Man, it's like having an atomic bomb sitting next to you in the dugout!"—Pete Rose, 1987

"I don't think he'll be Willie Mays. That would take some doing. But I don't see a weakness either. They say, 'Bust him high and inside, then curve low and away.' Said the same about me. It's how pitchers try to pitch to hitters they don't know what else to do with."—Hank Aaron, 1987

"Eric is blessed with world-class speed, great leaping ability, the body to play until he's 42, tremendous bat speed and power, and a throwing arm you wouldn't believe. There's an aura to everything he does . . . I'd paid to see him if I had to."—Dave Parker, 1987

"The best I ever played with, against, or saw."—Darryl Strawberry, May 1987

"He's electric."—Davey Johnson, April 1997

"He was, simply, the club's most exciting addition in years. Indeed, his community work and clubhouse presence made it easy to envision him becoming the city's biggest African-American sports hero since Eddie Murray."—*The Baltimore Sun*, June 18, 1997

"Cal Ripken hasn't missed a game in 15 years. Brady Anderson plays [hurt] ... In the past decade Rafael Palmeiro has missed less than 40 games ... Then, there's Eric Davis, who ... may be a better baseball player than any of them ... when he's healthy ... men have gotten hurt more seriously, or had their careers ended. Davis, however, breaks and heals, breaks and heals, then returns to play with wild abandon."—*The Washington Post*, May 14, 1997

"On September 15 Eric Davis returned to the lineup—a truly emotional moment for everyone on the team and in the stands at Camden Yards. I don't think there were many dry eyes ... when Eric walked to the plate the first time. This was a different kind of ovation ... one of respect for him as a person. After all, he was still getting chemotherapy."—Cal Ripken, Jr., *The Only Way I Know*

"When Eric got that first hit, after coming back, 30 people [in a Johns Hopkins Hospital ward] started cheering. They knew who was at bat, what it meant. I thought of the thousands of chemotherapy patients ... and what Eric Davis means to them."
—Dr. Jonathan Simmons, October 1997

"He's my hero."—Rafael Palmeiro, October 1997

"Eric Davis, this [ESPN 1997 Comeback Player of the Year] is for you. You really came back from something. Man, that was awesome!"—Roger Clemens, February 1998

"First time I faced him was in 1984, Al Lopez Field in Tampa, Florida. He doesn't look like he has the power he has. I didn't know anything about him or that power. He took me out to right-center field. He kept that drive, kept his faith, and now, to see him come back and do the things he's done . . . it's just re-markable."—Dwight Gooden, August 1998

"What's easy to forget about the inspirational comeback of Eric Davis is that, in the early stages of the ['97] season, he was the Bal-timore Orioles' best player."—*The Washington Post*, May 10, 1998

"He *is* electric. Something good is going to happen when he's in the game . . . When he's on the other team, he plays so hard, wants to beat you so bad, you tend to say, 'The hell with him.' But what a great teammate . . . cheers more than anybody." —Ray Miller, July 1998

"He's upbeat. He loves playing the game. It rubs off on other players. It's just a contagious thing that he has—something that not everyone brings."—Lenny Webster, July 1998

"I've never seen anybody as hot as Eric Davis is right now . . . I've never seen a baseball hit any harder than he just hit that home run . . . it sounded like a firecracker had gone off!" —Rick Cerone, Orioles' broadcaster, Detroit, July 1998

"Pound for pound, the longest hitter of current times may be Davis."—*The Washington Post*, 1998

"Knowing what he went through probably saved my life." —Darryl Strawberry, 1998

"In the summer of 1998, the city of St. Louis had Mark McGwire, and Chicago had Sammy Sosa. But in the second half of the season, over the last 70 games of the year, Baltimore had Eric Davis. Charismatic. And when you put up the kind of numbers he did ... let's just say that he made a believer out of me. I told him that I would've liked to have had the opportunity to play with him. You need a team full of guys like Eric, not only in terms of ability, but also character. Marvelous."
—Jim Palmer, 1998

"He's one of the greatest unsung heroes of the '90s, and his heroism goes far beyond baseball."—Kurt Schmoke, Mayor, Baltimore, Maryland, 1998

"Eric provided one of the most stimulating stories in baseball ... as he bounced back from one of life's greatest challenges with perseverance and determination that were inspiration to athletes everywhere."—Walt Jocketty, General Manager, St. Louis Cardinals

"What? You mean the St. Louis Cardinals got Eric Davis to go with Mark McGwire, in 1999!? Look out National League. Look out *world*."—Jeffrey Hammonds, Cincinnati Reds, 1999